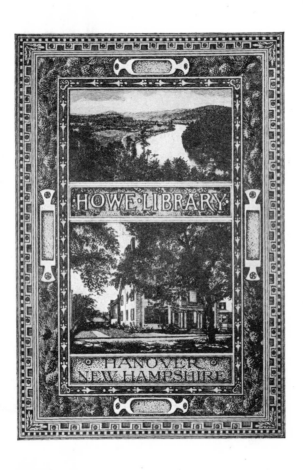

NO MAN'S LAND

ALSO BY JOHN HEMINWAY

The Imminent Rains

Illustrated by Jonathan Kenworthy

NO MAN'S
LAND

The Last of White Africa

John Heminway

E. P. DUTTON, INC. | NEW YORK

Published in the United States by
E. P. Dutton, Inc., 2 Park Avenue, New York, N.Y. 10016

Library of Congress Cataloging in Publication Data
Heminway, John Hylan
No man's land.
1. Africa, East—Biography.   2. Africa—Biography.
3. Heminway, John Hylan.   . I. Title.
CT2116.H45   1983   967.6'04'0924   [B]   83-5503
ISBN: 0-525-24196-5

Published simultaneously in Canada by
Fitzhenry & Whiteside, Limited, Toronto
COBE

Designed by Nancy Etheredge

10 9 8 7 6 5 4 3 2 1

First Edition

For Isabelle

CONTENTS

ix

CONTENTS

PREFACE
AND ACKNOWLEDGMENTS

Soon after the start I knew I could never fathom Africa unless I saw it through the eyes of those who lived there by choice. But loving Africa is like falling for chert and whistling thorn. The prospect, the dream, seems so easy. Some devotees even talk of Africa as if it were a person—a heaving fleshlike bundle of heart and quirks. Sometimes Africa is a she. And sometimes she becomes a paradox of romance—a streetwalker with a heart of gold, the Delphic oracle disguised as a fool, a beggar with huge cash reserves.

Loving Africa as I did, as a land mass, I loved the sum of its parts. When I was sixteen, I spent months with the game. I dreamed of becoming a game warden, a professional hunter, even a missionary, as long as I could be with animals. But soon I saw that I could not separate the animals from other Africas. I said, for instance, that I loved Africa's people. But then as I grew older, I decided I really loved certain tribes, while I was indifferent to others. Not unexpectedly, I soon found individuals among my pilloried peoples whom I liked best of all. Little by little, I came to see animals and people as the bounty of African earth.

Growing up anywhere is difficult. In Africa, adolescence is double jeopardy because there the deflowering of childhood idealism can be dangerous. In no other land I know of do expatriates dwell to such a degree on the environment. Nearly from the moment they start forming words, white children in Africa learn to say to themselves, "I love this place." They commit themselves to this lifelong devotion without comparisons, in full knowledge that Africa probably does not like them. The structured chaos between man and land, man and game, black and white is so all-consuming in Africa that when it fails to live up to childhood promises, the passion turns to cynicism.

I, who had the passion, discovered early that if laughter was the black man's secret weapon it should also be mine. I discovered too that Africa was never just animals, but bad winds, blind ambition, development schemes, rubber stamps and no team spirit. I tried to like these shortcomings as much as I liked the animals. Laughter helped. Only when I learned to smile at chaos and myself, chaotic as a result, could I say I really loved Africa.

Not being particularly wise or particularly mature at age twenty-two when I finished my studies and wrote a travel book about Africa, I did have the sense to make one reasonable decision. Since I was not born in Africa and since my stays there were never permanent (much to my sorrow), I chose protection by seeing Africa through others' eyes.

Loving the sum of the parts, at second hand, has led me into an Africa even more alluring than before. At first the effort for me was like trying to appreciate a desert—easiest to understand when a nomad and his camel come into view. You strain to hear. When at last you catch the chime of his camel bell, the desert becomes tactile. So too Africa. I could truly love Africa when I had a reference point.

Some may find bizarre the notion that I chose Black Africa's rarest creature—the white man—as my focus. To the white man, Africa is a no man's land. He can never own it. He may never never find peace there. He may think he has, but as long as he stays, he will always be between two frontiers, never certain from where the next shots will be fired.

The white man can keep few secrets. Today in Black Africa he stands alone, without counsel. He cannot risk being misunderstood. He knows he must be on his best behavior. He knows he is on trial. The only deception he can practice is the art of buying time.

The black man's testimony, in my view, is not so explicit. The African is, after all, the seignior. He can practice censorship, deception, favoritism. He is not on borrowed time. He has all the time in the world. He can parade through the streets without clothes, and he knows hardly anyone will dare remark. He has little reason to be self-critical or impartial. He need never see his land in perspective; those occasional times when he offers insights into Africa are when his actions, his life, ring with their own eloquence. For me to report on the black man's perception of Africa was to write Neptune's fully authorized memoirs. If I was looking for the lovesick, heartsick, deathwish view of the sea, I knew I would have to interview shipwrecked sailors.

No one should be surprised that, for the most part, I admired these shipwrecked sailors of Africa. This book is theirs. I am in their debt for hospitality, warmth and honesty. All the people in this book are real, though in some cases I have changed their names to protect their privacy. The following list should bear testimony to my belief that Africa is the friendliest of all places. I owe much to many—from a beer to an idea to a lifelong friendship. In addition to white Africans, I include the names of those who made this book possible, outside of Africa, and who, in some cases, believed in it even when I lost heart.

Latham Leslie-Moore, Richard and Meave Leakey, Terry and Jeanne Mathews, Liam Lynn, Paul Ssali, Harry and Bridget Oppenheimer, Alan and Joan Root, David and Carol Hopcraft, Gavin Lamont, Adrien Deschriever, Anne Spoerry, Dr. Alan Walker, Mary Anne Fitzgerald.

John and Angela Sutton, Hank and Mary Slack, Bud Morgan, the late Gloria Johnson, Alan and Jacquie Price, Joanna and

Danny McCallum, Ian and Chris Parker, Peter Beard, Esmond and Chrissie Martin, the late David Sheldrick, Daphne Sheldrick, the late Frank Minot, Sandy Price, Peter and Sarah Jenkins, Charles Miller, Jonathan Kenworthy and many, many Africans, wonderful hosts and good companions.

Jack and Gini Heminway, Hilary Newton, Lucia Realini, Bea Kenyon.

Bob Shnayerson, Philip Herera, Stan Hart, Theron Raines and Joe Kanon.

While they all helped make this book possible, only I can be blamed for its conclusions and mistakes.

NO MAN'S LAND

LETTERS
FROM THE OLD MAN

The beach was softening the tires of my car. Below the berm, the sand, crystalline and sugar-perfect, billowed and shimmered eastward until it reached the spit where the jungle and the breaking sea merged in a tangle. Directly in front of me, above the tidal wash, knot birds, just returned from Siberia, wheeled and bunched and, even closer at hand, mangroves, like headless waders, exposed their oyster-encrusted ankles to the sun. The old man would later point out that no sensible person, particularly not an Englishman of the "old school," would have violated the law of the tropics by being abroad at noon on a cloudless day on

I

the East African coast, without a hat. "But there," he said, characteristically reducing the crime to a question of background, "you're just a damn-fool Yank."

Only on a neap tide could a car, specifically a Land Rover, reach the island through the shallows, and then inexorably, as the Indian Ocean rumbled and moiled over the coral, the car and its occupants would become prisoners, until the next tide, of the island, the old man and his staff of six, the entire human population of the "Sultanate" of M'Simbati.

Mary Anne, my companion, and I were willing to take the risk, although the hotelkeeper in Mtwara forewarned us that the "Sultan" was certifiable, that he routinely expressed his contempt for the world by firing on strangers, that he was known to talk to the sea, that he even planted coconut trees with the middle eye of the nut facing Mecca. I had just graduated from Princeton, and for the last four months Mary Anne and I had cruised through ten thousand miles of southern Africa "collecting" characters for a book. Twelve hours on an island too beautiful to believe with an authentic British eccentric, even a dangerous one, seemed a golden opportunity.

I cut the engine near where the palms gave way to a cluster of casuarina, oleander, frangipani and purple bougainvillea. Camouflaged within their lacy shadows, the walls of an arabesque fort appeared. We waited for the overheated engine to stop backfiring. I opened the door. Standing in the sun I wondered. All of a sudden the fort's teakwood doors opened and Latham Leslie-Moore approached. All he wore was a massive Panama hat, and, around his waist, a short length of bright cloth called a *shuka*. In one hand he carried a walking stick, pointed at the end to serve as a weapon, and in the other, a gnu-tail flyswatter. His legs and arms were lean and well muscled, but his stomach was all by itself—a massive, handsome affair, well rounded, nicely browned and very sure of itself. I remember noting that his face, trimmed with a meticulously combed beard, bore a striking resemblance to portraits of a middle-aged King Edward VII.

After a studied, almost military approach, he examined the car, myself and, with special care, the beautiful Mary Anne, sitting in the front seat. He was now ready to speak. "I want you to know that the last time I had anything to do with anyone was at the Battle of Agincourt." His eyes checked mine to gauge the effect. "I've told the 'boy,' " he continued, "to set extra places at luncheon." He opened the door of the car for Mary Anne and, having kissed her hand, led the two of us into the cool shadows of his great home.

It has now been nearly twenty years since that day on the island. I could never have guessed then what our friendship might one day become, nor could I have known at that moment the twists and hurts and devotions that men will endure for a dream of Africa, nearing extinction. I was twenty-two; Latham was more than three times my age. Rarely, during all these intervening years, did the old man miss an opportunity to remind me that he was spiritually born in the age of the long bow, coinciding with those mythic days when he fought side by side with Henry V—that his abdication from worldly affairs had much to do with the demise of chivalry, and, more appropriately, with the deflowering of the British Empire. But as determined as he was to remind me of the banal world we had inherited, I never failed to be awed by the old man's talent to persist, and to laugh in it.

During that first encounter in 1966, Mary Anne and I forgot about other commitments and stayed for over a week. I remember particularly how the shuttered windows and the thick lime and coral rock walls, crenellated at the top, made the interior of the house refreshingly cool. In a book, published a year and a half later, I wrote: "It was as though I had walked into an English country house. Leather-bound books covered the walls of both the library and the sitting room, and in a corner was a set of Waterford decanters containing sherry and brandy. On a side table there was a highly-polished eighteen-pound shell standing next to a silver christening cup. Both rooms were lined with pictures of old friends—women with wasp waists in high-necked dresses and men in stiff white collars. The ceiling of the house was supported by mangrove poles and sleepers which had been appropriated from the Tanganyika Railway. Two swallows that nested in these beams flew back and forth through the Arab doors."

Twenty-five miles from a town, over two hundred miles to

a capital, the interior of the house gave me the illusion that if I stared hard enough through the windows I may have conjured the rolling hills and serpentine walls of Hampshire.

Every evening, after the sand had cooled and we had returned with scuba gear from exploring the giant clams, helmet shells, augers and cowries offshore, we slumped in the sitting room, the huge Zanzibar doors flung open to allow free passage of dogs, birds and the intoxication of the frangipani. " 'Rocks'— that absurd American necessity"—were always waiting for us in a silver dish, and one of us, either Mary Anne or I, usually felt compelled to drink a toast to paradise.

But "paradise" owed as much to the old man as it did to the island. He was hardly a misanthrope. The notorious gun was not to be seen, and his only worry about us was that we might leave too soon. He fretted incessantly about Mary Anne's sunburn and often offered to rub oil onto portions of her back she could not reach.

Time was important. The island life demanded a routine: dawn awakenings, vigorous activity before the heat of the day, prompt meals, the old man's afternoon siesta, tea, snorkeling over the reef, the BBC World Service and finally some star watching. Latham's wristwatch seemed unnecessary, but I discovered it was his bond with the world as well as a kind of sentinel to guard over that law of solitude that deals with yardarms and strong drink. Throughout our days together few events failed to suggest a tale. His voice, sometimes fading, sometimes drowned beneath his explosive laugh, recalled a time when commands were given without apology, and privilege inherited. I had, it seemed, stumbled onto a living time capsule.

Latham was born in either 1891 or 1893, depending on the story. His earliest memories were of Smallfields House, a sprawling country estate, from which his father presided over a family fortune buttressed by large land holdings in Tipperary. With careful words Latham conjured the very flicker of the candlelights the night his father won a bet by jumping his favorite horse over the dining room table without upsetting any of the crystal. And on another occasion, he recalled the boyish thrill of seeing his very first automobile. As required by law, a footman ran ahead of it, waving a red flag. For a time, Latham served as

4

a pageboy to Queen Victoria and claimed he could still feel the slap of her hand when he once was caught misbehaving.

The Irish Revolution brought an end to those privileged days. His father's estates in Ireland were repatriated, the family's fortunes reduced to a bundle of worthless deeds, and Latham was left to his own wits before he even had a chance to be sent up to Eton. In his late teens he set sail for Trinidad and thence to Mexico where he worked as an oil rigger. Two vacations were spent in Hollywood where, under the stage name of Larry Larsen, he acted as an extra in several Mary Pickford and Douglas Fairbanks films. ("I had only what you Yanks call 'bit parts.' I was no ruddy star and I knew sweet Fanny Adams about acting, but I did have fun.") When he returned to England, still penniless, there was a brief period when even poverty could not prevent him from enjoying the most luminous orbits of society. Once when I suggested that his African wardrobe would have caused a stir in fashion circles, he replied, "Yes, I know I am the best-dressed man in Africa. I was that in England, where I was considered the most elegant man-about-town. I was the introducer of the colored evening dress with knee breeches and buckled pumps, silk stockings, white tie and white waistcoat, of course. I had two of these: one royal blue and the other plum-colored. Terribly smart we were in those days!"

He had returned to England to serve his king in the Great War and as he watched his friends, the cream of English youth, die in the trenches beside him, their presumptions and ideals buried with them, he somehow determined never to forswear the life they left behind. True to this childhood promise he lived an Edwardian life for the next sixty-four years.

Under the command of General Gough, Latham fought his way through France until at Amiens he succumbed to mustard gas. "Doubled up like a hunchback," he returned to England in 1918, was told by "a bloody pillroller" that he had six months to live and immediately set sail for Canada to work in a logging camp to prove the doctor wrong. When he returned a year later, completely cured, he concluded that the new England was too squalid and confined for his taste. By now, he had become intrigued by the African territories, acquired from Germany as spoils of war. They might be "just the ticket" for someone who knew a thing or two about agriculture. A few months later, at the Arusha Club in Northern Tanganyika he, predictably, ran into an old school friend. "Having a devil of a time teaching the wa-Chagaa to plant coffee," the friend said over a drink at the bar. "Don't suppose you could muck in for a few weeks, do you?"

Latham raised his glass. "Delighted to lend a hand, old boy." So began a career that was to last nearly thirty years.

As an agricultural officer with a beat sometimes several thousand square miles in size, Latham was rarely in one spot long enough to become settled. For years his chief mode of conveyance was a bicycle, propelled on the uphill stretches by an African running behind, pushing with a forked stick. Latham flatly objected to driving an automobile or traveling in "a flying machine," since "the noise is unbearable and the smell absolutely appalling." He governed his movable kingdom with quips for the deserving and horsehide, the *kiboko,* for the disobedient, according to the custom of those absolute days. When a prominent Indian in Mikindani invaded his privacy one afternoon to proffer a bribe, Latham summarily threw the bewildered man off a second-floor balcony into a thorn tree. "The Indian community never forgave me for that one," Latham proudly remembers. "That chap should have known better than to disturb my siesta."

His was a job fit only for those who could abide the loneliness. For two years during World War II he never saw another white man. "Who cared, really, since one could always be assured of the occasional home leave?" Latham returned to England only twice in thirty years—visits that consisted of highly concentrated rounds of house-party weekends on great country estates, skiing trips in Austria, sails along the Scottish coast. Once, when in London, he exercised his pet lion cub on a chain outside the Guards Club and down Piccadilly. Stopping at the Ritz, a hotel that met with his disapproval (for reasons he never cared to disclose), he asked a terrified headwaiter for a table for two and then, having seated himself in one chair, and chained the lion to the other, he fixed his eyes on the trembling waiter and commanded: "The steak for me and a plate of bones for my friend."

When Latham first cast eyes on the island of M'Simbati in 1933 he vowed he would one day own it, and, twelve years later, after its owner, Pershottam Neranji, died, it came up for sale at auction. Clandestinely, by advancing the Boma clock twenty minutes, Latham rigged the bidding to begin before all the other contenders had arrived, and with very little difficulty he acquired the island for a little over $2 per acre. A team of several hundred ma-Wia tribesmen were soon clearing the bush, erecting buildings, planting cashew and coconut trees, and a few years later, after Latham's mandatory retirement from the Colonial Service, he moved into the twenty-four-room house called Wind's Whisper and settled down to a squire's life, with just enough of a government pension to survive the seven years needed for his trees to bear fruit.

He had now solemnly made up his mind never to return to England. "I lived at Wind's Whisper," he recalled decades later, "for twenty years in peace with everyone, just developing the estate, fishing and entertaining my guests. Some came for only a few days but others stayed for months. One lady was there for a year and a half. It was one of the most beautiful places anywhere."

Latham proudly observed at this time that by now he had served under six kings and queens—from Victoria to Elizabeth II. While a servant of the Crown he had taken and given orders on behalf of the God-given powers of his monarch. When in 1959 Britain finally decided to yield to "the winds of change" and dissolve its rule over Tanganyika, Latham believed that his lifetime devotion to the Crown was, by rank cowardice and disloyalty, being dissolved. I never knew Latham at this time, but I suspect from later remarks that independence was the greatest crisis he ever had to endure during his long life. His government, after all, was passing its sovereignty of the land he had settled into the hands of people he had once ruled. Latham foresaw nothing but trouble.

Rather than bow to the inevitable, Latham promptly took action. He formed his own government—a sultanate—and in a mock-formal ceremony involving an oath made over a silver Arab dagger and a Persian rosary to uphold the laws of the prophet Muhammad, the Koran and Queen Elizabeth, he and his houseboys declared that the island of M'Simbati secede from the mainland. "I have the honor to inform Your Excellency," he announced in a bulletin to the retiring governor of the Colony, "that on the last stroke of midnight, December 31st, 1959, this island of 640 acres seceded from Tanganyika Territory by the unanimous vote of all the islanders." The next day he wrote Secretary General Dag Hammarskjöld for permission to join the United Nations.

M'Simbati's bizarre claim soon gained attention in the press, and letters praising him for his novel defiance of progress poured into the island mail pouch. Even the *East African Standard* was moved to lavish rhetoric on the would-be sultan: "Today the English do not want to boast, or to be reminded too often about their rough island story, but the path of duty is still the way to glory and especially when the path is trodden alone . . ."

"My object," Latham wrote in answer to queries, "is to remain under our Queen and stay loyal to our country, thereby keeping a tiny white island in a sea of black barbarism, to carry on the civilization of hundreds of years of culture that has been the heritage of our race." To prove that he was in earnest, a new flag began to fly over the fort. Its upper left-hand corner was reserved for the Union Jack, to symbolize the island's reaffirmed pledge to the Queen; the rest consisted of three bold stripes, one emerald green, one sea blue, the last blood red, signifying that "the emerald green island of M'Simbati will forever be separated by the blue sea from the bloody shores of Tanganyika."

It was Latham's finest hour. In one of the many press releases he issued, the sixty-nine-year-old retiree assumed a menacing note: "Let no man think he can take advantage of a survivor of General Sir Hubert Gough's Immortal Fifth Army, that fought the battle of the Somme, Messines, Ypres, Polecappelle, the Menin Road, Paschendale and the epic retreat of March 1918 where outnumbered four to one by the Germans and outgunned six to one, we fought them to a standstill in eight days: the greatest fighting retreat in military history and the turning point of the war. I learned to fight for freedom there under the inspired leadership of our famous general and, by Allah, I will fight again if necessary. The spirit of the Fifth Army lives on."

Owning Lilliput was essentially good fun. Almost every situation provided its Sultan with an occasion to wag, if not the lion's, someone's tail. Just before Christmas one year an American journalist chartered a dhow for the island to witness for himself this bizarre experiment in self-emancipation. When he reached the beach he was greeted by the poker-faced ruler. "Where is your visa and landing card?" Latham demanded. The journalist, not sure of the tone in the old man's voice, handed over his passport and was told that the chief magistrate of the island would have to be consulted. After a wait of ten minutes in the sun, the journalist saw the old man returning through the trees. The magistrate, according to Latham, had handed down his verdict: "The punishment for not carrying an M'Simbati visa is a three-day confinement to the island." It just so happened Latham wanted some company over Christmas.

On another occasion, a pilot dropped a message for Latham weighted down with the only object apparently available in the cockpit of the plane—a ham sandwich. Because the event occurred on the first Friday in Ramadan, Latham decided to make it an international incident. He immediately dashed off the following letter to the Tanzanian government: "When the [flying machine] was over the Mosque . . . while still at a very low altitude, a port hole was opened from which a hand protruded and threw out a packet . . . It contained pig products . . .

"I do not know if it is the intention of Your Excellency's Government in Tanganyika to precipitate a Holy War on the continent of Africa but I cannot conceive of a method more likely to do so than to pelt members of Islam while at their devotions with pig products from the air . . .

"I have refrained from bringing this to the notice of the Sheikhs of Islam in Zanzibar, Mombasa and Dar Es Salaam until I have a reply from Your Excellency."

After eighteen months of M'Simbati's "independence," the new Tanzanian government decided to act. Latham had a knack for engaging the attention of the press in his opera-bouffe revolution, and the new black nation must have begun to find the situation embarrassing. ("Julius Nyerere had no bloody sense of humor," Latham recalls. "What more do you expect of an ex-schoolteacher?") A gunboat was dispatched from Dar Es Salaam, and one day in November 1961 Latham and his staff of six were forced to watch as the M'Simbati flag was lowered for the last time. "A sad evening," Latham recalls. "The end of my finest leg-pull."

Even the last British governor of the Colony had seemed moved by the old man's dedication. In a letter written late on the night before his departure from the ex-Colony, he was unable to disguise unofficial admiration for the old man: "I cannot leave Tanganyika [he wrote Latham] without thinking my farewells to the country's most southerly outpost. I send you my best wishes for Christmas and the New Year and for a long, happy and undisturbed continuance of your sojourn on M'Simbati Island. I am sending you a little fluid sustenance as a parting gift. We shall think of you . . ." A bottle of Scotch was enclosed.

For the next six years Latham resumed life as a commoner. Highlights included a squabble he had with *The Illustrated London News* when their covers began appearing in color rather than in black and white. "A bloody disgrace," Latham announced and promptly canceled his subscription. Now, alone most of the time, he found marginal pleasure in interrupting his evening pink gin with the news on the BBC World Service. The West was undoubtedly going down the drain, while, like the monarch of another planet, he observed it, unscathed. He had now determined never to set foot off his island again. He had instructed his "boys" that at his death his body was to be rolled in the M'Simbati flag and buried in a clump of coral behind the house.

Shortly after Mary Anne and I left the island, I began receiving letters from the old man. It is clear that he inherited from his Victorian childhood a habit of committing all thoughts to stationery. He felt comfortable with words. With his battered typewriter he could transform contempt into a sting, loneliness into company. During the seventeen years that have elapsed, there have been few months when he did not tell me of his moods, ambitions, loves and hates. At times, his letters arrived daily and today his file is explosive-looking, the frayed edges of hundreds of airletters bursting in all directions.

Shortly after I left the island in 1966, he began this correspondence by summarizing his philosophy: "To me, civilization ended in 1914. Since then it has been madness piled on madness. I fought in the wars and I know the politicians of all countries are to blame: the lust for power and the money-grabbing by low-born crooks everywhere including the States, England, etc. They have given power to these savages in Africa long before they were ready for it and look at the mess the continent is in now . . .

"I live alone on my island and I don't have anything to do

with anybody. I am disgusted with civilization, with crooked politicians, police, prelates and, most of all, the press: the four p's that should be exterminated en masse. [I suggest you] burn all flying machines, radios, propaganda machines; eliminate all Pop, Jazz, teen-agers, Beatles, etc. and come back to what it was in pre-1914. Then you may regain your sanity. At the moment I have no hope for the world. End of message."

In his next letter he presented a scheme for me to return to his world. He would sell me a plot of land next to his house and build me a small bungalow. He enclosed a set of plans he had sketched for the house. It would be called Dream Cottage and the total cost for land, construction and furnishings was estimated at $1,200. I replied that I was interested and I suggested that he contact the Ministry of Lands and Mines in Dar Es Salaam for title. While waiting for an answer, Latham's letters, addressed to me in New York, became more and more chatty. Mary Anne, he wrote, had stopped by on her return home to South Africa for Christmas. ("She arrived with a hat and so saved getting a spanking.") By Easter of the following year Latham still had not heard about the land title. There was trouble, he said, in the region. The hotelkeeper in Mtwara had been given forty-eight hours to leave the country. With surprising precognition Latham observed: "It's only a matter of time before they get around to me but they know I am ready for them and never far from a gun and am only too willing to use it." All belligerence and bluster, he continued, without so much as a change of paragraph, saying that he was teaching the little children of the island how to swim: "They love it now. The little ones sit in the shallows and play."

By May, Mary Anne, a desultory letter writer, had acquitted herself in his eyes by sending him copies of the pictures she had taken over Christmas. Now all was well, he explained. "There is one of me, standing on the shore, hat and fly wisk in hand and my walking staff in the other, looking just like one of those stone monuments on Easter Island . . ." He was hoping that Mary Anne would stop by again "but I don't think Papa trusts me too far with his beautiful blond daughter. Perhaps he is right at that." As for me, he had strong advice: "Don't get married. It's a mug's game. Keep single . . . If you marry you will never have a moment's peace afterwards. I have kept out of their clutches for 70 years and shall continue to do so until I am 80 and then I hope to be hanged for rape."

At last he had received a letter from Mary Anne. It told him about her adventures driving back to Kenya and her new employment there, working for a white hunter. "I think the woman is nuts," he reacted. "If she is driving about Africa alone in a clapped-out truck she is likely to end up in the bush and probably be killed by a lion or raped by a wog. . . . She said she was coming here again sometime. When? Quien sabe, and I hope she does as someone ought to take her in hand and spank her good and hard. She sent a snapshot of herself, looking like the wrath of God—her hair dyed two colors, dark at the top, and blond at the end. Looks bloody awful but it may be the latest thing in what you people call civilization. I hope she writes again as I shall worry if she is out on her own somewhere in this barmy bin that is East Africa today."

Life on the island was still untouched by time. "I have been pretty fit since you were here, but Anno Domini is beginning to show a bit. Can't walk very fast but I get there just the same." He had begun preparing for my next visit in September and advised me, if Mary Anne was busy in Nairobi, to bring out another blonde. He added: "I know you will laugh at me and say I am an old fogie and no one wears a hat but I can assure you that there are lots of actinic rays in the sun here and always the risk of a sunstroke. Having lived for fifty years in the tropics, and having seen scores of cases, I know what I am talking about. I don't want to bury you here and have to write your Papa that you were used as shark bait." He ended the letter with his usual battle cry: "Up 'em and stuff 'em, as we say in the Royal Navy."

Just as I was preparing to leave New York for my East African holiday, the news I had always dreaded arrived by telephone. Charles Miller, Latham's only other American acquaintance, read me a nearly illegible letter he had just received from the old man: "I am afraid this will be the last letter from the island. I am in the pub [the hotel in Mtwara] now, having been brought in by some 20 armed police-soldiers, beaten and kicked, handcuffed and thrown into the back of a Land Rover and bumped about over 30 miles of road into Mtwara. There is trouble expected from over the border and all this area has been declared a restricted area and I am not allowed to go back to the island again. I am waiting . . . to hear what the Gov't decides to do and if I shall be allowed to pick up my things.

"So this is the end of everything for me. All my life savings have gone into making a lovely place of Wind's Whisper and now the bush will reclaim its own. My lovely house will be looted and fall down, the birds will have to go elsewhere for their drinking water as I can't expect anyone to fill up the auger shells on the forecourt walls . . . I feel so sorry for my friends who have been to the island and loved it so much."

In his note to me, Latham tried to stop me from booking seats "in the flying machine," but by the time his letter arrived I was over the Sahara. When I reached Nairobi, a heroic picture of Latham framed the front page of the *East African Standard*. "Mr. Latham Leslie-Moore," the article read, "the 79-year old Briton who announced in 1960 that his island home of M'Simbati off Southern Tanzania 'would secede from Tanganyika' has been removed from the island 'for his own protection.' " The article reported that a government official had denied that the old man had been "manhandled." He had, however, alleged that the island was earmarked to become a training center for African "Freedom Fighters." Latham Leslie-Moore, the *East African Standard* reported at the end, "was known affectionately as the Grand Old Man of the Isle."

At dawn the next morning I boarded the regular Dakota flight for Dar Es Salaam. There, the British High Commissioner, sharing an inconspicuous office with the Canadians, claimed that there was little he could do at this time for the old man since the British were in such diplomatic disfavor. All he could promise him was safe passage to another country.

Frustrated, and now beginning to suffer from a recurrent bout with malaria, I continued my journey south in another creaking Dakota, and when it landed at Mtwara, I faced a phalanx of heavily armed *askaris*. Where was I going? one asked. How long was I going to stay? Who was I going to visit? The Russian-made guns played across my sodden shirt. My eyes had started to blaze with the fever; my hands, and now my shoulders, trembled.

A hand plucked at my shoulder. The harbor master, one of the six remaining whites in Mtwara, had recognized me from a distance as he drove by, and he now led me to his Land Rover.

"Mustn't let these lads have too much time to think. No telling what they might do." He ground the car into first and soon we were driving through Mtwara's main street, where I recalled the dust had once been thick in the air from the toing and froing of traders. Today, the dust had settled. The shops were shuttered and only one Indian, pedaling his antique Singer on the stoop of his *duka,* was visible; down the road a dog raised his head and hobbled on three legs into the shade.

"Just as well the old gent's out of town," the harbor master added, as we reached the edge of town. "He might just say something and get the whole lot of us into trouble." More armed recruits sprawled by the entrance to the hotel. "Wasn't good when that article hit the papers. We're all here on sufferance, you see. Nyerere's liable to declare the town a 'war zone,' and give us twenty-four hours to pack up. Best to keep still."

The old man had been removed from his prison in the hotel outhouse to an isolated structure that had been built for the Indian manager of a sisal plantation. Surrounding it, rows of this domestic sansevieria plant had been planted with maddening symmetry, and the spindly succulents formed a mechanical forest. The house had been neglected; its walls were crumbling and the tin roof blotched with rust. I stepped onto the unswept porch and into the dim interior of the house. I was already surprised the old man had not come out to greet me. He was sitting without a book in a broken armchair, and apparently he had not heard my arrival. With difficulty he rose. I had never before seen him with his hair uncombed. "Thank God you're safe," he said. I thanked the harbor master and as I listened to his departure I lay down on the couch, the cold sweat soon settling in pools on my stomach.

"Two victims of Africa—that's what we are. Bloody place," he said, staring at me. The old man tried to smooth his hair and draw himself into his old martial posture, but I could see he was acting. A midday council of cicadas in the sisal outside interrupted any further gratuitous remarks.

I stayed with the old man for three days. Each morning we routinely were driven into town to gauge the temper of the local generalissimo, but no one in government was willing to take responsibility for the old man's future. There were aimless searches through files, an occasional grin and once a lecture about the workings of a bureaucracy. This nation's manifest destiny was with larger matters, we were told—such as border disputes—not with old men, particularly white ones.

The remaining whites in town suspected the conflict with Portuguese East Africa might continue fitfully for years; the pleasure of the government, they believed, was generally not in sympathy with ex-Colonials.

For two days, Latham resisted these opinions. "What possible harm could come to an old man like me? Tell them I'll stay out of the crossfires. When I hear the old ratatattat I'll gather up the 'boys' and the dog and we'll all get inside with the door locked tight. Won't even look out the window to check on their fool war. Tell them that."

The town's only lawyer, Lilani, an Indian, who for safety kept the shutters of his office closed throughout the day, finally made up Latham's mind. "As a matter of fact," he said, "you have no recourse. And even if not one shot is fired, the war could continue unofficially for the rest of your life. There are laws here and also there is a government. One has more effect than the other. My advice is to think of financial recompense."

On our return to the sisal plantation that afternoon, Latham began talking of South Africa. "Lots of East Africans like myself down there. Probably would have a jolly good time." I was skeptical. Instead, I suggested the Seychelles. It was still remote, still a colony; land was cheap and the climate almost identical to M'Simbati's. "I've heard there are problems out there," Latham cut me off. "A cottage on the Natal coast would be just the ticket." He had made up his mind.

One moment sweating so heavily that my shirt needed to be wrung out, another moment shivering with an arctic cold, too tired to swat at the flies, I lay on the couch and wondered when the old man's remembering would cease and he could turn to the future with decisiveness. "Maya Lupescu [the houseguest who stayed a year and a half at Wind's Whisper] will be outraged when she hears the news. She loved the island. Taught the women and children to dance, and when she left, there wasn't a dry eye on the island." The old man started polishing the silver christening cup that had followed him everywhere since the days of Queen Victoria and had last resided on the side table in the dining room on the island of M'Simbati.

Soon after my return to Nairobi, the first of many letters arrived from Latham. He seemed particularly touched by the interest I had generated in his welfare from friends and members of my family: "I shall worry about you until I hear that you are fit again. I can't thank you properly for all you and your friends in the States are doing for me. It's very wonderful that complete strangers have taken so much interest and are willing to help." Evidently his mood was improving, for he continued: "How is my little Mary Anne? I hope she is behaving herself and being faithful to me . . . Smack her bunky for me." Five days later another letter arrived explaining that he had contacted a shipping agent about vessels bound for South Africa. He was still worried about the belongings left in the house: "Some I want to take South, some to go to auction in Mtwara and some for the boys as presents. They deserve something nice as they have stood by me through all this mess-up . . . It will be sad parting from them as they have been with me for so long but it's better to make a clean break now and have done with it. There is one thing the Gov't can't take away from me and that's the wonderful memory of my friends. . . ."

The news awaiting me when I had returned to New York was that Latham was still "on this Godawful spike *shamba*," and that Lilani, the lawyer, was being evasive, despite my many letters begging for news about the case against the government. Finally at the end of January I received an air letter, blooming in several hues of South African stamps. The typewriting was clear and exuberant. Latham had found a cottage, just as he had hoped, on the Natal coast, thirty-two miles north of Durban. For the time being, however, he was in a hospital having all the ailments he had neglected on the island attended to at last. The skin cancer under his eye had been removed and "I have had all my teeth out and am living on scrambled eggs, while waiting for the new snappers to arrive . . . then [the doctors] will have a dekko at my hind legs."

The only querulous note concerned the island. He still had not heard from Lilani. Rather than receiving a financial recompense, he would have preferred to return, but with the Freedom Fighters in residence at his house, he was sure such a return would not be possible for a while. "I can only hope Mariamu and all those boys who were loyal to me and who stayed on are safe."

His observations of civilization in Durban were typically terse. "This is a hell of a city," he wrote, "more blond teen-age tarts in mini skirts than you can shake a stick at."

Latham left the hospital in February and soon celebrated with a letter to me: "I kidded the doctors into giving me a Monkey Gland injection before I left, and they fell for the gag." He was now being treated everywhere as a celebrity. His arrival in South Africa had coincided with the publication of Mary Anne's article in a South African magazine, and now he wanted me to note that recognition, long overdue, was at last his. "It's the story of the year here, and a best seller in Durban. I was pestered in the hotel by reporters and broadcasting people, and spotted in the streets by scores of people who asked if they could help, and 'what happened to your dogs,' 'did they get the flag,' etc., etc." For a while the past weighed very little on the old man. The present was far too exciting. Mary Anne, down with a bad case of jaundice, was back at home in Johannesburg and able to feed the old man letters and hope at his little cottage near Chaka's Rock. "It will be fun," Latham wrote, "if she does come down here for a few days. That will shake old Chaka off his rock . . ."

Toothless, slightly crippled and thoroughly unnerved by all the "mod cons" (particularly electricity) in his cottage, Latham had suddenly become very curious about modern people. Having gone without company for so many years, he now was delighted whenever he heard a rap on the door. "Hate the whole bloody world," he generally announced to the curiosity seeker, and in the same breath, added, "May I offer you a dry sherry?" A blazer, bought in London in the 1930s, had been unearthed in one of the closets of Wind's Whisper before he left, and with khaki trousers and regimental tie or ascot to round out his wardrobe, he paraded along the little street of Chaka's Rock, often mistaken for a retired brigadier general. Yellowed ivory-handled brushes had also been salvaged from the island, for he was vain about his full head of hair and his saber-pointed Edwardian beard. Latham rarely discussed loneliness in his letters, but it was clear that now, without the coconut and cashew trees, without the children learning to swim in the shallows, without the retinue of retainers and the homespun wisdoms they once shared, he had become uncomfortably idle. His solution to these occasional bouts of aloneness was to send his Zulu houseboy out to the nearby parking lot to see if there were any interesting license plates. East Africa or Rhodesia would do. Whenever the houseboy's report sounded promising, Latham adjusted his attire and ambled amidst the "trippers," casting disapproving glances on the noisy and vulgar, while leaning rakishly on his cane within earshot of likely conversations.

On one of these rambles, Latham happened upon some German-speaking campers. The last time he had been in "the land of the Hun," he explained, was in the spring of 1938, hard on the heels of Hitler's Anschluss when Austria had unwillingly been absorbed into the German Reich. At the time, Latham was on leave from his duties in East Africa, and he and "a dear lady friend," believing that Hitler's threat to the Jewish citizens of Austria was "a bloody bad show," had decided to help some of the refugees flee across the Alps. Each night, his rucksack loaded with provisions, and traveling mostly on skis, he escorted parties of Jews, from Saalfelden to Innsbruck, arriving in the early hours of the morning. Here the refugees were met by another clandestine guide, like Latham, and secreted across the border into Italy. It was all good fun and a splendid opportunity to thumb one's nose at "old Adolf."

Gazing out to sea, Latham recalled to the gathering crowd the thin dawn across the Alps, the whispered conversations with these homeless victims, the cries of the children. He remembered one child whose crying had reminded him of the yip of a fox. Worried that the sound would carry across the snow and be heard in the valleys by the overzealous Gestapo, he dipped a finger into his bottle of Schnapps and then stuck it down the throat of the offender until its crying stopped and it fell asleep inside his rucksack. "Hell of a stunt. Not sure where I learned it either since I knew nothing about bloody children." Throughout the long march, he and the mother of the child talked in whispers, she describing her doctor husband who had been forced to remain in Vienna, he conjuring up his life in Tanganyika Territory. At last when they reached the final staging post and Latham handed the child over to another bearer, he turned to the woman and said *"Auf wiedersehen."* ("Till we meet again.")

Later, back at the hotel, sipping hot coffee, he pondered those parting words. "What a bloody fool thing to say. How could we possibly ever meet again?"

His story was ended, but his audience, he perceived, was still waiting for more. He twirled his cane and just as he set out to return to his cottage, a gray-haired woman approached him. She was a German-speaking Jew exiled in South Africa since the early days of World War II. "Do you know who I am?" she asked.

"No."

"I am the mother."

Latham did not, at first, believe her. He studied the face, the mannerisms, and soon he thought he could spot a resemblance, even after thirty-three years.

"But how did you recognize me?" the old man stammered.

"Because you have a lovely and very distinctive voice, and besides, you made the same grammatical mistakes this morning as you made the night we walked together over the mountains. Your German has not improved."

In March there were problems with money. "Those bloody people," Latham wrote, "have not paid in my pension and the bank here will not give me an overdraft." I had never known much about Latham's finances. Most of his savings, he once explained, were invested in the island and the annual crop of copra and cashews provided him with an occasional bonus to see him through rough times. In addition, I thought he had been able to squirrel away some savings—its size and location always undisclosed. When I visited him at the sisal plantation I had badgered him for more information in order to determine his needs, but during these grillings he grew remote and vague. Once he mentioned the existence of a family trust, but when I probed, he flung his hands into the air, claiming that he had never approved of the trustees ("a bunch of old blind men"), and in protest, during the 1940s he had burned all the trust papers and told the old men "to stuff it." If Latham was destitute, it was surely by his own lofty hand. Admiring the spirit, I sent him a check in March while Mary Anne forwarded him some of the proceeds from her article. By the end of the month, Latham's finances were once again healthy.

In the next letter a quixotic note was sounded. "A very dear friend" was staying with him while her young daughter convalesced. He avoided mention of her name or the nature of their friendship. I became more and more curious and asked him for details in his next letter. "My charming guest has lovely gray hair and green eyes," he responded mysteriously. Finally in late April, he added a clue: "My charming guest will be going back to Rhodesia on Friday and I shall miss her very much but I hope she will be able to come down again later in the year."

Throughout June he was silent about "his charming guest," but there were other distractions: "I seem to be getting well-known here. A couple of women—I think they are Lesbians—came here, armed with one of those damn black boxes [presumably a tape recorder], half a dozen kinds of cameras, flash lights, etc., and wanted to have the island story for some radio broadcast. . . . I gave them lunch and one of the bints went to their car and dug out six cans of South African beer and we knocked them back with the sausages. They are going to let me know when the broadcast will be on the air and what rag will be publishing the story. I imagine most of it will be censored. I expect to be asked to leave South Africa soon if this goes on . . ."

Latham was suffering from the South African winter. He wrote: "It turned very cold here a few days ago and I nearly froze but remembered an old 1st World War trick and put both legs in a sack of grain. Mitzi [his dachshund] came in too so we both kept warm with a blanket round our heads."

By July he was slowly agitating against his adopted country. He had received a letter from Mariamu on the island and he was worried about her health. He had thereupon written to everyone he knew in Mtwara to look after her. Clearly he was homesick: "I wish to God I could get back there to live again." The problems with his "hind legs" had recurred and he would have to go into hospital briefly "for the pillrollers to have another dekko at them. There is some American stunt to open an artery and then pump gas down to clear the damn things. Be a hell of a show if they put too much in and I blew up."

When he was back in his cottage a few days later, mending, he finally answered my questions about his "charming guest." Her name was Hermes and she was "lovely with gray hair, green eyes, a laughing mouth and very beautiful hands. At the age of 75, I am in love for the first time in my life . . . Up 'em and stuff 'em, old timer." In his next letter he corrected an error I had made about her eyes: "She has green eyes, not blue, silver hair and a voice like the tinkle of little bells, a neat trim figure and very lovely hands and what she sees in an old wreck like me, I don't know but we love each other and are very happy."

In the accompanying photographs I could see there was a considerable gap in age between the two. Smiling and supportive, she seemed all he described as she held him by the elbow before a whitewashed wall. The look on her face suggested public admiration, but I thought I detected something patronizing, a trace of bemusement. She seemed to pretend she was not in charge, humoring him as "his paramour," yet a certain steeliness in the way she held him said to me she wanted no uncertainty about their relationship. Unaware of the subleties, as he stood by her side, Latham was glowing with pleasure—the Sultan once again.

Throughout the autumn he was busy making plans for a Christmas visit to Hermes in Rhodesia ("The only way to get there is in a flying machine and, as you know, I have never been in one and I am scared to death. I shall ask the driver not to go faster than 25 miles an hour"). When he was once again back in South Africa after the New Year there was an uncharacteristic period of silence. When a letter at last arrived in the spring he explained the problems: He was far too busy with other letters. "As I must write pages and pages every day to my Hermes, I have had a special board made that goes on the arms of my chair where I can sit with my leg up on a pouf. The board has a half-moon shape to fit my tummy. I can reach the keys of the typewriter, write all day and obey doctor's orders."

Letter writing was the perfect escape from South Africa where the whites were becoming more and more odious. "Thank God the Easter holidays are over, and the masses of revolting humanity with their disgusting offspring are going back to their hovels in Johannesburg . . . One has to be careful here. The South Africans are very touchy and can't tolerate being contradicted on anything. As for their politics—well, I know nothing at all. Safer not to . . ."

I had always hoped that South Africa would only be a short penance for Latham and that one day Lilani, the lawyer in Mtwara, would surprise him with permission from the Tanzanian government to return. In our correspondence we both reminisced about the scimitar-shaped beach, the coral gardens and the sunsets that Latham forever dubbed "Rose Du Barry Pink."

His exile was now into its second year, and the yearning for the island's isolation and peace had begun to consume him. Lilani failed to reply to our queries. Perhaps, we wondered, he had been evicted along with other Asians. Perhaps he had grown timid about pressing charges against a government that had near-absolute powers. Or perhaps Lilani had forged a few signatures and taken possession of the island himself. Easy to imagine the worst.

"I hear now and then from Mariamu but no real news of what is going on there," he wrote. "It is too dangerous to write anything still . . . I think there is a chance they will let me go back when this damn terrorist affair is over but what the place will be like I don't know, nor do I know where Simba and the other dogs are now . . ."

In his letters, Latham was master of the mood change. Almost without pause he lectured me on my new job with one of the television networks. He wrote: "I can't think of you being assed about by those people. You would probably brain the Director the first week there, but the Starlets may be an attraction." He asked whether I could find an elderly millionairess to adopt him "as a pet and keep me supplied in monkey glands and hormone implants and also supply a nice yacht. We can then tour the world looking for blondes for you, leaving the millionairess in New York to look after the babies." Full stop. New paragraph. "Have you heard," he inquired wistfully, "that our little Mary Anne is engaged to be married to an Englishman?" Another paragraph. "South Africa is slowly killing me. The damp and the cold have got into me and I can hardly walk about. Nor does apartheid agree with me at all . . . disgraceful bloody show. So as soon as Hermes finds a cottage for me in Rhodesia I shall hop onto a flying machine with Mitzi in a box and go to a country where the sun shines, the birds sing, the bush is full of game, the people charming and my Hermes beside me."

For the next eight months there were no letters from Latham. Suddenly in the spring of the following year a letter arrived, full of apologies. He had moved from a rented flat in Salisbury to a small cottage on Sir Malcolm Barrow's dairy farm, and because most of his day was spent fixing up the cottage, looking after the garden, cooking for himself, feeding his eight budgerigars and keeping an eye on not just the dachshund but

Sumva, a cross between a Rhodesian Ridgeback, boxer and Alsatian, he had little time left over to write. Hermes visited him now only once a week because she was working at the university. "It's as cold as the fringe around a polar bear's bum now and each evening I light a roaring fire, about the time my legs give out and all I have strength for is a noggin . . . Yes, I hope you will be able to make the trip down here and stay at Ruware with me as I think you will like the place. The peace and quiet is quite something. Only some bloody fellah in a flying machine passing overhead disturbs it. Now and then one hears a cow mooing or a dog barking . . ."

An old friend had recently invited him to his house to see a film taken on M'Simbati many years before, and I realized that Latham's idyll in Rhodesia would never totally match the prospect of a return to the island. "It was splendid to see the island again," he wrote. "That lovely sand beach, the dhows and the Natives I knew so well. There was even a shot of me in my *shuka*."

One month later his dream ended: "The awful news of M'Simbati, that we all loved so much, has shaken me to the core. They kicked out Mariamu and all my people, and the whole place has been given to the local wogs. Mariamu wrote me from Mikindani but I don't know what I can do. I have written the British High Commissioner but I don't expect they will do anything. It's awful to think of Mariamu perhaps destitute and unable to go back to her own country. So this is the end now."

I offered to intercede, to write letters to the Tanzanian government, to demand reparations, but the old man saw this final blow as the climax to a continental scheme. There was nothing anyone could do. He had fought, he said, "a rear-guard action." Without resupply, he and all the other ex-Colonial servants had been left by the British government on the beach, to be forgotten.

Over the next few years, making films for the network, I had little time to keep up with Latham's letters. In any case, he was content being in Rhodesia, with once-a-week visits from Hermes. Occasionally he wrote, predicting the decline and fall of the West. Bobby Kennedy's murder bothered him: "It was ghastly and if your Gov't does not take drastic action now, you are going to have a revolution on your hands. Not just rioting. The real thing." Much later, he commented: "What is going to happen in the States over the Watergate Affair? Sounds rather a dirty show to me." For a brief period he was in the hospital ("full of cripples and nut cases") on account of the recurring problems with his legs. He noted that "the idea of cutting them off with a circular saw has been abandoned for the moment."

Once again I began to sense discontent. If he could only sell his cottage in Rhodesia, he said wistfully, he would move to Mozambique and "learn the lingo, drink the local vinho tinto and catch a fish now and then." He was sure that by plunging his legs into seawater, they would be restored and he would no longer be a burden on others. Hermes's visits had become less and less frequent, and his mind was turning once again to the island. Perhaps if he were in Mozambique, I theorized, he imagined he might find a dhow and a good boatman and ghost across the watery frontier to the island where once he had been so free.

In 1973 my letters to Latham were returned marked Addressee Unknown. I was now based in London making documentaries for a natural history film series. Finally, I wrote Charles Miller for help in locating the old man, and on Thanksgiving 1974, when I returned to Great Britain from an overseas filming location, Charles's letter was waiting for me. Yes, he had just heard from Latham. The old man had written him a rambling note, partially incoherent. Apparently there had been trouble in Rhodesia and he was now living in Dorset, England, at a house called The Old Fox. I cabled Latham immediately and his reply arrived two days later. He was delighted to find me so close at hand. "I had an awful thought that someone in the Congo may have taken a yen to you and put you in a pot."

Yes, there had been trouble. In fact—although he did not admit to it—his whole world was clearly in shambles. Hermes had committed him to hospital and, while he was under strict doctor's orders not to move from his bed, she had obtained the deed to his house, transferred it to her name, sold it and run off with the proceeds to Southwest Africa. Latham's only comment was, "As my Great Grandmother used to say, 'I am not amused.' "

Against this backdrop of deception, Latham had managed to board an airplane, having at last made up his mind to return to England after thirty-seven years. His first view of the land of his birth was through the windows of an ambulance bound for Dorset. There he became a paying guest of old East African friends who rented him a room on the second floor of their thatch-roofed house. Festooned with cardigans and scarves, he was, according to his account, now doing his best to adapt to the British climate. He rose early, as was his custom, to write all his friends and acquaintances of the last seventy years, advising them of his new address. Revived by a cup of Earl Grey tea, he set out on a marathon walk—the cold be damned. Midday was saluted with a pink gin at his desk and in the evening he joined his friends in the drawing room for the second drink of the day, for dinner and, no doubt, recollections. Although he had never seen a television before, he disapproved of the contraption on sight, often demonstrating against it by retiring early. As always, his was a lonely life. His hosts kept to themselves and his main pleasure was sending and receiving mail. He pleaded with me to come one day, pick him up at The Old Fox to "down the odd Pink Gin or so with lunch at the local pub." Please, he insisted, bring a blonde. "Tell her that I am 82 . . . so she won't be disappointed." He clearly hoped I might conjure up Mary Anne, who was still living in Kenya.

Instead, I brought Valerie (an invented name), a brunette. She was tall and laughing, intense about art and eager to meet the great Edwardian gentleman who appeared so often in my stories. We took an early-morning train one Sunday from Waterloo Station and, at Dorchester, hired a taxi for the town of Piddletrenthide. The narrow, slippery High Street and the eponymous pheasant on the rattling sign above the door gave the Poacher's Inn the mark of Thomas Hardy. The old man had chosen well, I thought. When I opened the frosted-glass door, I realized I had not seen Latham in eight years. South Africa and Rhodesia, high hopes and grand larceny had interrupted our friendship, and now I hesitated, wondering if the old man's advanced years and his new status as a refugee from glorious M'Simbati would change my regard for him.

Anticipating that this was a moment not to be forgotten, the old man was impeccably dressed, straight-backed, the beard jutting beyond the silver-handled cane as though his profile was intended for a bas-relief in the crypt of a great cathedral. Seeing me from his distant corner, he rose slowly, his rheumy eyes seeming to melt. "Dear boy," he said, shaking his head in disbelief, not daring to release my hand. For a moment, his voice was sing-song, and when he cleared it his eyes suddenly fell on Valerie. He leaned over to kiss her hand with a gentleness reserved for porcelain. When at last he straightened himself to his full height, he began to slip back into his chair, as though a rug was slowly being pulled out from under him. His eyes never once left Valerie. "My dear, dear thing."

The owner of the pub, working the tables, knew the old man from previous visits. "Stand at attention when speaking to an officer," Latham barked at him all of a sudden. The owner, using his tray as a kind of ornamental sword, snapped his heels, arched his back and looked solemnly into the paneled wall. Semisatisfied, Latham turned to me and, in a loud and conspiratorial whisper, said: "Softer than porridge—these bloody N.C.O.'s."

Our luncheon was full of laughter. The old man effortlessly knocked back three pink gins while Valerie and I dithered with our Bloody Marys. We talked of Mary Anne, the island, South Africa, bloody Harold Wilson, bloody weather, bloody trade unionism (never of Hermes and the unpleasantness in Rhodesia), and after a lunch of thick soup, paté and coffee, I looked at my watch and hurried to say good-bye in order to catch our return train. "What is it," I asked the old man, still enthroned, both hands clasping the handle of his cane, "that would make you most happy?"

"One thing," he said without considering. I sat down to hear him better. "To return to Africa. It's where I promised I would leave my bones."

My parting words to Latham were, I recalled, muddled—something about not forgetting. They were uttered in total ignorance of the complexities of transporting an indigent old man to a black African country for final retirement. I had easily convinced him, by ill-conceived assurances, that Kenya would be ideal. Now I would have to obtain passage, a place for him to stay and official permission for him to settle in Kenya. Six days a week for the next two months I received a letter from him, begging me for news. The weather in Dorset had turned arctic and with only a small electric heater in his room, he had begun to suffer. His hosts, unaccustomed to sharing their house with anyone, had also grown cool, and it was clear Latham felt himself imposing on a friendship that was no more. He fired scores of questions at me in each of his letters, most of them relating to Lamu, the island off the coast of Kenya where I hoped to find him a cottage. Convinced that there were too many matters to be settled by mail, would I, he inquired, come to Dorset for a whole weekend? And, oh yes, would I be bringing Valerie?

On a mid-January Saturday Valerie and I drove to Piddletrenthide. The old man, waiting for us at the same table, was wearing his Charterhouse tie and double-breasted blazer. In numerous letters preceding the visit he had promised that there would be two Bloody Marys waiting for us, fires blazing in the rooms. He was as good as his word. In addition, the owner of the Poacher's Inn had been coached that we were prominent celebrities, verging on royalty, and during our stay, a whisper made the rounds of the hotel staff. Wherever we went eyes followed us with awe. One chambermaid curtsied. "To the most beautiful girl in the world," Latham toasted us at our table. "And the luckiest man in the world." I looked at Valerie and agreed.

During the weekend I discovered there was little room for compromise on the old man's future. He insisted on returning to East Africa by sea ("And I would insist on an outside cabin, please"). In Lamu the cottage would have to be on the beach with at least one guest room. And he would like to leave for Africa within the month. When I tried to help him with his continuing pension problems by seeking the assistance of the local vicar, whom we met on one of our Saturday walks, Latham cut him short: "Sorry, old boy, I'm Muslim."

That evening when we assembled for dinner downstairs, Latham was wearing an even more elegant tie. Carefully tiered on the table in front of him were several parcels wrapped in brown paper. One contained an album of pictures that he eagerly showed Valerie. Since each photograph suggested a story, it was not until much later, after coffee and brandy, when the table candles had become mere stubs, that he finally closed the book and looked at the other parcels. "I have a little Christmas present for you, long overdue, darling," he said, holding Valerie's hand and looking into her brown eyes. Out of a box came a Queen Anne silver tea caddy and a pair of Chinese tortoiseshell dishes that had once decorated a side table at M'Simbati. "Bon-bon dishes for you, darling." Valerie leaped from the table and gave the old man an enormous hug. I saw tears of pleasure coursing down his red cheeks.

The final package contained presents for me. The first was a pair of admiralty charts of the waters around M'Simbati. While dated 1874, they were, according to Latham, still the only accurate renderings of the shoreline. "Lieutenant Commander Gray, Royal Navy, onboard H.M.S. *Nassau,* must have bloody well known what he was doing."

The old man reached inside the parcel again. This time he produced a flag. Unfurled, the emerald green, sea blue, blood red stripes with a Union Jack in the left-hand corner were still as vivid, as cocky, as if they were flying over Wind's Whisper. "I can't," I said.

"What the bloody hell am I going to do with it if you don't take it? When those customs people in Kenya see it in my case, they'll throw me in irons and call the UN."

The M'Simbati flag must have traveled with Latham, along with the photograph albums and guest books, all the way through South Africa and Rhodesia. "You can't give things like that away," I insisted. "What happens if you're allowed to return to the island. Then what?"

"Then you personally can bring it down and raise it yourself. I'll be the first to salute."

I thought for a while, swirling the remains of my brandy in the glass. For a spell I did not notice that the old man had also produced his passport and had carefully laid it in front of him on the table. "One last thing," he asked. "What's your most permanent address?"

He carefully inscribed it onto the second page. Later I stole a look. My name filled the space inside the passport cover under the heading: "Person/persons to be notified in the event of death."

Back in London, I wrote Latham, thanking him for his gifts, praising him for gallantry and mentioning briefly that I had had a disagreement with Valerie on our return to London, and that we had decided to go our own ways. I had been smarting from too much togetherness and if anyone was to blame for the separation it was I. Now, both alone, no one was very happy.

"Johnnie, old boy," he replied, "I am very distressed about the trouble with Valerie. I thought you were the greatest of pals and I hate to think that you have had a tiff and now both of you are unhappy. . . . If there is anything that I can do to heal the breach, please let me know. I know too well what unhappiness is. I have had a lot of it in the long years that I have lived . . . I love my friends and I will do anything to make them happy and you and Valerie are the only real friends that I have now . . . I seem to be the last survivor of the Battle of Agincourt, when I left my bow and arrow on the battlefield and went off with another buddy, to the local *estaminet* and did some wenching there. Now those good old days are over for me. The heart is willing but the flesh is weak."

For the next few months I was away in Africa on a filming reconnaissance. While there I inquired about cottages in Lamu and prepared the way for the old man's arrival. Latham, meanwhile, kept busy at his typewriter. His application to the Principal Immigration Officer in Nairobi was a document of great dignity: "While in Tanzania, I got on well with the African and with other nationalities. I had a lot of African friends in all parts of the country, and they knew that my sympathies were with them. . . . In view of the above I am writing you to request that I be issued with an Entry Permit, Class L, so that I can go ahead with my preparations regarding booking a passage by sea, and bidding farewell to my friends . . ."

Latham felt that my letters to the various shipping companies were inadequate and he started writing them himself, enumerating the many advantages of having him aboard one of their ships. Despite his age, he insisted, he was as fit as anyone. Furthermore, since he was fluent in Swahili, French, German and Spanish he would be a positive asset in the officers' mess. Not receiving any replies, he wrote to me in desperation: "Just tell them that I have traveled thousands and thousands of miles, in all kinds of ships, except luxury liners, and I have never been seasick in my life. Also, that on one side of my family tree, I can trace my origins back to the days when we swung by our tails from branches, and on the other side, I am related to the mountain goat which jumps from precipice to precipice and back to piss. No need to worry about my falling down and breaking a leg."

Valerie reported to me on the telephone that his letters to her had become daily rituals, after our last visit to Dorset. Later she allowed me to look at several paragraphs. His first letter had begun "Valerie darling." In the next one he opened with "My darling Valerie." From then onward his greetings were almost invariably *"Carissima mia,"* and his closing words *"Yo te beso los ojos, mi corazon dulce. Con todo mi amor, Latham."*

For those who did not know Latham, these letters might be misconstrued—the work of a prurient imagination. No doubt her fresh beauty, elegant manners and laughter had stolen his heart, and almost every paragraph was evidence that he spent most of the day doting on her ("Between writing to you, I have been composing a song for you but I am stuck at the moment for the last lines. I will sing it to you *sotto voce* next time we see each other. Perhaps you will be able to help . . .").

I understood his infatuation. He had spent so much of his life in isolation that the doings of other men and women had come to assume for him epic grandeur. People were either beyond contempt or above suspicion. Rules pummeled into his backside by a score of Edwardian nannies had never been put to a test during intervening years. With so much time to ponder and embroider he had come to perceive women, particularly those who were well born, as flawless. Men he understood better— they were liable to temptations and deceits—but women, given the correct chemistry of birth, were demigods.

There was one dramatic exception to Latham's rule: his own mother. According to his pieced-together story, his mother had clearly despised him. He grew up knowing that a few days prior to his birth she had tried to induce a miscarriage by racing around Hyde Park on her most skittish horse. From the minute he was born she abandoned him to the care of nannies, avoiding the very sight of him at all costs. His brother and sister were apparently doted on. He was mocked. Now, after some eighty years, I could still see Latham's hurt. Only a psychologist could tell me whether his view of women, his decision never to marry, his life as a recluse had their roots in his loveless Victorian childhood. I can remember asking him several times why his mother had singled him out for such cruelty. He always replied with an enigmatic smile as though there was indeed more to the story, but that it was one secret he intended to keep. In the meantime, he had found a goddess to redeem his childhood: Valerie.

In one January letter to her he began: "Your lovely letter

arrived just now (12:30 P.M.) and you have cheered me up so much, so I went at once to the windowsill where I keep my stock of Gin, poured out an East African–size drink, looked towards where I thought London ought to be, then drank to you and said, 'Carissima mia, yo te amo,' and I hope your ears were burning at that moment." Later, discussing her activities at Sotheby's, he inquired: "I wonder if your boss would put me up for auction as the last survivor of the Battle of Agincourt—the only true Victorian living outside of a museum?" His letters touched on many subjects. In answer to Valerie's generosity in helping with his passport expenses, he insisted he would pay her back: "No back chat please or I shall put you over my knee and spank that portion of your anatomy that is most fleshy and least sunburnt, designed by the Almighty for the express purpose of spanking. Compri?" Later, in a reflective tone, he said: "I was beginning to give up the fighting after I left Rhodesia. My legs were giving me hell at times and I felt that no one cared a damn about me any longer, until John brought you down to the pub and we met. You both have put new life into the old carcass and now I am ready to do battle once more. Up the rebels."

Latham made no secret why he was determined to return to Africa by sea. "I should like to go round the Cape and then up the coast. Perhaps," he mused, "I can ask the Captain, when we pass the mouth of the Rovuma River, to go in a little closer so I can again see my lovely island."

When I returned from my assignment in Africa, Latham reported in a letter that he had nothing but bad news from the shipping companies: "The Powers That Be in Mombasa say that I am too old to travel on their cargo ships. They think I might fall overboard or trip over the ship's cat. Did you ever hear such tripe? So now, it looks like some larger steamer but if the Middle East War starts up again, then I'll have to walk to Kenya. I am willing to sign on as a deck steward. Anything to get back to East Africa."

Feverishly, I persisted with other shipping lines. Most of them had accommodations for occasional passengers bound for Mombasa but all of them refused to carry anyone over eighty. On the other hand, Latham could make the journey as far as Durban on a passenger liner. But from there it was anyone's guess how he could reach Mombasa.

At last I made the only decision. I purchased him an airplane ticket to Nairobi and waited to be soundly rebuked. Instead, Latham accepted the news fatalistically. At that moment he had become distracted by a battle being waged against civil servantdom. At the age of eighty-two he had been denied an "over eighties' pension" to supplement his minimal Colonial Service stipend. The National Insurance Commissioners argued that he had not lived in England for the last ten years and therefore was not eligible. Latham's reply pointed out the anomaly in the argument: In 1945 the then governor of Tanganyika had personally asked him to stay on in the Colony after ultimate independence "so as to give a tone to the place." For Latham that command might just as well have been handed down from H.M. The Queen. "How in God's name could I serve my Queen and at the same time comply with the Pension people? If that, Johnnie, is British justice then they can fight the next war without me."

Having terminated all further communication with "the bloody bureaucrats," he began steeling himself for the flight in the "flying machine" scheduled for June 4. His Class L Entry Permit into Kenya had been granted, and Mary Anne had recently cabled me from Nairobi confirming our arrangements for the house in Lamu, and saying that she and her husband would meet Latham in Nairobi, entertain him for a week or so at their house and then transport him down to the coast.

Since the two days in London prior to his flight were to be his first view of that city in thirty-eight years, I tried to make the visit a landmark. A car and driver met him at Waterloo Station and a whirl of heavy social engagements kept him occupied from early-morning kippers to the last brandy of the night. He took great pleasure in decrying the decay of London. He was at pains to recognize anything as we drove from the station to his hotel. He claimed he was confused about how all the cars could fit into the streets, horrified by the din and, most of all, outraged by the coarseness of the language he claimed he heard on the streets. But as much as he pretended to be scandalized, he was equally fascinated, and whenever a woman came into view, his manners suddenly became swashbuckling and courtly.

Without doubt, the highlight of his visit was a dinner party given by Valerie at her flat on his first night. He arrived in his chauffeur-driven car, behaving as if he were on his way to Lillie

Langtry's for a *cinq à sept.* He was somehow sure that Valerie's father, the ambassador, would immediately challenge him with an "Exactly what are your intentions with my daughter?" So he would have to be discreet. A horde of Valerie's friends, her mother, her father and sister, met him at the door. They had all been hearing about the gallant gentleman who swore by pink gins, and now they wanted to see him for themselves. Soon he forgot the forthcoming dawn duel in Hyde Park. He located a central seat and luxuriated in the attention of all the women who settled themselves nearby, some on the arms of sofas, others on the floor. He told his tales with wild abandon, hardly stopping for dinner, and much later, when we were the last to leave, he whispered to me that Valerie was still the most beautiful girl in the world and that she and I had made a wise decision to be reunited. I never told him that these two days of togetherness had been solely in his honor.

On the next evening Valerie and I took him to the theater and then to one of the more elegant restaurants in London. For him Hermione Gingold in *A Little Night Music* had a "common" voice, and the restaurant, its excellent food and sumptuous decor be damned, catered to a rather "low-class" clientele. "In the old days," he claimed, "we would have asked anybody who didn't lower their voice at another table to leave. Simple as that."

The old man's spite for London was, in fact, his pleasure. Years later, in recounting his two days there, he grandly peeled through names of smart hotels and restaurants as tokens of the many worlds he had inhabited and as further proof that "civilization" was no longer to be found in the West. At the airport on the morning of June 4, as I prepared to say good-bye, I suggested I get some books for him to read on the airplane. "Not necessary," he replied. "I plan to do a lot of talking."

As I drove back from the airport, I thought I had made a mistake. The old man was returning to the Africa he called home, but to a country he barely knew. In Kenya it would be difficult for him not to be confronted by the realities of a nation that cared little about the past—particularly his past. How many years did he have to live? Would his last days be miserable? What would happen when he could no longer move around? Who would then be responsible for him?

Predictably, Africa did not receive Latham with the welcome he expected. It seemed to conspire against its own best champion and for a year afterward I blamed myself for having advocated his return. Mary Anne and her husband, however, were the best of allies. In Nairobi, they entertained Latham like the sultan he had once been on M'Simbati. They drove him to the coast, hired a plane for the last leg, and when they discovered that the Lamu airfield was underwater, they diverted to another airfield on the mainland where they hired a 1924 Model T Ford truck to transport him the remaining distance to the island ferry. By the time they reached Latham's new home, a thatched house on the beach, he claimed he "was strong enough only to mix everyone pink gins" while the others cleaned the kitchen and shifted furniture. Whatever the renting agent had promised me by letter she had failed to provide, and the house, according to Latham, was in a state of ruin. Instantaneously, his rueful view of selected womanhood had set a new target: the rental agent. Within a few days he worked himself into a lather of carefully controlled outrage. Essentially, Latham's complaint was not that she had failed to live up to her side of the bargain but that her manner with the African was not that of a civilized human being. "As you know," he wrote, "I am fairly tough, but to use 4-letter words all day long to the African is just outside the pale." Later, he wondered aloud why nobody had done "the noble thing and slit her throat."

Soon most of his letters were consumed by spleen. The rental agent was "at the moment," he wrote in late June, "in Nairobi Hospital. I don't know what her complaint is but there is a clear sign that mental disturbance comes into it somewhere." In conclusion, he wrote, "The woman is as crooked as a dog's hind leg."

Lamu had traditionally attracted European eccentrics. As long ago as the 1890s, remittance men had found a home in this peculiar Swahili town where everything short of murder (and sometimes including murder) was accepted behavior. Twenty-six bordellos for a total population of six thousand gave it some glamour, and its reputation, enhanced by lonely beaches, still continues to attract Europeans who find comfort amid the seedy decadence of another culture. Since Latham's house was well outside the town limits he need never have worried about the others. Nevertheless, the proximity bothered him. For a while he met only one other European and she was, he claimed, "as tight as a tick." Latham believed that white people had obligations of behavior in Africa and that his fellow residents in Lamu were, by and large, unaware of such traditions. In one letter he proudly proclaimed how he was perceived by the other expatriates. "I heard that I am not liked as I pay 5/-a kilo for fish. The others want to beat the fishermen down. I don't play that game. I know the risk the fisherman takes at night if a sudden storm comes on . . ."

For the next two months Latham's rage seemed to subside. I always hoped he would sound happy in his letters, maybe comparing Lamu to M'Simbati, but his legs, suffering from age, kept him more or less housebound. Nearby there was an attractive hotel catering to discriminating travelers who wished to avoid well-worn tourist trails, and I hoped Latham would acquire the habit of stopping there in the evening for a "sundowner." But by now he was experiencing another of his periodic "cash-flow" problems and he could not afford such luxuries. His principal pleasure was a gift from Mary Anne—a cat who was forever "in the family way." Latham noted in resignation that she had "a common taste in mates."

It is certain he dreamed of his island far to the south. There was always a chance, he believed, he would be allowed to return and, secretly, I was sure, he was preparing for that day. In the meantime, there were other dreams. One of his few friends in Lamu was an Arab, and in the course of their reminiscings, Latham discovered that a piece of land, beyond the hotel, high on the great dune, was available for purchase. He immediately sent me a description of the plot, and a few suggestions as to how I should proceed. He would undertake the building of my house. It would be a large and rambling affair and would have an unbroken view of the distant coast of Africa, the headland on Manda Island and the Indian Ocean on nearly every side, breaking on the reefs. "At night you can stand on your veranda," he promised, "and pee into the sea and listen for the splash . . . Peace, perfect bloody peace." On one side of the house, there would be, of course, a wing for Latham. "Then I could live there and look after the place for you, make a garden, keep the odd chicken, and when you come down with a sample of your blondes for a nice rest at the seaside, the place will be spic and span. I don't think you'll regret it. It's by far the nicest thing I've seen since M'Simbati.''

I replied that the idea sounded very tempting but that I had neither the money to build the house, the blondes to fill it, nor the wherewithal to take regular holidays to Lamu. I suggested we delay the purchase. Perhaps I could find a partner.

My reply went unnoticed. "Now a suggestion in regard to the construction," he began in his next letter. "Thick side walls, for there is a strong wind all the time. The roof should be made of Bangalore tiles, as all the Arab-type roofs here with *makuti* poles as supports are N.B.G. [no bloody good]."

At the same time, Latham had developed an interest in world news. The best excitement all summer was the Israeli commando raid on Entebbe Airport. It was "about the best show that has ever been pulled off. Idi Amin must be biting the carpet over it." In October he wound himself into a fine rage over the British handling of the Ulster insurrection: "The trouble there is the British are pissing their pants with fright and are quite useless to deal with a schoolboy rising let alone the Irish. During the General Strike in '26, I was home from East Africa and rejoined my old mob, the Gunners. I had command of a battery of 18-pounders and I took them through the East End of London with the guns loaded and hoping for trouble but the bastards only threw dead cats at us . . ."

Latham had at last found a friend. Anne Spoerry, the Flying Doctor, had a house nearby and on her occasional visits to the island, she stopped at his house to check his legs. "I think she likes me," he wrote, "as we talk French together and I tell her all about Paris when M. Escoffier was the chef at Chez Henri."

Sometime during the next year I planned to be in East Africa on a vacation. Friends from America were joining me and I promised Latham a visit at the termination of a train trip we planned, from Nairobi to Mombasa. Latham, however, did not approve of our mode of travel: "From what I have heard there is about one engine running on the whole system. If your guests are prepared to push the ruddy train you may expect to arrive somewhere in the bush a week or so behind schedule. Don't let me deter you but I hope to God you're not on the ruddy train when she goes over the cud somewhere. In the words of the 1st World War song, 'I don't want to lose you.' "

In December Latham moved into a small house in the nearby village of Shella, thereby terminating any further association with the dreaded rental agent. In his new home, rooms and plumbing were laid out for Arab use, but after minor modifications, the old man seemed happy at last. "At least I can bar the door," he noted. The rent was in line with his modest pension, and for the first time since he was at Lamu he became more or less solvent. In a letter thanking me for a contribution, he mentioned that he had rewritten his will to make me his sole beneficiary. Startled, I told him that he should think of others. A few days before Christmas, he replied: "I am sorry that you were worried about my leaving my bits and pieces to you, but I have no living relations. I am the last of a long line of odds and sods who have served their Kings and Queens for generations in the armed forces of the Crown. Now I am the last and the name dies with me. As you are the only real friend I have now, I thought you would like to have my things, although they don't amount to much."

In my last letter before my vacation I told him that it was time I started thinking of settling down. My continuous traveling was beginning to tell. In his reply he agreed with me: "You are not in the same place long enough to pick the ticks off your backside." Then, not so subtly, he began crusading for his favorite girl: "So you are going to settle down in 1976. You, Johnnie, are the luckiest bloody man I know. There you are with the loveliest girl in the world, Valerie, and you are looking for someone else. You go and see Valerie and ask her, and I'll bet a dollar to a doughnut that she will say 'yes,' and then see that she does not change her mind by you doing something with a blonde and she gets to hear about it. Marry the girl before someone else asks her, and then you will carry out my toast to you both at dinner at the Poacher's Inn: 'To Valerie, the most beautiful girl in the world, and to Johnnie, the luckiest man alive.' My toasts always come true."

The very next day, brooding that he had oversold the idea of marriage, he wrote to me again, to show that he was still a hell-raiser: "If you want to amuse the girls, take a French letter and fit it over a sherry glass which has been filled with Eno's Fruit Salts and water. Then watch the girls' faces. You can tell at once the ones that do and the ones that don't." He added that he had booked accommodation at the hotel for me, but "I could not tell them if you wanted a double or a treble-bedded room."

On February 22 my friends and I flew to the hotel for a brief lunch, bound for the north. On arriving, I wrote a note to be delivered to the old man. It read: "Don't think you are paying enough taxes. Please see me at the hotel.   [signed] Harold Wilson."

I followed the note up the hill, curious to see if the old man really was comfortable in his new home. The street was only wide enough for two fully laden donkeys to pass, and the open sewers abutted against the walls of the houses. Ruins of coral-walled Arab mansions were now used only by fruit bats and hunting cats; small children, their lips crusted in snot, ran along beside me until we came to a square. Here there was only a tin-roofed store, and veering to the right, the road, seething with the smell of coriander, became narrow and dank. Because the walls on either side sometimes rose three stories high the street was mostly in shadow, and lichen grew between the paving stones. When we reached the door to the old man's house I let the messenger precede me while I waited. Three minutes later I opened the door. Latham's walled garden was hardly larger than a closet. On the far side, stairs ran into his kitchen, which led to the sitting room. When I entered the room Latham was still seated, and once his eyes were able to pick me out he shook his head in feigned exasperation. *"Hodi,"* I yelled.

"Karibu, you old devil," he replied. *"Karibu. Karibu."* ("Welcome, welcome, welcome.")

 Four porters carried the old man down to the hotel in a makeshift sedan chair. Dressed in his Panama hat from the island and carrying his ornamental fly whisk, he was like a monument—a white Jomo Kenyatta chiseled out of pre-Cambrian stone. In one of his letters he had boasted: "I am greeted by all the Africans, who already know quite a lot about me, *'bwana Mzee Kidevu'* ['The old gentleman of the white beard'], which is a great mark of respect." Today, however, the young boys scurrying beside this human talisman had another name for him. In piping voices they cried out: *"Bwana baado kufa"* ("The old man not yet dead"). With a different alliteration and meter the greeting soon became a question: *"Bwana, baado kufa?"* ("Old man, aren't you dead yet?") Laughing with pleasure, Latham yelled back: *"Baado."* ("Not yet.")

My friends, waiting on the veranda overlooking the beach, had been primed to meet the old man, but the spectacle of his arrival, the living anachronism, took them by surprise. "He had such naughty eyes," one noted.

Once Latham was on his feet, he carefully studied the group. All of a sudden, his eyes froze on a tall dark-haired girl standing apart from all the rest. Valerie had joined me on the trip, in a spirit of reconciliation, and we had both decided to keep her presence a secret from the old man, until the very last moment. The effect took the wind out of him. He stood motionless trying to catch his breath and then with a sweeping hug he clutched her against his chest and closed his eyes.

We were only with Latham for two hours, but he never forgot the visit. The men seemed to make little impression on him, but the faces of the women, particularly Valerie's, clustered around him at the luncheon table became fixed in his memory. He wrote all his correspondents about the event, and even his letters to me over the next few weeks seemed full of a new testiness, as if he had rediscovered his own sex appeal. From advice handed out to him at lunch, he had begun to tape-record his memoirs. Writing, he had insisted to me, was never one of his strong points, but storytelling he enjoyed. "I know my limitations. I am a good raconteur and have a good speaking voice and can keep people interested." But as soon as he started working with the recorder, new problems arose. The machine, he claimed, terrified him, and because the children were always "howling in the streets" in the day, and the cats always "making love overhead" at night, he could find the right time to concentrate.

In June, there were new problems with his legs and he admitted wanly that he felt "like the last rose of summer." The bureaucratic machinery responsible for forwarding his pension check from England had failed him, and through no fault of his own, Latham was broke once again. "I don't wish him any bad luck," he said, referring to a member of the Pension Board, "but I hope his balls turn to bombs and blow him to buggery."

He was sure that my reconciliation with Valerie would now be permanent, and try as I might, I could not convince him that the differences that had always separated us were, in the last reckoning, permanent. While counseling me to see more and more of her, in spite of the ungainly truth, his letters to her were full of avuncular advice. "If you have not gotten rid of your cold," he urged, "try my old father's cure: hang a stocking on the end of your bed, drink hot rum until you see two stockings. You are cured . . . A message from my old heart, darling Valerie." There was no doubt, he continued, that the reason for her feeling out of sorts was her ceaseless round of London activities. "Give your nerves a rest." he pleaded. "Have you moderns never heard of M. Emile Coué, the famous French doctor who came over to England in the First World War and cured thousands from shell shock? They had to say a simple thing every morning and night: 'Day by day, in every way, I am getting better and better.' They had to say it ten times morning and evening. Just those very simple words put thousands and thousands of badly shell-shocked men on their feet. I know. I was one of them."

By now I had made my long-promised visit to Kenya, and Latham did not waste a day to send Valerie a complete description. He disapproved of the film production manager who had accompanied me but was impressed by the talents of a painter staying at the hotel with us. The fact that this painter, David Hemmings, was best known as an actor made no impression on Latham. He had nothing but contempt for modern movie-making: "They haven't made much that was good since Chaplin and I were the only Englishmen in Hollywood before World War I."

In the same letter he complained to Valerie that I had asked him, during my visit, to start writing short stories. "What John-nie does not realize is that I am an old man," he pointed out. "I honestly do not think that I am up to doing something quite new at my age. Just to take an instance. I told you once about an extraordinary love affair I had during a 10-day leave in Paris during the First World War. You say it was one of the loveliest things that you have ever heard. Yes. But I could not possibly write about it, could I? To start with, I should be breaking faith with the lady and as far as I know she may still be alive . . . Again, how could I possibly describe our love, that beautiful house, garden, the whole amazing affair? How could I sit down in cold blood and write about it? It's just not possible. Why should the public know about a thing as beautiful as that?"

By November, Latham had finished his tape-recording sessions and, having abandoned my advice about short stories, he was beginning to take an interest, albeit critical, in the odd visitors who occasionally stopped at the hotel in Shella. "It's been quiet and lonely since you all left. The hotel seems empty and the only person I saw there was a Dutchman. All he drank was a Fanta, whatever that is. He wore a very small peaked blue cap, at least three sizes too small for him, sitting on top of a mass of gray untidy hair. He had patchy whiskers all over his face, a sweat shirt and very tight shorts. Around his neck he wore oddments which I took to be a camera and meters. He looked just like the old stage type of German spy, circa 1910. I forgot to mention he had glasses and false teeth. The boots were the type you climb Alps in. All he needed was an Alpinestock and a chamois tail in the back of his cap and he would have brought the house down at the Pavilion."

Over the years, letters to Lilani, the lawyer, in Mtwara had not been answered, and now the East African papers were reporting the discovery of titanium on the island of M'Simbati. The old man asked me to write the mining moguls of South Africa for their intercession on his behalf. He imagined himself someday returning to Wind's Whisper as the Titanium Baron. All my letters to government officials, however, never drew a reply, and I had to disappoint him once again. Latham's dream of leaving his bones on his island now seemed remote.

The old man began working on two other campaigns. One was to leave Shella for a higher climate in Kenya. He was sure that the sultry weather at the coast accounted for the continuing problems with his legs, and anyway, he was lonely. As soon as I told him that I had written the owner of a small up-country hotel asking whether the old man would be accepted as a resident guest, Latham wrote me impatiently: "I shall ask the owner if he will allow me to have a dog. A little dachs would be perfect. May I have a table to myself in the dining room? Can I have a radio and listen to the other stations? Not Moscow. Can I keep a bottle of gin in my room or must I go to the bar?"

In December, when Latham heard that he had been accepted

at the Sportsman's Arms in Nanyuki, he was in an exuberant mood in what he proclaimed to be his "last letter from Lamu": "I shall be as happy as a dog with two cocks and a street full of lampposts. And if I can't get well, I will ask you to come and cut my throat . . . I hope this is going to be my last move. Too old now to amble about with a couple of dud legs. Incidentally, the Post Office here is just too wonderful. I have just gotten a post card from Valerie dated July 29th. Vive le Jet Age."

Latham's second cause had to do with my proposed film about the early days in East Africa. In his letters he had begun to audition for a part, believing that he could lend some authenticity to one of the characters. He began this campaign subtly: "I don't suppose there are many of us old-timers left now—those who know how things were done and can talk the King's English and dress properly. The moderns will ruin the film." Later, noting that I had not risen to his bait, he became more direct: "If you do give me a part, I imagine that all I have to do is to be absolutely natural, just me as I am today. I can look the part and I have the presence and above all the right voice. This may sound rather snobbish but we may have something to be snobbish about." In the end I had to extinguish Latham's hopes altogether. The film still was not set, the unions were uncooperative and acting had changed since the days when he (and Chaplin) were cantering down Hollywood and Vine. With fierce pluck, Latham hit upon an alternative plan: "I know you will do everything you can to get me on the show as Tech Adviser and I can do that job as well as anyone as I have been in East Africa for over 50 years and know just what went on in those days . . . Anyway, if you don't have me, you will have to put another old man on the job, otherwise the modern long-haired pansies will ruin the show . . . I should hate the film to be a burlesque."

For the first two months of the next year I did not hear any more from Latham. Others wrote to say that he had been flown up to Nanyuki by Dr. Anne Spoerry. The hotel, where he now resided, was operated by an urbane Indian; it had other elderly residents and I hoped Latham would find himself new friends. His silence may have been caused by the news about Valerie. He now knew that after all the stormy partings and reconciliations we had decided to start new lives away from each other.

Not until the middle of February, after I had absently for-

42

gotten both his and Valerie's birthday, did he write about his new home. "Yes, I like it here—very quiet except when bus-loads of bloody tourists arrive. They demand everything at the double. God, what people—East Germans, Poles, Checkos, Bashi Basuks . . . I have got a nice little cottage at the bottom of the garden . . . The food is very good and lots of it and I am getting a tummy like a poisoned pup . . . There is a nice little bar and the barman now knows the right way to make a pink gin."

I arranged for a friend of mine, a member of the House of Commons, to write the British High Commissioner in Dar Es Salaam asking for an investigation of Latham's claims to the island. Latham added to the request a four-page description of his long-ago life, and an accounting of his loss. In the end, the British diplomatic corps could do very little. The Tanzanians shrugged their shoulders, Lilani could not be located and the southern coastal district was still off bounds. My hope of a personal investigation was out of the question.

But at least the old man had regained his old martial spirit. His current *bête noir* was the Voice of America. In May 1977 Latham addressed its headquarters in Washington, D.C., in a letter reminiscent of those he wrote during the island's independence: "I am writing to request that you take the broadcast, the 'News in Special English,' off the air. The broadcast is an insult to our beautiful language and Mr. Al Ross, the narrator, cannot speak English, mispronounces words and has an abominable delivery. His voice is American with a common New York accent. No Englishman ever spoke English in such a way. . . . If you wish to instruct the American public in the art of speaking English properly, then may I suggest that you request the BBC in London to send some of their broadcasters to America to teach you. I wonder what the American public would say if the BBC put on a news broadcast in 'Special American' with some Englishman gagging it up in a common New York accent and mispronouncing words? Mr. Ross would be better employed on his farm planting groundnuts [peanuts] and looking after the pigs (hogs to you) than using up my valuable air time with his stupid talking. . . . I am sending a copy of this letter to an American friend to insert in the American press in the hope that some good may come of it."

Caught once again in these global crossfires, I made a

halfhearted attempt to see that Latham's letter made the rounds in America. As it had on other occasions, his anger soon abated. He was now excited to know that some American Air Force personnel were about to become fellow residents at the hotel. "They are making a new airfield," he explained, "complete with hangars and control towers so they can park their huge jets here for the duration of the next war. The hotel will cheer up when they arrive in March. I shall parade in front of the Commanding Officer and ask for a job as an interpreter—American/English/ki-Swahili. I am looking forward to seeing their faces when they ask for coffee and they are given the stuff that Din [the hotel owner] charges 6/- [eighty-four cents] for. . . . Someone is going to shoot the cook."

When the Americans finally arrived, Latham introduced himself and made several new friends, particularly among the wives and girl friends of the pilots. He had now decided that the hotel was really not up to standards and that he should not accept any more alleged insubordination from the hotelkeeper, "a low-caste Indian." "Din dislikes me," he said with sweeping conviction, "as the Indians hate British Army Officers." By encouraging the friendly Americans to take sides in his private war, the demands for better food, service and coffee became more strident, and soon Shamsu Din was bridling whenever he laid eyes on the old man. In my letters I urged conciliation and berated the old man for stirring up trouble when he could ill afford to find a new home. My advice went unheeded and Latham became jubilant in the company of all the young warriors: "The American Air Force boys are still here but are getting a move on now to finish the job and be out before the Cubans, the Abbos, the Somalis and the Russians come down here on their way south to have a crack at the Rhodesians and South Africans, with the kind permission of Jimmy Carter, of course. . . . That only leaves a few old sweats from the 1st World War, like us, to repel them. I can swear at them in Spanish and wave my gimpy leg. You could come into action wearing your new 10-gallon Stetson, riding your latest bronco, with Jimmy Carter, leading the 7th Fleet, having sailed up the Tana River via Mombasa, waving his flag—for Women's Lib and Human Rights. It will so demoralize the Cubans that they will retire on Nairobi, taking all the fluff with them, so as to deprive the Americans of a nice bit of tail. The

7th Fleet will then insist on returning, via Cairo, and going to the Waza and then onto Marseilles and seeing Madame Cleri and finding out what the latest French movements are."

Latham's flight of fancy abruptly ended, and he proceeded more cautiously: "No news here except we are waiting for the locust invasion from up north."

When my proposed feature film about the early days in Kenya was canceled Latham was nearly as disappointed as I. Shortly afterward I left London for the United States. Latham felt that I had abandoned the film project too hastily, even though the decision had not been mine but that of financial experts. Almost every one of Latham's successive letters alluded to the rare opportunity still awaiting me in Kenya: "But, my old buddy, why not do the film out here with the local talent? Mary Anne has an Indian cameraman who she says is the best in Africa. There are lots of pretty girls. Then how many of the old sweats like me are there who would jump at the chance of doing the old days again, just for the hell of it? The train is in some yard in Nairobi. All it wants is a drop of oil and a good push and it's off again, hell-bent for Mombasa. . . . Most of us are old soldiers. We know what an order is and how to obey it. We were brought up on discipline . . ."

In February 1978 a violent blizzard blanketed the American Northeast with nearly a yard of heavy snow. When Latham heard on the BBC that a state of emergency had been declared across Rhode Island, he somehow felt that I was in grave danger. He cabled Valerie in London to call the American embassy and plead to have a helicopter flown to the little village where I live. He then sent a frantic letter to my father in New York and another to my sister, living not far away in Rhode Island. His letter to me was the shortest one I had ever received from him. All it said was, "Please let me know how you are and if there is any damn thing I can do from here."

I cabled him immediately to reassure him, explaining that I had waited out the storm by working feverishly on a screenplay and that there had been plenty of provisions in the house. "I got the wind up after that BBC broadcast," he explained. "I have been having kittens ever since. I had visions of you and Hilary [my sister] and her little boy, snowed under, no light or water, air getting fouler by the hour, eating tins of army rations. All the time you were as snug as a bug in a rug knocking back the odd rye . . ."

In 1978, Latham began suffering more than usual from the infirmities of old age. His legs, he explained, were not responding to any treatment at all. The head coach for an English rugby team, staying at the hotel, had tried massaging them; the Italian doctor in the local Roman Catholic mission had given him five different pills and a new ointment; and in desperation Latham had even gone on a crash diet, denying himself his precious pink gin in the evening. All had been in vain, for in September he was in the local cottage hospital, despairing that he would always have to walk like "a crippled crab."

The only medicine that had any effect on Latham in 1978 was a cause. Whenever he found a victim for one of his querulous campaigns, his legs immediately healed. His sense of survival seemed to verify an aphorism from his schoolboy days— Pompey's exhortation to the crew members of his galley as they feared for their lives in a storm: *"Navigare necesse est, vivere non necesse—"* ("It is better to sail than to live"). Equally with Latham, matters of health were of little consequence next to goals of the heart, principles of life. In May, for instance, one such issue sustained him enough to keep him walking for four weeks. He had become outraged that a film company, engaged in the remake of *Tarzan,* had canceled their bookings at the Sportsman's Arms because, he presumed, the accommodations were found to be inadequate. He had been looking forward to some new faces and their change in plans was, no doubt, a disappointment. "Hell's bells," he complained. "What do these people want? What is the matter with tents? An English film company in 1930 filmed *The Blue Lagoon* at Mikindani [in Tanganyika] and lived in tents on the shore." In a titillating aside he mentioned that "The leading lady spent a lot of time in the *boma* with C. P. Lyons, the District Commissioner, as they did not film at night in those days." My curiosity whetted, I asked Latham for more details about the D.C. and the leading lady, and in his next letter, still cheered enormously by the pusillanimity of the *Tarzan* film crew, his story took a sudden twist. He claimed that he had forgotten the name of the leading lady but that "she was blond and got terribly sunburnt as she refused to listen to us old-timers who told her to rub olive oil over her exposed parts. In consequence she was burnt to hell and she was out of the show for some days, and had to live up at the house of C. P. Lyons. . . . I used to come in from Mpapura on my motor bike, 18 miles along a footpath, and dress her with olive oil. C. P. Lyons was too busy in the *boma* during the day and he was always too drunk in the evening to do anything except pour another pink gin. . . . Have you noticed that people never listen to advice from old-timers about anything?"

By the end of the year the snarls from Latham about the hotel management had become cries of outrage. Din, "that unspeakable cad," "the untouchable," "the Indian coolie," had at last given the old man notice to leave his establishment. Apparently there had been words and, according to Latham, Din had publicly insulted him, saying that he did not want his "1st Class hotel becoming a 3rd-rate boardinghouse for crippled old men." By now the American Air Force had also left and Latham had no regrets about his eviction since "there is no one to talk to here." On the other hand, he had no place to go, although he approached this crisis with cavalier unconcern. I furiously wrote to a number of homes for "distressed gentlefolk" in Kenya, hoping that someone would come to our rescue. Unknown to me, Latham calmly put his name up for membership to the local sports club. A few days before Din's eviction notice came due, his application at the club was accepted. As soon as he moved into his new cottage on the club grounds his mood turned to elation. Not one but two ladies were in residence at the club. They were both widows, within striking distance of his age, had lovely manners, good speaking voices and enjoyed his stories. At long last he did not have to complain about the company. Every morning when the air was clear, he reported, he could spot the distant snowcap on Mount Kenya from his doorstep. The view seemed to give him strength for his "five-furlong canter around the flower beds."

Latham was now preparing for my next visit to Kenya. I had promised to bring one of my documentary films to show to his friends at the club, and before I had time to comment he had arranged for the film to be shown to everyone living in and around Nanyuki. He wrote to the East African Women's League, advising them that they could raise money for their cause by sponsoring the event. "May I suggest," he added to the secretary of the League, "that all children be barred from entering as the only film I ever saw at the Club was completely ruined for the audience by a mob of screaming children. The children were mixed—some white, African and Indian. The worst behaved were, without doubt, the British." In a letter to me, Latham confided that he really wished the film would "make the kids yell and the women have kittens."

In describing me to his new friends I had become known as "the well-known American author and film producer," and when I finally arrived at the club for the Saturday gala in mid-April I sensed that I was being devoured by all the eyes in the dining room. Each of Latham's lady friends held silent domain over her separate table, and whenever I lifted a spoon to my mouth or twirled the red wine in my glass, I felt I was being filed into one scrapbook after another. Celebrities, it seemed, rarely stopped at the Nanyuki Sports Club. "You mustn't do that," I whispered to the old man. "I'm not famous."

Latham threw his head back and laughed, exposing a set of pink gums still too proud to wear false teeth. "You make me cry."

The old man was dressed in his double-breasted blue blazer and Charterhouse tie ("circa 1908"), and his hair, now snow-white, was so carefully slicked down that it seemed to drain into his trim turn-of-the-century beard. As part of our continuing charade, I had begun to address him as "The Earl Of Nanyuki," a title he much enjoyed. Apparently, he had not been entirely successful in discouraging mysterious rumors about his noble parentage, and the eyes that followed my every moment inevitably settled on his gallant features. Among his peers—all two of them—he was still very dashing. The survivor of General Gough's Immortal Fifth Army, the Sultan of M'Simbati held himself with that distinguished bearing I remembered so well when he only wore a *shuka,* a Panama hat and a gnu-tail flyswatter.

Much of my purpose in seeing the old man in Nanyuki was to discuss the island. "Latham," I began, "I think I can get to Mtwara now. The war's over. The place's no longer restricted. Maybe I can locate Lilani and the deed. Who knows—with a coat of paint and few bits of furniture, you might be able to return to Wind's Whisper, and sit on the beach where you belong."

For a while the old man was excited. We both recalled the coral gardens and the view of a great seagoing dhow beating its

48

way around the headland. But soon his mind rebelled. His voice became a whisper. "Can't you see," he said, "it's too bloody late." He carefully laid his coffee spoon in the saucer. "When they kicked me off the island in 1967 you remember what they said? It was 'for my own protection.' Remember? My question to them was: 'Protection from whom?' " His words were final. He eased his chair back from the table. "They won, didn't they?"

"Not entirely."

I doubt if the old man heard. In any case, we never talked of the island again. Having helped him from his chair, he leaned on his cane to steady himself for the final leg of our journey, into the theater where my film was to be shown. "The ancient monument is breaking up fast," he muttered, as we left the dining room. He led the way out into the night, down a footpath and into the theater. It was a bare wooden room with hard, unmatched seats.

In the ceiling some light bulbs had blown out, others were flickering. Since no one else had arrived, we chose the best seats. Our conversation had returned, as it often did, to his memories of World War I. We both agreed that Siegfried Sassoon's *Memoirs of a Fox Hunting Man* had said everything that needed saying. "The winners, especially the winners, lost," I said. My truism, however, was not entirely to his satisfaction.

"I'll tell you something," Latham interrupted. "You know when the world changed? I'll tell you." He paused to look over my shoulder at the white farmers and ranchers now filling the theater. "It happened long before the war. It began changing the day Keir Hardie walked into the House of Commons wearing a cap. Nothing was ever the same after that. He purposefully insulted *us* by not wearing a top hat."

Soon the old man noted with pleasure that the theater was nearly filled to capacity for my film. I perceived this moment to be a kind of valedictory tribute for him—the large audience was not just a triumph over anonymity but a symbol of our mutual success in fighting the enemies of his old age over these last fourteen years. Strangely, he never knew or would know how important that battle had been for me too, how much I had learned about private principles, amid abuse, pain and loneliness. Somehow he saw gratitude proceeding in only one direction.

"You've heard about Valerie," I said, breaking the silence.

The old man knew that she had found someone else. "I think she'll be happy married to him."

"Johnnie, old boy, you missed . . ."

The audience, seated now, suddenly hushed. Latham leaned over for the last time. "I think it best if I give you a few short words of introduction."

I tried to stop him, but from out of his pocket he pulled three pages of typewritten notes.

Several months later I again accepted an assignment in Kenya. Latham had written me that he was not feeling well, that bit by bit his body was "breaking up like an old ship on a reef." By now I had become used to these complaints, and when I reached Kenya I fully expected to see him, leaning rakishly, as always, on his cane.

I stopped in Nanyuki with a photographer en route to our assignment in the north, and when I entered the Sports Club, the manager hardly looked up from his bookkeeping to tell me that Latham was in the cottage hospital. "Dunno," he replied. "Sometimes it's his legs, other times his gut. He's becoming too much to handle down here, you know." I had heard these complaints from the manager before, so I made ready to return to my car. "You're going to have to start thinking about the day he's no longer able to get out of bed," he continued, still not looking at me. "Let's hope the other thing happens first. Get my drift?"

I did get his drift. I found the cottage hospital on the other side of town. The trellised bougainvillea had been well maintained since colonial times and there was a large terrace where patients could sit and enjoy a view of Mount Kenya. As always, Latham somehow knew I was coming. He was in his room, half propped in bed, dressed with a *kikoi* around his waist and another one, as a kind of shawl, around his shoulders. His ivory-handled hairbrushes, dating to schoolboy days, lay on the bureau. He looked like a paramount chief, greeting me with an I-told-you-so laugh. Immediately he wanted to know about my photographer who, because she was a woman, was no doubt another of my romantic entanglements. I explained our professional association, but Latham was unconvinced. He began asking the lady about her background, no doubt to see if she was sufficiently well bred for me.

I broke off the audition to ask Latham for a story. He accepted my gauche request as a compliment. His voice had recently become the object of his greatest vanity. It was, he felt, the one asset that would never fail him. "Women," he explained, "particularly women, find my voice irresistible. Reminds them of Charles Dickens at one of his readings. Do you see what they mean, old boy? It hypnotizes. Haunts. Their eyes even glaze over."

With my urging, Latham described to the photographer the events leading to his acquisition of the island of M'Simbati in the late 1940s. His voice was strong and calculated, alternately whispering and booming. In a tone of calculated outrage he then refused to recount the tale of his ten romantic days in Paris during World War I. "There are confidences still to be kept," he insisted after sixty-three years. "The lady may still be alive."

With a little coercion Latham agreed to a photograph. He hobbled out to the terrace, balancing unnecessarily on the photographer's arm. Having bellowed greetings to a few of his fellow inmates, as we returned, and then settling himself into bed, he suddenly blurted out that he did not believe he would reach the age of ninety. "Everything's packing up," he said. "I can remember what happened thirty years ago, but yesterday . . ." Latham looked toothless and wan. "Come back," he said, noting me look at my watch. "Please come back. There's so much to talk about."

I never did return. Even at the end of my assignment, when I might have found a day or two to spend in Nanyuki, I evaded Latham. At the hospital I had indeed noticed that he was fading. He hated accepting his infirmities and I was uneasy, I discovered, hearing about them. I now knew that nothing I did could halt the inevitable—not a return to his beloved island, not a Harley Street specialist, not even the surprise materialization of Valerie. Neither he nor I enjoyed feeling helpless. Our friendship of fourteen years had been one of hope. Whenever life became miserable we took charge and made it better. When he lost the island he undertook no less than six changes of landscape in search of the perfect home. Now there was nowhere left to go, and I, for one, did not have the courage to sit with him and admit final defeat.

It was as if after many years of trekking, we had finally reached the wrong sea.

After I had been back in wamerica for two weeks I received one last letter. On the envelope my name was hardly decipherable and the note inside, although typewritten, was nearly illegible. I read it several times and finally pieced together that Latham had met a lady lion-trainer ("She teaches them manners"). Since the lion-trainer was from California, she was certainly "the right girl for me" ("One of the few Americans that I know who is full of brains and a good-looker as well . . . she likes me as I am something out of the common. I tell her stories of years and years ago. Of course she adores my voice . . ."). The letter never once touched upon Latham's health, nor explained why the old man's typing, normally so clear, was now incoherent. A few days later I learned a little more. A cable from the club manager explained that Latham was back in the hospital "regrettably short of funds, would be grateful for help." A letter from Mary Anne, arriving simultaneously with the cable, explained that he had been placed in hospital with recurring pneumonia, "but he went in later than he should have and came out earlier than he should have because he was worried about the payment . . . Latham is more or less bedridden and everybody's goodwill and patience is pretty short. . . . [The manager of the club] has told me he would be happy if I could find him somewhere else to live. But there really isn't anywhere else . . . I'm telling you this so that you know how things stand. Latham is pretty depressed and would love letters from you. So sad when you get to that stage."

I cabled the money to the manager, somehow convinced that if I sent it to Latham he might pass it on to someone he considered more destitute than himself, as he had once done in the past. I then sat down and wrote him the letter that had been so long overdue. I told him that while he may think he was in hospital with pneumonia, those in the know recognized that he was really in prison for rape. I lied to him, saying that I would contact his friend, the lion-trainer.

I told Latham that I had been thinking of the friendship between us two men—how it spanned two centuries and many more generations, a couple of oceans and a continent or two, and that, in the end, it proved the durability of two youngsters who refused to grow old. I told him not to let me down. To fight once again and prove everyone wrong. "Yours until hell freezes over," I ended, imitating the battle cry he so often used.

My letter took over two weeks to reach Nanyuki. During this period a nurse at the hospital, I learned, called Mary Anne in Nairobi to tell her to come quickly. Many months later, in a letter, Mary Anne described that visit. "He was delighted to see me but I was shocked because for the first time ever he had really—almost literally—given up the ghost. He was very weak and feeble and really did want to die. He kept on asking me if I could slip him five milligrams of morphine. I would have loved to have been able to help in that way, but when it comes to the crunch, my conscience wouldn't allow it. He was in no real pain and, in fact, there was nothing particularly wrong with him. He was just fading away. . . . I made him his Earl Grey tea in a special china teapot . . . and he ate a bit of scrambled egg and that was about all. Typical of Latham, he took everything in stride with great courage and no complaints. I had come to pack up his things at the club because I knew that he could never return there. And I thought it would be difficult suggesting a permanent stay in the hospital. But he brought up the subject himself. He said, 'Darling, I'll never get out of this place now so it's best to settle my account with the club.' So I packed up all his things. There were rat droppings all over his room and they'd nibbled away at his papers in his desk. Those people at the club just hadn't bothered at all looking after him. And Latham never complained. He still had a snatch of his old humor. . . . After I had slept in his room at the club, I went into his hospital room the next morning and asked if he had slept comfortably. He winked an eye and said, 'But it wasn't the same as it would have been if I'd been in the bed with you. . . .'

"At times he was optimistic and looking into the future—he wanted me to inquire from you about a wheelchair. Should he get an electric one or one that used petrol? I told him that I thought an electric one would be better. And he inquired about getting a better room in the hospital for 'later on.' But he hardly recognized anything or anyone at the end. I put up some of his old pictures of his family. He didn't even recognize his brother."

Mrs. Paterson, Latham's elderly friend and fellow resident at the club, also wrote to say she had gone each day to the hospital to cheer him up. When she spotted my letter one day in his post box she rushed immediately to his bedside, since on every occasion he had been pleading for news of his American friend. But when Mrs. Paterson reached the hospital, Latham had fallen into "a deep sleep, almost a coma, and I couldn't read it to him." Fully expecting to see him the next day, she opened the letter and read its contents, to prepare herself for the declamation. "I hope you won't mind," she wrote me. "Now I have destroyed it [the letter] and, of course, I will never mention any of your confidential news."

She had destroyed my letter because at nine in the morning of the day she planned to read it to the old man, she had received a phone call from the hospital saying that she was too late. The date was the eighth of June.

On the eighth of June I was in Canada on a remote salmon river with friends. The fishing had been as bad as anyone could remember over the last two years, and anglers were beginning to note with gloom that the great days of the sport were now ended. The cable from Mary Anne, followed by another from the club manager, arrived late on a Tuesday evening.

I did not cry. Nor did Mary Anne who wrote to say: "Johnnie, he was happy to go. He had had enough. He couldn't read anymore and he didn't even want to listen to the classical music on his tape. So I didn't shed any tears. I was happy when I heard the news. I am sure you were too." Valerie did not cry for him either. In her letter she said, "We must all be relieved for him. His mind was encumbered by a body that had served him well but was weary of the world. Thanks to you he is resting in a country he roved in more robust days and where he would now wish to be, far from the England he could dream about without facing the reality of its changing face and the turning of tides and fortunes."

I could not cry that Tuesday night, nor early on Wednesday morning when I went out to try my hand at what was proving to be hopeless.

Within ten minutes I took my first salmon. Within an hour I had my limit for the day. I suddenly turned quiet: it was not so much that I had been lucky to achieve the impossible. It was that I now knew Latham had been personally responsible. While I boated each of those fish I heard his booming voice. He was laughing. I remembered once hearing him tell how he had come

54

to Canada, not far from this river, just after World War I to recover from his wounds. His doctors had given him half a year to live; he had defied their wisdom by surviving a further sixty-one years. I could hear Latham laughing through the balsam, up and down the moiling river, accompanying the four notes of the whitethroat, like the opening of an important symphony. The laugh seemed to say, "Free at last."

I cried then for Latham. I cried the next day when I learned through a distant relative of the old man that Latham had indeed been the bastard son of Edward VII. I cried not for the recognition of his all-too-apparent nobility but for the secret he had borne so long, so effectively, if for no other reason than to protect the other man who had served him well as a father. I cried the following day when I heard that, in his will, Latham had left me all his photograph albums, covering those two centuries from Smallfields House in Hampshire through two world wars, through a thirty-year career in the African bush, beyond his island exile, to his final years as a fugitive. Of all Latham's scanty possessions, the M'Simbati flag and those photograph albums were the ones he prized the most. Now they were mine.

I wept that I had failed so miserably ever to bring Latham back to his island. I wept for a friendship the likes of which I would never see again. I wept for a letter that had arrived a few hours too late. I wept for an Africa that would soon forget the old man.

And it would never be the same.

Terry Mathews is, to me, neither the best sculptor in Africa nor the best known. He sells his wildlife bronzes handily but they have never stirred many waves in art circles. His following is composed mostly of African aficionados rather than the cognoscenti.

But of the three sculptors who have a reputation in Africa, Terry is the most obsessive. Unlike them, he does not suffer from the excesses of ego. Nor has he come to believe that he bears a message. Perhaps there was a time when he was more presumptuous, but today he is mostly a victim of his own gnawing self-doubt. His works rarely satisfy him. They are irritants,

THE WHOLE
SHOOTING MATCH

daily acts of penance for life in a land that seems to have brought him little long-term joy. He was once a hunter, then a safari guide, and today, not quite retired from either avocation, he balances and juggles life as an artist. With such a patchwork existence, Terry seems the perfect victim of this beautiful land: all-consuming, pained, unable to explain himself, conscience-ridden. And all the time he is appealing for his honesty, almost too ingenuous for his own good and natural in the way an African drought or flood would be natural.

Terry Mathews cannot escape having once been a hunter.

Even as a sculptor he has a hunter's point of view. He will not think twice about pointing at a piece of clay and showing you the best heart shot. Even though today he cloaks himself in occasional conservationist clothes, he will still assure you that everything he ever learned was from the chase.

He is tall and his blond crop of hair belongs on a youngster half his age. The black eyepatch gives him the roguish look of the Hathaway shirt man, but even from photographs of him taken before his accident he clearly has always worn the smile of a swashbuckler. Today his trim lines are rounded. He makes up for a disinterest in strong liquor by eating well; middle age, much to his disappointment, has begun to show in the engraving around his eyes and on the back of his neck.

For all the sometime glamour of his looks, he remains exceedingly unsure. The hunting stories he tells are almost always immodest about the game, reticent about himself. While companions from his hunting days may boast of his deadly accuracy with a gun, Terry will prefer to tell of prodigious events that happened far from a gun sight.

This morning we are drinking black coffee in Terry's studio. The swirl of commuter traffic on Nairobi's Uhuru Highway can be heard even from here. I ask Terry what was his greatest hunt. Scratching his uncombed hair, looking sadly at all his works in progress, he lets me wonder for one long minute. I sip my coffee. At last he talks and the story he chooses echoes, it seems, that prevailing state of incompleteness.

Terry is twenty-one and about to shoot his first elephant. He has paid dearly for the license, but if he is successful that £15 investment will launch him into his chosen career of professional hunter. For four days he and a friend have been scouring the Ukambani country in Southern Kenya. Today, at last, they spot four bull elephants, asleep on their feet, in the shade of a lone tree. The wind and the terrain are all perfect. Terry drops to a crouch and creeps forward, holding the .404 off the ground, his neck hurting, his nose sniffing for a change in the wind. At thirty yards, Terry raises his gun and sights in the earhole of the largest elephant. Terry has heard much about brain shots and he knows them to be the best recipe for assassination. Slowly, he squeezes the trigger.

Bedlam. As the elephant's forelegs collapse and it falls onto its stomach, Terry's companion adds two rounds of .577 lead to the elephant's brain.

While the three other elephants scatter, the two partners shake hands and offer congratulations, in the manner of hunters. As the men head for the carcass, however, the three departing bulls suddenly stop in mid-flight, look back and, slowly at first but with increasing speed, return to their fallen comrade. From a safe distance, the hunters watch in bafflement as the three elephants lift the carcass to its feet and march it off into the distance.

Terry fires off four more rounds into the wounded elephant's brain, but the shots only raise puffs of dust on his skin. By dusk, having followed the bizarre retinue for four hours, Terry sits on his haunches, soaked in doubt. He lights a cigarette and wonders what he did wrong.

At first light on the following morning, Terry rediscovers the elephants' spoor. Between the surefooted tracks of the "stretcher-bearers" is a furrow, rimmed by blood, where the corpse was dragged. Here the two hunters come upon a place where the corpse fell; a pool of blood six feet wide is flecked with splinters of pumicelike bone. Here is where the others raised him up. Here he fell by an anthill. Surely, this parade will soon end. But the blood becomes a trickle and then vanishes altogether; the furrow dug by the trailing legs also disappears. From time to time, the hunters can see where the "dead" elephant lost his balance, where he stood with support of his comrades and finally where he proceeded without any help whatsoever. The spoor shows that the four elephants have now joined a larger herd of cow elephants and young. On the third day of tracking, Terry climbs a small hill and sees, far in the distance, a herd. He approaches and with his field glasses he examines each one individually. One of them must have a gaping head wound. Terry looks for congealed blood, for a telltale unsteadiness, for a sunken stomach. For two hours he scans the elephants and, in the end, he sees nothing.

The hunt is over. Terry, age twenty-one, with a career now in doubt, in debt and no longer sure of his heavy rifle, or any rifle, returns home.

Today Terry stands at the window, looking into a tree for a

weaver nest he first discovered yesterday afternoon. "A wounded elephant, I was sure, would never be able to feed." He sips his first coffee of the morning. "That was, of course, my mistake. Today, I'm sure my wounded elephant was in that herd feeding, just like the others. Elephants feed when they're wounded. Age twenty-one and I was a horse's ass. What didn't make any sense to me then makes perfectly good sense to an elephant."

Terry lifts his black patch, rubs at his damaged eye and laughs, almost quizzically. From the sound of it, the joke was on him. The elephant won.

The day has hardly begun in Tsavo National Park. The young hunter, nearly twenty years Terry's junior, is today taking a photographic client to a gap between two hills. It is called Thabagungi, and for the last hour of bumpy driving, the client has been hearing about a rhino dubbed Sidney who, according to the animated young man, "owns" this gap. "Unlikely anyone else knows that old buck rhino by the name of Sidney. Just me," the guide says proudly. "We're the best goddamn enemies you ever saw. Wait and see." The young man is evidently looking forward to being charged and giving his client his money's worth. "I can't remember a time I ever visited this place I wasn't seen off by the old low-down varmint." The guide has affected a very successful American accent for the amusement of his client.

Today the car passes through the gap unchallenged. The young hunter looks everywhere for his old friend. "Maybe he's down by the river," he says. His Texas twang has now vanished; once again he is British Colonial. They drive to the Galana River and look through the heavy growth for a lone rhino. Instead they find a carcass. The skin is mummified, stiff like an old tin roof. Either the rhino was killed by drought or by poachers. "Probably goddamn poachers," adds the hunter. He, who last night had boasted of the distinguished list of trophies he could claim, kicks the dry bones. "It's Sidney all right," he says. The hunter crouches in the bush, staring forlornly at the clumsy square skull. "You don't know what this means to me."

Clients tend to see their white hunter as a father. They boast of him, when he is out of earshot, and, when he has returned, tell him things around the campfire they might not tell their own father. He looms in their imagination. They are proud of him, and should he happen to visit them at their homes in the northern hemisphere they will make sure that as many of their friends as possible meet him and see for themselves his invincibility.

Such attitudes among Terry's clients clearly embarrass him. He talks of a career change. He speaks of hunting not as a series of triumphant successes, but as discoveries. While Jeanne, Terry's wife, may worry about the government, the weather, the press and the safari market, Terry tends to see conditions and changes in Africa as inexorable. He is still not certain he has chosen the right career. He is not even certain Africa is the best place to live. He once even bought a flat in London, near the foundry where his bronzes are cast, but it has never become home. He clearly loves Kenya, but he, like so many whites, lives here indecisively, sensing that it is not a legitimate place to settle but knowing he has not yet found the right excuse to leave.

Terry's clients might also be embarrassed to hear Terry talk with such scant conviction. When he says that he hopes to conduct his last safari this year they will probably silence him, reminiscing instead about the thorn scratches—their only reward for looking for a set of corkscrew horns—or the triple heartbeat when something mountainous and armor-plated came at them like a locomotive or the quiet hush at dawn, lying in a warm bed, and the clattering of the tea tray and the whispered *"hodi"* at the screen flap of the tent and the sight of a new sun rising over what now seemed a youthful land, when last night it had been antique. Magic, they might say. And don't forget that smell of wood smoke—must be the acacia bark burning because you only get it in Africa. Magic, they will whisper again, not noticing that Terry is smiling politely and not listening. He was their sorcerer.

The chairman of Philip Morris told how he gained all his confidence from Terry. Bing Crosby raved about all the "birds, animals, flora and fauna Terry knows by name," and a network executive searched for metaphysical words to explain the knowledge of life he acquired from Terry in Africa. "Retire?" they exclaimed. "If so, Africa's finished. The end of the game. Glad to have known it when I did, but you won't see me back there if Terry's gone."

When Terry talks of the end, I wonder about the loyal gunbearers, camp helpers and cooks who have rattled across half a million miles of Africa in his company. Who will they now work for? Will they treat his retirement like a change in the climate?

Clearly, however, Terry has only told *me* of his plans. The notion must have occurred to him this morning, and he is trying it on to see if it fits. He mentions it as he might mention his most spectacular meal, his favorite hotel or that little girl who became a voluptuous women when "they took the railroad tracks off her teeth." Terry is just like us—wracked by life's softnesses—yet his clients, blind to the self-doubt, ascribe a mythic quality to him, as if he need only say one word in Swahili or identify one plant with its Latin name to prove that he owns the sunset and the wood smoke. But Terry, who knows that sunsets are imperfect even in Africa, does not have the heart to correct anyone.

Meanwhile, down at the Hunters' Bar, they are calling for cold Tusker Export, although noon is still two hours away. Brian Campbell, one of the most senior members of the fraternity, pushes open the glass door and a cheer rises from the bar. This morning he was seen on Kimathi Avenue escorting a pert little blonde wearing a pink halter top, hot pants and blood-red high heels. She must have been no older than eighteen. How does old Brian, pushing seventy, get all those centerfold clients? But Brian shakes his head, for once not amused by the legend making. He orders two beers, downs the first in one quick inhale, sips the second and says, not quite sure whom he is addressing, "Buggers won't renew my work permit." He thinks about those words, knocks back the second beer and in one fluid movement nods to the bartender for replenishment. "For all these forty years," he says to the man next to him, "for all these forty years I always looked forward to the luxury of picking my own good time to retire. Now some bloody bureaucrat in some bloody ministry has chosen that time for me."

62

If only Terry could believe in compliments he might be more satisfied with the elephants he is modeling. "Too bloody passive," he complains about one. For a second he seems ready to destroy it, but with an adroit change of heart, he bends a wire foreleg, raises the trunk, slaps on clay, and suddenly the cow elephant's muscles are tight with apprehension. What once seemed no more than a huddled clump of wire armature is now an infuriated mother torn between escape and a charge. Her youngster is just behind her, scurrying to keep up. The idea is not very original, the execution perhaps conventional, the proportions, for the moment, excessive, yet the effect is startling.

Terry is still discontented. He turns to another pedestal where four bull elephants are grouped around a tree, trying to penetrate the human stench on the wind. They are instantly recognizable: the elephants Terry came upon one midday twenty-five years ago. I can hear their ears still clopping like tent flaps. Is there enough time for a shot? Will they charge, will they run bellowing into the dense bush or will they sleep on? "I remembered it all yesterday," Terry mentions. "Probably if I had any guts I'd smash it up today and start over." He walks to a corner of the studio and opens a closet door. "And there again I could always put it here."

Inside the closet are at least fifty clay models: kudu and giraffe, black marlin and sailfish, giraffe and zebra. The smell is like kindergarten.

"My rumination closet," Terry adds, none too pleased with what he sees.

She is an old elephant and in five years she would probably die quietly. Instead she will be executed today. The park warden, David Sheldrick, watches her from a distance of thirty yards. He has handed down many such sentences before, but for reasons known only to him, he delays this one for a last look.

The sun is almost directly overhead. The elephant stands next to a muddy pool, reaching for water with her trunk. Having successfully inhaled, the trunk travels to her mouth where the water will be emptied, but en route it spills out, leaving the old lady with a wet chest and nothing to drink. Again she tries. Once more, failure. With water in great abundance all around her, she will soon die of thirst. Her temples are sunken, her ears sway awkwardly, broken at their bases, and her skin, like an ill-fitting stocking, is wadded around her knees. She leans forward to take a step, but unable to move, she remains rigid at a teeter-totter angle—three tons of pachyderm ready to fall with the slightest breeze.

Through the open sights of his gun, David Sheldrick can see on her shoulder four small holes dripping pus. No doubt she suffered these wounds from poachers' arrows. The acocanthera poison must have been old, its effect blunted, because now after two weeks she is still alive.

David Sheldrick could have killed four elephants in the time he is taking to put her out of her pain. In the last year he has already done away with forty-four such derelicts. Poaching in Tsavo has now become a chronic problem because of the soaring price of ivory. Last night in the cool of his veranda Sheldrick alternately blamed the market, the Orient, high-level government corruption, the middleman. He holds no brief against the Walliangulu poacher, who, in Sheldrick's lexicon, is to be praised for his cunning and bushcraft, and condoned as a mere victim of fashion. The dilemma for Sheldrick is that he, the most vaunted park warden in all of Kenya, is powerless to do anything about real enemies. He can only chase after the fellow with whom he most identifies. When he entertains prestigious conservationists at his house, he must rail against this little guy, "the poacher," when all the time he wishes he could handle a bow and arrow as well, or know as much about bush poisons. With his forty-fifth elephant of the year, in the twenty-third year of his stewardship of one of Africa's most profligate paradises, David Sheldrick has begun to hate his job.

He squeezes the trigger. The elephant tumbles onto her forehead, then rolls onto her side. The moment she hits the ground her body explodes and black infection flies in all directions.

"Poor old girl," Sheldrick says. Suddenly, he decides not to lower his gun. He fires another round into the elephant, then another, pulling the trigger until he has exhausted all his cartridges. "Poor old bitch," he says with relief.

Terry, still working on a rebellious elephant foot, has decided to skip lunch. As he dabs, he explains why this morning he considered retiring from the safari business. "I'd rather not accept a deposit if I'm not sure what, if anything, we'll be allowed to hunt next year."

But Terry is clearly speculating, not handing down a decision. Money is money, and any client determined enough to risk the vagaries of Kenyan politics is welcome to offer Terry a deposit against a safari next year. The issue that puzzles him has to do with the other lives that this uncertainty will disrupt. Several years before, he took on a young man, Alick Roberts, as an assistant, and soon Terry will have no work to offer him. Even worse, one of Terry's sons is threatening to become a professional hunter too. How do you tell a boy that the profession that has yielded such pleasure and so many rewards to an older man is now a dubious prospect for anyone else? Why does he not have the nerve to admit that Africa is no training for a career anywhere else in the world?

Terry turns up the phonograph volume to let the city limits hear the Carpenters tell about a country fair thousands of miles away. He chews on the end of his modeling tool, and then, struck by the first really good idea of the morning, he pounces on the clay herd, scratching here, nibbling there, like an oxpecker.

But the notion comes too late, for in mid-execution the door opens and the only redhead of Terry's five sons enters with the tea tray. Jeanne's instructions were quite clear: The thirteen-year-old was not to bother his father, to return downstairs on the double. So instructions are immediately waived and the boy pretends to be riveted by the elephant. "Off you go," Terry says. Five minutes later, when the door finally closes, Terry adds: "The snakeman."

He looks at the white door, delaying having to face the elephant leg. "Just like him, I was a snake collector, a budding herpetologist," he recalls, buying time. "In Uganda where I grew up, my world was birds, eggs, snakes, with an emphasis on snakes. My mentor was our neighbor, Charles Pitman, the chief game warden of Uganda. He had a three-sided veranda, and on it a museum of skeletons, eggs, fossils, feathers, skins and stones—the only possessions we both agreed were of any value.

One day at the ripe old age of nine, I brought Pitman a snake, tucked inside my shirt. 'Just a harmless typhlops,' I said. I can hear the roar of his voice still. What a rocket he gave me. How was I sure, he asked, that it was not a Gaboon viper? 'Never, never, never take liberties with snakes you cannot identify.' "

Terry is smiling with the long-ago memories. "Do you think I'd have any success passing on that lesson?" Terry points to the door, indicating the spot where his son had just stood. "That's the chap. Just the other day he reaches under a petrol drum for a snake he is sure is harmless but what turns out to be a black burrowing viper. Charming, what do you think? Little bugger very nearly died."

Terry is about ready to laugh. Dangerous snakes and little boys are at the very heart of the African idyll, and he is proud of young Philip. But best of all, for the last five minutes Terry has avoided the elephant leg and all those other obligations having to do with young boys soon to become young displaced men in Africa.

Radcliffe, one of the other park wardens, is fast asleep in the Long Bar in the back of the New Stanley Hotel. No one can remember ever seeing him in Nairobi except on official business. Radcliffe's contract with the national parks, renewed for the last seventeen years, has not been extended beyond this year. A week ago he met his successor, a full-blooded Kenyan ("He's a good chap, mind you, but he just won't be able to say no, poor bastard. All his cousins and brothers will be wanting part of his windfall.").

Last night, staying in a friend's guest cottage in a Nairobi suburb, Radcliffe's wife once again started going on about retirement in Lancashire and about part-time work for Radcliffe as a gamekeeper on an estate. That's when he began his beerfest. This morning he even forgot to pick up his wife after her hair appointment, her first in nearly a year. Now he has absolutely no idea where she is, and vice versa. "England bloody England," he mutters, half asleep.

A few moments before, he had to stop himself from shouting at the bartender for giving him a Tusker Export when he had asked for a White Cap. That was unforgivable behavior for a white man, he decided afterward, but now he is fast asleep. "England," he had thought. "I could stand the weather, all right. Even though the silly bastards talk about it all the time. It's not that. It's the other business. You spend your lifetime learning to run a five-thousand-square-mile slice of real estate in the middle of Africa. Next stop where? What are you supposed to say in that bloody manager's office, drinking tea, waiting for the 'how very interestings' to cease so you can get around to qualifications—weapons, command of an illiterate field force, elephant control, bush flying, orchid growing in an arid region. And once you have covered that ground, then what? 'Oh, I say, let me read to you from my latest citation, awarded to me on the occasion of my fifteenth anniversary in Kenyan National Parks: ". . . respect from conservationists for his relentless and innovative campaign against poaching . . ."' And I was just beginning to see results." Bloody Africa.

While other patrons shout insults and stories at each other, Radcliffe, alone at a corner seat, senses only the slow tick of his heart. With his chin on his chest, he could be dead. A thin trickle of saliva, the first sign of the long rains in a dry riverbed, reaches his chin and drops onto his shirt.

It is clear that although Terry will forgo lunch, he has declared a lunch break. He looks forlornly at the elephant, letting one story lead to another.

Shortly after he had qualified as a professional hunter, he relates, he was hired by two very senior and highly respected colleagues to help lead three Americans after big game in Tanzania. He was the youngest of the professional hunters, and each evening as the others added up their bag, it became clear to him that he was also the least experienced. While they regularly killed four and five species in a day, he only managed, at the most, one. Twelve hours of daylight never seemed adequate for one decent hunt after one good trophy. "What am I doing wrong?" he asked himself finally.

On the fifth day of the safari, the clients were rotated and

Terry was assigned a Mr. Quimbley, who was dying to collect a second buffalo since his first had not been a very good trophy.

Buffaloes are not nearly as thickheaded as they look. To hunt them often requires as much patience and silence as a leopard. The first day passed without a shot being fired. On the second, Terry and Quimbley came upon a large herd gathered about one fine trophy buffalo. Terry decided to take the most strenuous of two options—the one requiring a stalk of several miles, through a sunken riverbed, into the wind. After two hours on his stomach, Quimbley was at last in position for a shot. The herd was now uneasy, sensing an irritation on the wind. It milled and stomped, all its eyes faced in the direction of the two hunters. Quimbley's Abercrombie and Fitch shirt was now ripped in three places, his hair was matted with grass seeds and wait-a-bit thorns and his love handles, made possible by a prosperous Cadillac dealership in Brownsville, Texas, were now nearly vaporized.

Once Terry had spotted the trophy animal amid all the others and had made his client do the same, he had one last look at him. Quimbley's tinted Polaroid glasses were fogged, a heavy heartbeat was tripping his fingers every third second. "Right," Terry whispered. "Go for a heart shot."

Quimbley twisted in pain from the recoil of the .375. The buffalo reeled against the undertow of the females, hesitated and then thundered off to lead them, and as it turned, it swayed and fell, spinning in one last attempt to work its way around a bush. Cautiously the hunters skirted one bush and then another, until finally they could see blood flecking the dead buffalo's nostrils. But with relief came a disappointment: One tip of one horn was broken. Terry shook his head. "It's my fault," he said. "It's imperfect."

"What are you talking about!" exclaimed Quimbley. "This is the greatest trophy I'll ever own." His first buffalo, he explained, he had shot from the Land Rover at a distance of five yards, at a speed of about twenty-five miles an hour, and the animal died after every bullet in the chamber of his rifle had been discharged. "I did exactly as I was told."

Suddenly Terry realized why all his colleagues had been returning to camp each evening with four and five trophies. Those two legendary white hunters were no better than third-class meat hunters.

Terry is now by the window of his studio. "Everybody these days talks about principles. The so-called principles of hunting." Terry turns to me. "My ass. There never were any principles in hunting. I doubt whether there were even four or five hunters in the whole country who knew how to conduct a hunt without their Land Rover and their African tracker. And even the good ones, sooner or later, got lazy.

"We called it a sport too. Really. What kind of sport is it when a client pays a man to follow the spoor, to select the trophy, even to help him shoot it, to protect him from anything with teeth or a sting and in the evening to provide for his entertainment? It's like someone at a country club, hiring the tennis pro for a partner and then going on to win the club championships. Sport, you call it?" Terry rubs his eye under the patch. "And now my son wants to be a white hunter. Believes it to be a noble career."

The best hunters in Kenya generally avoided the Hunters' Bar in the Hilton, and soon after its creation by the Professional Hunters' Association it became the lair of those out of work—the ones who liked to boast about trophies and trysts. Liam Lynn, the Irish white hunter, will never have anything to do with the Hunters' Bar unless, of course, he is very thirsty.

Today he is just that. His thirst began the evening before, lasted through the night and allowed him to go without sleep and breakfast. Even after he has consumed two bottles of Martell brandy, Liam still retains the unique talent of being able to entertain listeners with the awful truth.

Today, at lunchtime, he is lurching as he pushes open the glass door. His clients, just arrived from Philadelphia, are waiting for him in one of Nairobi's hotels. His safari crew has already been posted to one of the hunting blocks to set up camp, and a chartered aircraft is standing by to fly Liam and his clients there in comfort, but poor old Liam looks as if he will never make his way even to the bar stool. He spots someone else's clients sitting at the banquet table, and he weaves toward them. His eyes have fallen on the daughter of these nice eager people. She is a sixteen-year-old blonde with the hopeful looks of a recent convert to the sexual revolution. At first, the parents are not quite sure how to deal with Liam, but their hunter, John Painter, lets them know he is all right, one of Kenya's more lovable rogues, a great success as an elephant hunter but rather his own best enemy whenever he arrives in Nairobi. Liam considers this introduction a bit excessive. He leans onto the daughter and whispers, in a voice loud enough to be heard throughout the bar, that John Painter was well known to have wet dreams. "No," says the girl, quite horrified.

"And did you hear what came of his last wet dream?" Liam continues, his County Antrim brogue stronger than ever.

"No," says the girl once again, this time her face flushed with color.

"On his last wet dream he produced Uganda. The Republic of Uganda, that is. Quite a splash it was too."

John Painter is howling with laughter. The girl is still too nervous to laugh. But the parents are looking pained.

At the far end of the counter, one of the regulars of the Hunters' Bar yells: "Liam, tell us about your .458."

The Irishman affects a look of excruciating pain. "Awful thing," he grumbles. "Makes a terrible bang in me ear." Clearly Liam does not want to talk about guns or be egged on by any bullshit artist in the Hunters' Bar. He looks at the sixteen-year-old. His leer makes her smile. "How long have you been a virgin?" he asks at last.

John Painter, as tough as any hunter in the profession, blushes. "Tell us about elephants," he pleads, desperate to change the subject.

"Elephants," Liam says with a look of contrived puzzlement. "You mean those things with the big ears and long noses?" He has at last made the girl's parents smile. "So you call them elephants, do you?"

Suddenly, Liam no longer wants to keep up the patter of his one-liners. Even his interest in the girl has waned. He looks at his watch. "Time to leave. I've only a half-hour left on my twelve-hour deodorant."

Painter successfully changes the table talk to one of Kenya's more sober subjects—the calculation of death figures. "What does it look like?" he asks rhetorically. "Last year one client accidentally shot by his hunter, another killed by a rhino. The year before, one professional killed by an elephant, another taken from his tent by a lioness, and then what do you think, about half a dozen maulings and gorings? Quite a few record years . . ."

Liam has been listening with interest. "I'm always pleased," he says, "to hear about hunters being killed by elephants. It restores my faith in Africa."

"The most dangerous animal in the bush is the client," Terry continues, looking to clear the air at three in the afternoon. He has finally come around to the subject of the black patch over his eye. He explains that he was bird-shooting near a place called Selengai with a wealthy New Yorker. "He was forty-five yards from me when a guinea fowl flushed, flying low, behind me. I suppose he should have known better than to fire, but he did, and I had just enough time to move my head slightly. Had I not, the pellet would have gone directly through my eye and out through the soft part of the orbital bone, into my brain. That would have been it. As it was, I had pellets in my forehead, pellets in the back of my hand and one pellet that obliquely entered my left eye. When I was brought back to camp I got on the radiotelephone to Jeanne in Nairobi. The reception was terrible, but she heard me say there had been an accident and to send the plane as soon as possible. Three hours later it flew us back to Nairobi, and when we landed, Jeanne was on the tarmac staring through the window at us, knowing only there had been an accident, not sure if it was me or the client or the gun bearer, sensing, in the way women do, that from now on things would be different."

" 'Are you all right?' I remember her asking.

" 'Yes,' I said. 'But I doubt whether I'll ever see out of my left eye ever again.' Incredible, wasn't it, how I could sense even then that my career as a professional hunter was already behind me."

The wound took a long time to heal. There were expensive

operations, a career left in disarray and a lawsuit against the client, who at the time of the accident had tried to disavow any liability. The compensation finally won by Terry in court was adequate to launch him on his new career as a sculptor. Still, he suffers from headaches and from a memory of the seamier side of human nature.

"The funny thing," Terry adds, "I still feel like protecting that client. I keep his name a secret. I avoid telling the story. Strange, isn't it, to feel that way about a so-and-so, just because he was once out in the bush with you."

One and a half hours out of Nairobi, there is a narrow canyon called Hell's Gate. It is near Lake Naivasha and, because of its starkness, it has escaped many of the unpleasantnesses of modern life. There is a farm on the floor of this canyon, and on the cliffs there are nests of important birds that attract important bird watchers. Rock climbers are also attracted to these cliffs and on weekends the canyon reverberates to the sound of metal pitons being hammered into rock. But on most weekdays Hell's Gate is bothered by few human beings. Left alone, it is the very embodiment of geologic history, of earthly eternity.

Late this afternoon at exactly 5:25, the Nyanza swifts—little birds more acrobatic than swallows—brush through the canyon like a freshening wind. Before the sky blackens a pair of lammergiers, an uncommon species of vulture, drops onto a high cliff not far from where a Verreaux's eagle stops her flight, her wings beating heavily, and deposits a dead hyrax into her nest.

All these subtleties of nature mean much to an old man who lives on the valley floor. He came out to Kenya from England fifty-six years ago. Ten years ago when he was hired to manage the Hell's Gate Farm he was sure he would never have to look for another job in his lifetime. But two years ago he was fired. The owners eased the shock by letting him stay on in a little farmhouse as a kind of honorary caretaker. But now he will never leave, believing the cliffs and the plains would erode without his care. During the day he drives his vintage Land Rover from one end of the canyon to the other, taking count of the game, checking on the water, glaring at intruders. Now, standing outside his house at dusk, a lantern in one hand, waiting for night, he studies the dirt track with mounting disapproval. A sportscar is approaching at a furious speed. As it passes through his yard, it scatters the chickens, whirligigs the dust. To the old man the vehicle is ignorant of who made the road, how old the cliffs, what a bloody marvel a lammergier's egg.

The old man signals for it to stop. "I'll build a ditch across the road if you keep that up, and then you'll see, laddie." The dust now envelops old man, sportscar and boy in a hungry cloud. The kid does not have the sense to turn down the Stones on the eight-track stereo.

"Sorry."

"You'll do nothing of the sort," the old man replies, not having heard. Fists, soft like washrags, rain through the open window on the boy. The old man's face turns an evening purple, flushed with fury. He would like to be truly violent but all he can muster is the ineffective pattering of his fists.

The boy crushes the gearshift into first and the car bursts out of the farmyard like an airplane, nearly dragging the old man behind.

He regains his footing, slaps the dust from his great balloon shorts and waits for the whine of the car to fade. Looking up, he can tell the swifts are still flying, even though the moon has not risen. One by one they black out the stars.

A minute ago the old man was thinking only of the kid and his sex palace and the rock-'n'-roll music. Now nothing matters. He watches the evening lights being turned off and on. The old man stands there, not noticing the chill, feeling only the passing of a mood and the mysteries of a black sky.

At dusk Terry is still in the studio. He looks toward Nairobi where the lights are coming on across the skyline. In one blaze, as if it had just been blowtorched, the conference center comes to life. Terry is reminded to turn on the lights in the studio.

This evening the prospects for making any real progress on the elephant group seem diminished by the nonstop crying from downstairs. It is a child's wail, powered by what must be a superhuman set of lungs. Terry studies the elephants. Even though his very livelihood seems threatened by a petulant three-year-old, he is only thinking of elephants. Tiny footsteps clatter up the stairs. "Oh, no, you don't," Jeanne yells from the downstairs hall. The crying changes pitch: It becomes a low howl.

"I'm convinced," Terry says, searching the clay for a clue, "that elephants have a concept of death. I've seen them go to a waterhole where the bones of another elephant are lying. They touch them, play with them, carry them off a short distance and then drop them. They've even been known to take the tusks off with them, into a forest, and bury them. Makes you think, doesn't it? Have they been studying the ivory market? Paying last respects? I wouldn't believe anyone who claimed he knew the answer. All I can say is that they're bloody marvelous. Dammit."

Terry picks up the smallest of the elephant group and pulls it apart limb by limb until all that is left is the bare armature. "Now," he says, "I can start again with a clear conscience."

"Umm," said Tony Dyer, president of the East African Professional Hunters' Association. He cleared his throat, buttoned and then unbuttoned his blazer, and finally stroked his curly hair. "Umm," he stated once again, this time with even greater conviction. The hunters, their wives, girl friends, sons and a phalanx of impatient waiters, all assembled in the Casuarina Room of the Nairobi Hilton, coughed and looked for safety at the chandeliers.

This evening was the occasion of the last Hunters' Ball ever and it was Tony's reluctant task to serve as its toastmaster and master of ceremonies. Tony is the undisputed spokesman for the East African hunters. He himself was once a prodigious name in their ranks—a leopard specialist, so it is said—but when he was still young he retired to manage a large family ranch. A hunter, yet no longer a hunter, he was considered invulnerable to pettiness, jealousies, vogues and greed. An impartial arbiter he certainly has been, but now with the government threatening a total ban on the use of firearms for any purpose, Tony seems powerless to lobby for his association's goals. Still, Tony is the ideal figurehead: He has not one enemy.

Tony's right foot was now tapping. As he started to unbutton his jacket for the third time a voice from a distant table yelled: "Start the music."

In fact, Tony did have something to say. Last year there had been no ball, for it was felt, even then, that hunting was doomed. But the profession endured for yet another year and, in a mood of blind whimsy, a committee was formed and a Hunters' Ball to beat all Hunters' Balls was organized. On this evening Tony, it seemed, wanted to say something about false hopes and unrealistic expectations, but a man who has spent all his life miles from cities often finds addressing large groups distressingly difficult. He looked for the perfect words. He searched the moldings around the ceiling. He studied the faces of his older colleagues, most of them sitting in the first row to hear better. He saw their bemusement. "Umm," Tony said with a little more dignity. He looked beyond the first row at the younger faces. He noted their enthusiasm, maybe even heard their whispered tales of great elephants still to be shot. The Acrilan ties and regimental blazers glistened from every corner. Tanned forearm and muscled shoulder were tonight constrained by shirts too white and by wives with too high an expectation of gentility.

"Start the music," an exuberant voice yelled. Tony's lips were now forming words. He clasped the sides of the lectern with white-knuckled hands.

"Yes," he said at last. "I guess that's all."

The Pakistani band, poised for the last thirty minutes, assumed that those words were their cue. Immediately, the leader struck up "Yellow Submarine." From all sides of the room couples rose with a vengeance, and a veteran hunter, his arm stiff from an old injury, turned to his dinner partner and observed: "Mark those words of Tony. I think he's a lot more articulate than we give him credit for."

Terry has not said very much during the last few minutes. When he turned the lights on in his studio the elephant groups came to life. Watching them grow out of gloom is for me like being in a museum late at night, waiting for one's eyes to grow accustomed to the dark. For the last eight hours the elephants were stillborn. Now at last I can sense their fear and rage. What should have come to Terry so naturally has been a tumultuous battle. Every morning, he has said, he wants to achieve a state of sublime instinct—a half-conscious mood when his modeling tools play on the clay, independent of his mind. But today he thought too much, and for a while he even began to despise his elephants. Now, under the artificial lights, spent and discouraged, he has suddenly rediscovered what he should have been after this morning.

His thumb is as useful a tool as any. It compresses and shapes, twists and molds. Eyes appear out of nothing, just as suggestions. A leg is filled out and when it looks as if it dangles clumsily it is palmed close to the body. The whole process is not so much an act of creation, but a reduction to essentials. What is considered unnecessary is removed. Purity is restored.

Suddenly Terry stops. There is something he must say. He paces the room, looks out the window where the only sound is of cicadas, turns, checks himself and studies the elephants. He begins by saying that during the rainy seasons most professionals declare a holiday from the hunt. Some leave the country on holiday, others work around the house. Just last year, Terry decided to take his son Glenn, then twenty-one, hunting near the Tana River. The boy has determined to become a hunter and Terry could remember how lost he had been at a similar age when all he needed was "dangerous game" experience, and there was no one to give it to him.

All morning they have been following a lone elephant. The rain has been constant since dawn and now, every twenty minutes, Terry stops to wring water out of the black patch over his eye. Since the accident three years before, today will be his first encounter with any quarry that can fight back—not terribly advisable for a man with one eye.

Terry's shorts have annealed to his legs. Droplets of rain spin along the scratched barrels of his .458. In the black mud ahead, the swollen molds of elephant's feet have filled with water. He keeps to one side of them to avoid falling in. When he advances, all he hears is the squelch of his sandals in the mud. When he stops, he must wait for the thump of his heart to cease before he can hear the elephants.

Just as Terry replaces his eyepatch for the second time he

hears rumbling. Father and son freeze, their feet sinking deeper into the mud. Terry twists to the left, to the right, to see beyond a badly positioned tree. At the end of a tunnel, leading through commiphora bush, he can see two tusks. They barely move. Terry studies them, knowing that whatever they belong to is also studying him.

Suddenly the elephant's head turns. His ears fan out, the trunk periscoping above the bush, and then, without warning, he charges. His ears and trunk are tucked tight against his body and if he screams no one hears. Terry jams his gun against his left shoulder, pops off the safety and squints along the barrels. He sees only blackness. The elephant should be in full view by now but Terry sees nothing. He can sense the animal's bush-flattening rush, he can feel repercussions in the ground. He even suspects the displacement of air, caused by the elephant's charge. But down his sights there is only blackness.

"Dammit to hell!" Terry switches the rifle from his left to his right shoulder. At last the elephant is in full view, ten yards away and coming fast. Terry pulls the trigger, drops the animal with a brain shot and as it falls, mud rains down, coating the hunters in a black glue.

"I was scared," Terry says to me, plumping himself, exhausted, into a big chair. "Elephants had never done that to me before. I knew I should never hunt dangerous game, but, you know, I thought I could make an exception for my son. And now I'm shit scared. Not of them so much, but of something else. No, don't say I'm scared of myself. That's too goddamn easy. No. Something bigger. I wish I knew. You wouldn't believe the feeling. I have to keep doing elephants. Bloody elephants. It's awful."

Rolfe Andresen is one of the few professional hunters who really look the part: blond glistening hair without a trace of thinness, hatchet-sharp features, blue eyes that rarely blink, a large Adam's apple that remains immobile even when he talks and forearms as large as any body-builder's. He sits at the first table in an otherwise empty restaurant, talking to a colleague. Sometimes there seem to be tears in Rolfe Andresen's eyes.

He has been driving all through the day to reach Nairobi to find out what the hell has been going on. As recently as this morning he was conducting an elephant hunt. His client was from Texas and determined, like everyone else, to shoot an elephant. They had been following three bulls for two days. This morning they awoke two hours before dawn to be on the site where they had abandoned the chase last night. The timing was impeccable, in fact, for with the rising sun they had only walked half a mile before they spotted the elephants' backs, looming, like worn rocks, above a patch of bush. There they stayed, waiting for the perfect shot. Suddenly, at nine o'clock, the elephants began to move. The first one emerged: good but not special. The second was larger, but still the hunters believed the third must have been the biggest of all three. But just as he emerged from his concealment, Rolfe began to hear the horn.

Far away in the direction of camp, a car was approaching, its horn honking insanely. Rolfe stood up to look, confused and then angry, and as he did, the elephants panicked, fleeing the scene at a run. Rolfe was ready to hit the driver, whoever the bloody hell he was, and then he saw the vehicle was one of his own Land Rovers, the driver employed by him. Something must be wrong, thought Andresen. Had the camp burned down? Had there been an attack by *shifta* (bandits)?

The driver was breathless. Yes, he said, something *was* wrong. He had been listening to the "Voice of Kenya" on the radio this morning, and there had been a special bulletin: All hunting throughout the country had been banned.

"For how long?" Andresen asked.

"Permanently."

Tonight Rolfe Andresen knows that what his driver heard on the radio is absolutely true. He has decided to consider other matters over dinner with a friend, but all they can discuss are their professions, now seemingly ended. "We'll fight it," the other says. "We have documents. I can prove it's unrealistic." He stops to sip his soup. "Hunters keep the poaching under control. They check overpopulation of species. Their investments in licenses amount to over a million dollars annually for the Kenyan treasury. What the hell can this bloody government think it can gain from a ban?"

Rolfe Andresen looks carefully at his steak. He knows all the answers already. He knows he stands to lose a lot of money this year. He has no idea, for instance, how he is going to repay all the deposits he received for promised safaris. He refuses to divert the safaris to the Sudan. Uganda is a mess, and Zambia and Botswana had closed shops. And what about Tanzania? What about it? The potatoes are cold. "Waiter!"

Rolfe Andresen wants more vegetables. Yes, he liked the asparagus but they weren't enough and instead of the vinaigrette sauce he would prefer a cup of melted butter. "John, if you're not going to finish your steak, may I have it? The large-size Tusker, please. And, oh yes, pudding—lots of it—and a decent-size brandy for afterward . . . Coffee? Of course. And don't forget those chocolate-covered mints you're so famous for. . . .

"At last Nairobi has a good restaurant. Fuck the world."

One year later:

In Nairobi, the curio shops no longer sell ivory carvings. Instead, their windows are filled with wooden Makonde renderings of elephants. Some hunters are still busy knocking on government doors, believing that hunting will soon be resumed. Others plan to go to San Antonio, Texas, to stand before a forum of wealthy big-game hunters and expose corruption in high places in the Kenyan game department. Others have become car mechanics.

Looking down Mama Ngina Street, it is difficult to tell that the town is not as prosperous as it was last year. African women are dressed in bright *merikani*, all men carry briefcases and seem in a hurry to cash their checks at the nearby Standard Bank. Many beggers are overweight.

Far down the street, the crowds make way for a white man, steering an uneven course toward one of the airline offices. Even when he is close at hand the man is not instantly recognizable as Terry Mathews. The stomach is wasted, the blond hair dull, the cheeks hollow and yellow, the black eyepatch missing altogether. Once his voice had a distinctive metallic rattle. Today it is a hoarse whisper. How could a white hunter—once the true king of the jungle—now look like one of the hunted?

79

"Have to get tax clearance before they let me buy a ticket to London. Bastards," he says.

"What's the problem?"

"I'm not coming back." Terry begins coughing uncontrollably. "I've had it with the whole shooting match. I'm not coming back."

"You've got malaria."

"Yes, and hepatitis, and it'll never go away if I stay here. Bloody Africa."

"Did you ever cast those elephants in bronze?" I ask.

"Not yet." Terry fingers the toothbrush he carries in the top pocket of his bush jacket. "I've got all I need."

There is a cave in Tanzania that should only be seen at sunset, preferably by a child. The sun slashes through its oyster mouth a few minutes before dusk, illuminating the interior briefly once a day. A cave of such a design, you think, must have a secret, so you crawl deeper and deeper, your matches needing constant replenishment. The ceiling, you see, is black from long-ago campfires, and in the distance, you notice a remarkably flat wall. You crawl and once you are in the farthest recess you see the figures. They are dancing across one another with no thought of order, of proportion or, for that matter, of time. Here there is a giraffe, there a warthog three times its size. The wildebeest has eight legs, the elephant staggers under the weight of its ivory and through this African circus squirms a python as large as a savannah. On the left there must have been other figures but rainwater, bleeding down the rock face for a thousand years, has turned them black. You now need two matches, for the sun has dropped below the cave mouth, and at the far right you see the crudest figure of all. He is the hunter—merely a backbone, a few limbs and a space where a round face should be. His expression has been left for you to determine. He will, you muse, kill the wildebeest and the warthog and the elephant. And when they are all gone and his stomach hurts and after the smoke from the fire has drugged him to sleep and he awakes one afternoon, stiff and hurting, his eyes like yours will be drawn to this perfectly flat wall.

Or perhaps you were mistaken. Perhaps the warthog fled into an unexpected hole; perhaps the python was, on closer examination, the taproots of a giant fig tree; perhaps the elephant survived its wounds and fled into a secret valley. It little matters.

All that endures is an artist's enigma: He could not see the hunter for the game.

Today Terry has returned to the same Nairobi studio, still at it.

For years I had dreamed of making a long walk in Africa. The
idea grew on me while I was in Kenya's northern frontier making a film about man's first ancestors. There, where allegedly we
first started making stone tools and chasing after antelopes, I began to see distance as a personal challenge. Later, while I was
editing the film in a windowless room underneath London's Park
Lane, my thoughts turned once again to walking. I was obsessed
by the restraint of this polite city, aggravated by a concern that I
was getting nowhere at my job. Africa and a Pleistocene exertion
seemed a cure for all this. Most of all I hankered after a great

WALKING THROUGH FIRE

heart-wrenching view of the land I wanted so much to possess.

In March 1977 I flew to Nairobi, rented a small Cessna and piloted myself on a reconnaissance flight over several areas of country I had considered for a walk. The Aberdares were too confused, the northern frontier too limitless, Tsavo National Park illegal. Finally, I decided that I must walk the Kedong Valley, a small chunk of the Great Rift Valley. I cannot say exactly why I was so taken by the Kedong—in a sense it was just one more section of the copper-gray bush that covers so much of sub-Saharan Africa. On the other hand, it had rather neat boundaries.

It began at beautiful Lake Naivasha at an altitude of six thousand feet. From there the ground falls away in a neat flight of colosseum steps until the valley more or less ends at Lake Magadi, festering only two thousand feet above sea level. Wherever I flew I saw no car's dust, no tin roof, no fence. I flew low over the ground in the plum-colored light of a late afternoon, nudging the stick every time the ground dropped at one of those massive steps. Even in the cockpit of the plane I could feel the temperature rising on our approach to Lake Magadi. On either side, the walls of the Rift Valley rose to make the journey seem like a descent along a corridor into the bottom of the sky. My passenger, an African friend who had never before been in an airplane, whistled at one moment as he saw approaching the scar tissue rimming the shore of Lake Magadi. He knew this land well on foot, but he had never seen it from such a height. "Kenya is big," he said proudly. I agreed.

In Nairobi the next day I hired four porters without much thought to the consequences. Karumba, a self-described half-caste, seemed more Masai than Kikuyu. He rarely asked questions, seldom looked me in the eyes and considered no one, especially me, his equal. Not even his absurd striped trousers, befitting more a morning coat than bush fatigues, stole from his superior manner. He treated me as a guest whose job was merely to pay salaries and provide meals, and on both counts I was delinquent in my duties.

Francis, Karumba's friend, looked like a fool. When he toted his backpack, he reminded me of Quasimodo. Because his pug nose was so upturned there was not enough skin left over to cover his lower lip, so his face was set in a perpetual leer. But Francis was anything but a fool. He was far cleverer than Karumba, and when at the end of the safari he decided he should be paid more than the others, I somehow agreed. He took the money and, lest anyone forget he was overpaid, he leaped high into the air, sprang into the bush, whooped some more, the money high over his head, while he ran back to his village, chanting all the way. It was hard not to like Francis best of all.

Then there were Hoya and Filif, both wa-Kamba, both Jehovah's Witnesses and both uneasy with the pagan Masai. At night they would sleep away from the others, praying for all our souls.

Supplies were purchased in the afternoon with wild abandon and little forethought. By the end of the day the floor of the Land Cruiser was covered with four one-gallon jerricans for water, four military canteens, some sunburn cream, five tins of tunafish, four packets of dried apples, two cans of beans, two bottles of HiHo squash, three packets of powdered mushroom soup, a can of coffee and a nineteen-shilling hipflask of Vat 69. The porters would have to survive on six five-pound bags of maize meal, a small bag of onions, a canister of tea and four chocolate bars. When the trip was ended I noted that I had touched little of the food, having been far more interested in water than in protein. On the other hand, the porters left behind none of their maize meal, onions or tea. The other items: a not very accurate compass and a Shell road map, six years out of date.

By late in the day we are all assembled at our starting point—the foot of a volcano called Suswa. We should have been here at two in the afternoon. Now the air is cooling and we have only an hour and a half of daylight to make the shakedown leg. One hundred miles now separate us from Lake Magadi.

Among us we carry 190 pounds, much of it water and corn-meal. The first step is ominous, suggesting that this stunt may conceivably be more work than fun. Down into a sand river, up a loose embankment. But the thirty-pound pack is not as heavy as I had imagined. Across a bed of rocks—well, it's still easy. A zebra barks an alert. Going up an incline with my shoulders hunched forward, I fiddle with my hands: do they belong in my pockets, hooked to my shoulder straps or swinging uselessly? As I go downhill, the pack pushes me into a slow trot through a patch of thorns—pure African pleasure as they scrape against my bare legs. Horizons become important. They're all the same, but on top of each rise I expect to see elephants.

The pack makes me swagger and the swaggering makes me feel master of the load. Four and a half gallons of water: Is it enough for five people for three days? My doubts are growing. Soon the swaggering degenerates to a plod. "In hot country a man needs at least one gallon a day," an authority had said. I do not believe I could be so greedy, but now with night falling and the great land filling with shadows and secrets, I am uncertain. The mathematics are harsh: If a man limits himself to a forty-pound load in this country, he can be independent of waterholes

85

for no more than four days (one gallon weighing about ten pounds)—that is, if he carries no other supplies. But if he carries his own food, he is probably reduced to two days. And if he adds a camera and lens and spare shoes to his load, well, then, he had better stick to circumnavigating freshwater lakes.

This is the holy hour of Africa: The cicadas have ceased. The wind, wafting through the tall grass, ripples the hairs on my arms. All life in this country is coming out of hiding. The shadows have not yet deepened and colors are restored to their true tones. The bleached grass turns yellow and brown and even flaked gold; the far escarpment wall is a temple blue. In the distance, the high-pitched cries of Masai herdboys echo against a hill.

The wind suddenly pummels us. The hair on my head stands vertically and the thorns whistle—a low moan rising and falling, south to north. I dump my pack near a *boma* of cattle and in the dark wander aimlessly with the porters, hoping to trip over pieces of deadwood. After two hours we return with only a few scraps; the herdboys have already depleted the countryside. My heart beating chaotically with the thumping of the wind, I light nine matches with no success. At last, the tenth ignites; the thin flame digs its fingers into the ground, and the wood begins to splutter, sending blue sparks into the night.

When the fire is settled, the flames lie low, avoiding the cooking pots. The soup will be cold and lumpy, no matter what, so my bottle of Vat 69 is the solution.

The wind pitches dust and thorns at me, lying still on the canvas bed. Karumba's refrain above the plainsong voices is a constant *"Tabu safari"* ("A bad safari"). When anyone alludes to our destination, Lake Magadi, he mutters, *"Mbale sana, mbale zaidi"* ("Very far, much too far"). For Karumba, Magadi is at the very edge of the earth.

By seven-thirty in the morning the wind has stopped and the dust lies flat. A 747 breaks against the sky on its final approach to Nairobi. Just as wait-a-bit thorns bite into my ankles, I imagine breakfast trays being whisked away from the bleary-eyed passengers. By nine I know I have conquered the heat and the load. We have reached a Masai manyatta called Gejungeroo— the ground sodden with cattle diarrhea, flies slurping moisture from everyone's eyes, mucus icing on the upper lips of all the babies. But this is a fortunate place, for here there is water. We fill up, unwittingly, for the last time. No stopping now: south southwest. Until now my compass and Karumba have agreed that our goal is that fissure on the edge of the eastern escarpment. At midday Karumba asks to see my compass. We have climbed two steep cliffs that I never noticed from the air; paused to watch giraffe, kongoni, Thomson's and Grant's gazelle and the largest eland I have ever seen; we've crossed a lava flow that scraped my ankles. Suddenly the landmarks, blurred by thorns, are new and strange, altogether unlike the great walls I had assumed would closet us until we reached the soda wastes of Magadi. The worn steps that guided us this morning have disappeared, like elephants fading into the countryside. Karumba examines the compass and when the south southwest radial settles down on some commiphora bushes, he clucks in agreement to tell me that the compass has passed its test. He squats beneath a thorn tree, asking permission, and expects me to be as ready as he for the midday break.

Within an hour we are once again on foot, our loads noticeably lighter. But now the sun is painful, conspiring with the thorns to turn all exposed skin to fire. By six in the evening my legs are traveling out of habit alone, the soles of my feet swollen with blisters. "How far to Magadi?"

"Too far," says Karumba.

"Then what's that?" We stand on the crown of a fault that has been approaching us for the last two hours and an evening wind brushes past us, sailing across the emptiness to the south. Just beneath a distant heap of hills there is a reflection of white, like a peeled scab. "Magadi?" I ask again. For a moment, Karumba is silent, unsure of himself, but as he turns away, he nods inconclusively.

"Magadi," he intones.

"Then it's close. We'll be there tomorrow."

"No, not tomorrow."

"But it's within my hand's reach."

He walks off, laughing like an executioner.

After sundown, the wind turns cold, and we settle on a large thorn tree for a campsite, perhaps from the habit of looking for shade. A tree is a house, a roof, a second story, but for Hoya and Filif it is mostly protection against lions. During the last hour, they have been observing loudly that the lion spoor in the sand is fresh. Now they begin dragging thorn trees from all directions to build a fence. As soon as stars appear and Orion's belt swells to take center stage, they set a nearby bush on fire and the wind drives the great flames along the ground, until they lick dangerously close to the gates to the camp.

Lying on my camp bed, for the first time I am truly worried about thirst. I am not even sure I can sleep. Thirst is the underlying theme of all the early travel books about Africa, and watching the sky I morbidly run through the accounts I can remember. One particular writer haunted me, an early administrator in Bechuanaland (now Botswana). Months after my walk I checked the book (*Trekking the Great Thirst*, 1912) and found that my memory of Arnold Hodson's account was not far off. He wrote of a friend: "He was coming along this very same road with a Hottentot. The journey was awful, for they suffered terrible thirst, and both their riding bullocks died. They eventually arrived at this village in a terrible condition, practically at their last gasp, with swollen tongues and bloody lips, the latter having been cracked by the heat. There were plenty of melons in this village and also ostrich eggs full of water. Leroux and the Hottentot implored these people to give them water, but they refused and demanded £5 first. Leroux tried to make them alter their minds, but they would not, and eventually, being nearly crazy with thirst, he gave them the £5, which he luckily had on him, and got his drink. I asked why he did not take it by force, and he told me he was too weak at that time to kill a fly, and it is more than probable that if he had not had the £5 on him they would have left him to die."

The great problem with walking long distances for one who has become accustomed to riding in cars is accepting the slow pace. The distances do not approach; they recede. Pacing oneself is the bleakest exercise of the mind. Imagination, disguised as daydreaming, becomes an enemy. A giraffe unlimbers its legs; four legs become eight. I know I should stop and see why the giraffe moves so ponderously yet vanishes so quickly, but if I stop I will break the pace, perhaps never to be resumed. Mental isometrics. Filif is asking a question. Won't he be quiet? A strap breaks on a pack and I can feel my brain spinning with the tedium of delay. To resume the same pace is asking too much. Daydreaming helps self-control but is itself uncontrollable: It caters exclusively to the needs of a dusty throat. I squeeze my flickering thoughts into a vacuum and out pops a cold Tusker beer.

Ewart Scott Grogan, an adventurer who walked from Cape Town to Cairo in 1898, thought he knew why self-control was so much more difficult for Westerners. He wrote about his porter's talent for enduring great distances and heavy loads: "His mind is so inactive and blank that he can carry for miles loads that he cannot pick up from the ground, merely by sinking his entity. He becomes mentally torpid, with the result that the effort is solely physical. A white man, though physically stronger, would fret himself into a state of utter fatigue in a quarter of the time." I strongly disagree with Grogan that I am physically stronger than my porters. There is no doubt they can outdo me any time, yet Grogan is right when he says I fret.

I am thinking now of Wilfred Thesiger, perhaps the greatest desert walker of our times. Hawk-nosed and towering, he crossed Arabia's Empty Quarter twice on foot, explored most of Ethiopia's Danakil Depression and traveled for several years with the Marsh Arabs in Iraq. The last time I met him was at his camp on the edge of Lake Turkana. Despite his age (near seventy), he explained, he still enjoys a forced march of fifty miles through hot country. His pleasure is not so much in the trial of endurance as in the people; walking with nomads is the only way he knows to understand them. He wrote of this "comradeship in a hostile world" as a source of endless joy. "Many who venture into dangerous places have found this comradeship among members of their own race; a few find it more easily among people from other lands, the very differences which separate them bringing them ever more closely. I found it among the Bedu."

Thesiger's companions, when I met him, were Turkana boys who had accompanied him on other jaunts along the wild lakeshore. I caught him between walks and he was fidgety with the penance of having to stay in a camp for more than a few days. As we compared notes on the geography of the land, one of the "Turks" shouted that a calf was eating Mr. Thesiger's belongings. We leaped out of our canvas seats, rushed to his small sleeping tent and discovered that, sure enough, an emaciated calf had been on the rampage. A bag of cornmeal had been ripped open and the contents of the tent were covered in a fine layer of white dust. Worse, the hunger-crazed animal had gnawed on the strap of Thesiger's field glasses and had whittled at least two books into a pile of white shavings. Thesiger's granite face turned scarlet. He berated the camp staff for allowing the calf to break and enter; he shouted at the calf, which was now munching on the only blade of grass left in this hot country; he threatened to shoot it. When we eventually resettled in the canvas chairs in the mess tent, he relived the incident with artery-pounding anger. The responsibilities of permanence had undone him. He finally regained his composure and humor, but only after we had worked off his anger with a five-mile walk in the late afternoon. "I wouldn't have minded," he confided to me just before I drove away in the evening, "if the bloody calf had gone for the Dostoevski, but it only had an appetite for the Ayn Rand. Bad taste— that's what I call it."

Thesiger is no more suited to vehicles than to permanent camps. Legend has it that he once succumbed to the purchase of a Land Rover, the only sensible means of reaching the country where he wanted to walk. One day, finding his way blocked by two boulders, he took the course a walker would take: He kept on going. The boulders were five feet apart and his car slightly wider, but that did not deter him. He put the vehicle in four-wheel drive and mashed it against the two monoliths, until in the end his car was four feet, eleven inches wide.

A friend once found him striding along a track six miles short of the town of Makowe, on the Kenyan coast. A solid sheet of rain was falling and Thesiger was drenched. "Can I give you a lift?" my friend asked through the window of his car. Thesiger thanked him courteously. He had just walked two hundred miles from the Somali border, he explained; the last six miles were quite tolerable.

I think I would have accepted the lift. I am walking the Kedong Valley, nearly one hundred miles of it, precisely because there are no roads. Like Thesiger, I prefer to walk in the company of people not of my own race. With a fellow Westerner I would have been deaf to this African music. But unlike Thesiger, when I come upon a road, the symphony is ended.

A giraffe is watching us from a distance and next to it there is a Masai manyatta. Here there is bound to be water. My stride lengthens. But Karumba, master of the pace, bears to the left of the low mud huts. *"Hakuna watu,"* he says. ("Nobody here.") The place is empty; the Masai, without water for their cattle, are long gone. I had even prepared myself to drink their drink— fresh cow's milk and blood.

By ten o'clock we have passed three other manyattas. All are empty and even the game has gone. Overhead, a waterbottle bird keeps us under surveillance. Singing and belching, he reminds us that just because we are human, we are not so special. The long view that so encouraged me last night is now obstructed by the gray film of acacia tops.

By noon I declare our first halt. We flop down under a screen of thorns. I cover my face with my arm and instantly my face is bathed in sweat. "How much water is left?"

"Hakuna." I open my eyes to stare at the sun. Nothing? How can it be? Who drank it? The half-gallon that I had guarded was our emergency ration, and now it has vanished. I shake each of the other jerricans to see if a drop has been overlooked. No luck. The only splashing in all our packs comes from my canteen with a mere half-inch of water, and from the two bottles of squash concentrate. Filif, who knows how to ward off blame, says: "You drank too much last night."

Of course I did, but so did everyone else, mainly because all that cornmeal tempts one to drink a gallon at each sitting. The guilt lies squarely on my shoulders: I should have kept military discipline from the start, I should have outlawed the water-consuming cornmeal and I should have stood guard over the water.

Arnold Hodson, that raconteur of thirst, leaps out of me masochistically with yet another ghastly account. He tells how one day, while trekking through Bechuanaland, he stumbled upon the corpse of a dear friend, missing for many days. Hyenas and jackals had already had their fill, so the remains were barely recognizable, apart from a pair of socks clinging to the bones of the feet. Nearby lay a bottle containing the following letter:

Dear A,—Last night the cattle ran away. I have no more water. I despair. I left the wagon on foot in the hope of reaching Kokong, but my strength fails. My private papers and stamps send to my children in ———, and inform them that I have died of fever in the desert and am buried. . . . Charlie and the new Kalahari boy are mainly

91

*responsible for this. The thirst kills me. These are the last words of
a dying man.*

Your true friend, M.

P.S. *A little water would have saved me.*

Karumba is pressing to set off, but it is only one o'clock and the
sun, which I have never known so hot, will not let up until four.
Walking at this time of the day will only cook us, leaving us
with little strength for the rest of the journey. If, on the other
hand, we wait until four we will surely not be able to reach the
waterhole of Sonorweah by nightfall. I decide to walk for another hour, and then to declare half-hour halts until the sun cools.

Stopping is suicide, going is worse. The porters slurped
down the water that would have granted survival. They blame
the loss on everyone else, and we have only been gone two days.
My mind reels under blame and hopelessness, knowing that I
should have been firmer, and thinking how ridiculous it will be
to perish from lack of water after only two days. I am insane and
so is Africa.

My left eye sees only blurs, and I walk stiff-legged so my
knees will not crumble. I have nearly finished a package of glu-
cose tablets and a dried saccharine foam rims my mouth. I advance by picking out one large tree on the horizon as goal, and
when miraculously I reach it, I search for another beyond. On
and on I trudge, dehydrated and overcome by the endlessness of
the march.

The African midday has never been properly captured by a
camera. On film, landscapes flatten and become monochrome;
most cameramen say shooting at this time is worthless. In reality
it is a time of many dimensions, of heat haze receding behind
hills, a recessional in grays, in yellows, in glancing copper.

The ambient temperature I estimate at 104 degrees Fahrenheit. In direct sunlight, the air would be 140 degrees. The Kedong can be the hottest area in Kenya. The danger is of course
dehydration. The skin dries: When I pinch my arm it remains
pinched, like wax paper. And after the skin is parched, all the
organs that depend on water, such as eyes, start to fail, until at
last, the kidneys fail. Victims of dehydration will often die in the
hospital even though they are being fed all essential fluids. Once
damaged, the kidneys rarely respond to help.

Checking once again to see if a drop of water has been over-looked in one of the jerricans, my eye falls on the two bottles of undiluted HiHo Orange Squash syrup. There is no warning on the label against its consumption, and when I drink it, I reason, the packs will be lighter. It rolls about in its bottles like an angry sea, half invitation, half menace. I drink. It is wet, seemingly good for the throat, but the aftertaste is like cleaning fluid. The sensation begs for more. Now I hastily gulp down a finger of the odious liquid and then lie back to vomit.

At three o'clock I decide even rest is unbearable. Somehow I feel stronger. I even wish my pack were heavier so I could show off for the porters.

I see the road from a long distance. The sun is low and even the shadow of a tree can create a highway. But this road is straight, and it is raised, and its color is blacker than even the darkest basalt boulder. Only by stepping on it will I know for sure. Yes, it is a road—tarmacked, straight and built for a future with lots of traffic. My sandals glide across it, and I drop my pack and do a sort of run to make the others laugh. Karumba is saying that he had told me about this road, but, in truth, he had never said a word. He is as surprised as I. When finally I lie down in the soft sand on the shoulder I look about me at these four shagbaggers, dirtier than I, but not showing their dirt as candidly. I know that this road has saved our lives, and because it appeared so suddenly it will always be a special road for me.

I simply cannot believe I did not know about it. With my back flat against the tarmac I resurrect all my knowledge of this country. The map did not show the road clearly because the map was six years old. I had not seen the road from the air because I must have flown along a more westerly path than our foot route. But then, I had made every effort to follow on foot the compass heading I had set in the aircraft. I struggle with these concepts of higher mathematics until my mind grows weary, picking out clouds in the afternoon sky instead. Only later, after I had re-covered myself, did I discover that the compass was inaccurate by twenty degrees. I also discovered that the road had just been completed two months before. My mistake was clear: Just as I had flown the country by air, so too should I have driven it.

Thunderheads are building over the western escarpment and a yellow-billed kite circles low for a closer inspection of the five bodies beside the road. Perhaps the rains will break this evening. Certainly the heat could not be worse. Suddenly Francis sits up, points toward Nairobi, and soon I see two cars, a sedan and an overloaded station wagon, working this road as a *matatu,* a native bus. The sedan is slow to brake. Francis and I run to catch it, halted far down the road, while the others gain footholds on the station wagon. Our rescuer is the chief engineer of the mine at Magadi. He is being chauffeured home after a day in Nairobi. I can tell from the way he averts his eyes that he would have preferred not to stop. "The last person to walk overland like you, I buried by the side of the road."

"We're lucky."

"Mmm." The conversation, it seems, can go no further.

"I understand there's a club at the mine—the Magadi Club," I say, thinking only of a drink.

"Mmm."

"Any chance of getting a day's membership there so I can buy the chaps a beer?"

His eyes are fixed to the road. "Sorry, but it isn't that sort of club." I then look down at myself. My white shorts are now splotchy gray, my skin is red, and I would agree that I don't look like membership material. I was later to discover that I had lost twenty-five pounds in three days of walking. I wink at Francis, who has understood just enough English to grin. "There's another place," the engineer continues. "We call it the working-man's club. There's a pool where you can wash off, and beer, although it's not quite as cold as it is at our club. What's your name, by the way?"

I pronounce it slowly, and for the first time he turns to look me over more carefully.

"Hemingway. I'll be damned. I know your uncle. Back in 'fifty-three, I think it was. He was hunting near here." For a second, I wonder if I ought to put him straight—tell him that I am no relation—but the mood passes.

"That must have been his last safari, just before the two crashes in Uganda," I volunteer.

"A squarely set man."

"Built like an anthill, they used to say out here," I embroider whimsically. The engineer has not stopped looking at me since I mentioned my name. He is gauging my reaction to his next remark. "Terrible tragedy about his death."

"Awful." I lower my eyes. For a while we ride in silence and after a dignified pause, he adds:

"My wife's a great fan of your cousin—Mary, isn't it?"

"Margaux," I correct.

"That's right—Margaux. What a lovely girl."

"Mmm," I say, imitating my host.

"You had better come back to our house for a wash and a beer. Our fridge is the best at the mine. My wife will never forgive me if she heard I picked up a cousin of Margaux's and didn't bring him home."

As soon as the engineer looks away I nudge Francis to tell him all is okay, but he already knows. With the windows open I can smell Lake Magadi long before we are there. I had never known water with such a powerful smell and, although the stench comes from decaying organisms, it somehow tells me I am home.

GORILLAS AND THEIR PEOPLE

As long as I can remember, I had a dream of gorillas. They were horrific and strong—mutilated humans, in fact—while at the same time being alarmingly familiar. Best of all, they lived in jungles, the fantasy world of boys born and raised in big cities. Alan Morehead, in *No Room in the Ark,* evoked an atavistic memory of them for me. After tracking them on the Virunga volcanoes of southwest Uganda for several days, he recounted how he finally sighted a troop. He admitted then that he felt like a Peeping Tom. "Of course he would have," I thought to myself. "And so must I." From that minute I was determined to see gorillas. I convinced myself that no encounter with a lion, elephant or rhino could possibly match a sighting of a gorilla. Alan Morehead had shown me that to be a complete person I must let a gorilla into my life. The year was 1961 and I was all of seventeen years old.

During the summer of that year I signed on with school friends and a would-be explorer to look for gorillas in the same area where Morehead once had been. The crossing of Central and East Africa took us nearly two months and when we reached Kisoro, straddling the border of Uganda and the Congo, we were scrawny, sunbleached and filthy.

Unlike other Ugandan villages of a similar size, this one possessed both a white man and a hotel. The white man was Walter Baumgartel, an Austrian, who a few years before had proclaimed himself "the king of gorillaland." The hotel, euphemistically called Travellers' Rest, belonged to him and evoked his rough and quirky nature. For a ratpack of schoolboys, it was as good as its name. The shower was almost hot, the sheets real sheets, although not clean, and the food available in large quantities. For other travelers it was no such luxury. The guest book was punctuated with such remarks as: "The food would not be so tasty if the kitchen wasn't so close to the loo," and "I'd rather live under canvas than stay here again," and "Don't sit at Baumgartel's table if you value your sanity."

We had already been warned in Kampala that Walter Baumgartel was manic-depressive (I was too shy to ask what that meant), and that neither one of his extremes of temperament was much of a diversion for a guest. On the other hand, his hotel was said to be an experience we would never forget; its location one of the most breathtaking sites in all the world.

The grounds of Travellers' Rest were well-clipped lawns, shimmeringly green, and beds of succulents, posing as flowers. The hotel was on the brow of a low hill. In three directions, small farms climbed toward mountain walls, obscured by clouds most of the day. The walls of the hotel buildings were wood and bougainvillea, each one supporting the other. Baumgartel's major worry, so I found, was keeping the jungle at bay. Flowers bloomed overnight, moths were mutating from pupa to chrysalis in the blink of an eye, and the damp and rot seemed to turn even the newest object into something flaccid and familiar after a day or two.

But Travellers' Rest was nonetheless an invigorating place. The evenings, despite the rain, were full of cozy charm with the machine-gun rattle of rain on the iron roof and the popping of green wood in the lounge fireplace. The mighty cloudbursts unfailingly scrubbed the sky clean of clouds just in time for the mornings. For all Travellers' Rest's singularities, the one I recall with the most nostalgia was its tomatoes. No matter how appalling the dinners, the tomatoes were always a tour de force. Their color verged on purple, deep enough to make one's eyes smart. Grown wild in black volcanic soil, they needed no dressing, no salt, no pepper. They were already pungent and sweet, seasoned in the rain forest, so it seemed, with chicory and garlic.

Walter Baumgartel was beside himself with the pleasure of being host to this vanguard from the Children's Crusade. He was foremost a storyteller and in us he found the perfect audience— attentive, enthusiastic and thoroughly gullible. His waving arms told half his stories, evoking the looming volcanoes, girded by clouds. He spoke of them as the haunt of the mountain gorilla, an animal whose ferocity was only matched by a black leopard— the gorilla's natural enemy. It was clear that Walter Baumgartel planned to use the leopard as his alibi in the event we never saw gorillas. "I make no promises," he said more than once. And all the time he tortured our adolescent minds with intrigue of pygmies, gorillas, swirling mists and the occasional cannibal. Each morning he was a different person. Bleary-eyed from too many steins of brandy and looking uncomfortably fat, he would stand by the bar in silence, rubbing out stains on the counter with his elbow. One moment he would berate one of his African staff, the next he would deliver bear hugs to his cook, his waiters, the puzzled chambermaids. "You know," he said to his bartender after one of these sweet and sour outbursts, "I luff you like mein own childt."

By the time we set forth into the volcanoes I was prepared for disappointment. Our retinue consisted of seven barefoot porters and a fifty-two-year-old guide called Reuben Rwanzagire, who was then the éminence grise of gorilla country. His feet were hard as pine boards and sinewy enough to wrap around a taproot. Like Baumgartel, he had a vivid narrative style. One of his stories was about a randy female gorilla who had fought him to the ground. By sheer cunning and sinew, Reuben had been

98

able to slip out from under her and thwart her amorous advances. In telling the story Reuben required both an interpreter and a large clearing, for there was much coming and going, charges and cartwheels. He fell to the ground, fought his gorilla, growled through a toothless mouth and finally, after frantic bicycling of his legs, secured his escape. The performance drew a burst of applause from the porters, and a big grin from Reuben. He was definitely the caretaker of these mountains. When he smiled so did his men; when he moved they followed. Even Alan Morehead had quoted him as a major source of information about gorilla behavior.

The final staging post with the cars was at six thousand feet above sea level. From here on the first day we climbed to twelve thousand feet through slippery, tangled ground cover. On several occasions I was sure I would be unable to advance another foot. But the sight of Reuben, bounding without effort as his lungs reprocessed the smoke from the rawest of African cigarettes, gave me bravado. At last, near the top, in the densest of jungles and on a slippery slope, Reuben gave us the alarm signal. There were gorillas ahead, he announced in a whisper. He had heard them feeding. Now we must advance with the greatest caution. We crept on our stomachs, collecting mud in our pants pockets, until Reuben indicated we were but a few feet from the gorillas. We waited. Reuben smiled, delighted to accommodate us on the first day of our quest. Suddenly there was a deafening crash of falling trees as three mammoth shadows plunged down the mountain a few feet from where we lay. For elephants they were small. Still, at two tons an animal, they little resembled gorillas. I looked at Reuben. For a so-called naturalist who had just made a giant gaffe, he showed little embarrassment. He began to laugh, pointing to where the elephants had been, then holding his stomach to contain all the absurdity. He was beside himself: All the way down to our camp just the mention of the word *ndofu* ("elephant") was enough to make him explode all over again.

We slept that night in metal huts on the saddle bridging the two volcanoes of M'gahinga and Muhavura. The next morning when I awoke, the door of my hut would not budge. I pushed several times with no effect. Finally, imagining that one of my school friends was playing a practical joke, I gave the door one violent shove. There was a sudden explosion of big hooves on wet mud, and as I opened the door, I was just in time to see a Cape buffalo beating his way down the mountain.

Reuben and the porters had been out looking for gorillas since before dawn. Now they were back, whistling to us from across the clearing, telling us in hushed voices to follow. We kept to their footsteps and within ten minutes we reached a copse where Reuben showed us the beds of gorillas from the previous night. These were fashioned out of willowy bamboo and the "sheets" were made from layers of leaves. To prove the Posturepedic comfort of these beds Reuben reclined in one, curled himself into the umbilical position, yawned and gave us a demonstration of falling asleep. Once again the performance was too much for the guides, who howled with laughter and only stopped when one of their members pointed to the far side of a gorge where a strand of heavy moss, suspended from the branch of a tree, was waving much too vigorously for the breeze. Five pairs of field glasses were immediately pressed into service as five schoolboys waited for this, the rarest of wildlife sightings. At last, after ten minutes, a large black cylindrical sphere, the shape of a bullet, emerged from the foliage. A gorilla's head, Reuben assured us. Female too, he added with a leer. But from a distance of some hundred yards we could not even see its eyes. I then volunteered to accompany Reuben for a closer look while the others, well positioned, could film the first known instance of a white man being savaged by a gorilla.

The approach was on all fours, through stinging nettle that left large welts across forearms and face. When Reuben stopped, I stopped, and counted the drops of sweat splashing onto the leaves beneath my face. After twenty-five minutes I was not sure where we were. Above us, the sun was totally obscured by the mantle of high branches, and even the slope, which had been steep in one direction for the first ten minutes and now steep in another, was disorienting. Surely, I thought, we now must be near that bullet head.

I stopped to look back and as I turned there was a furious bark, nearly on top of me. No more than fifteen feet ahead of us a gorilla burst out of the leaves. She stood nearly my height, her head surely twice the size of mine, hers beveled by dark blazing eyes. True to the legend, she rattled on her chest with her fingertips, creating a sound both deep and hollow, like a bongo drum. Fear, bluff, anger—she ran the gamut in about fifteen seconds. She might easily have charged us, broken us as if we were matchwood, but she only seemed to want to be left alone. In looking back on that high-speed moment, I would willingly say I was scared. She was indeed frightening, but somehow my instinct was not to run. I was alarmed, too amazed in fact to take a picture, or, if I had held a gun, to take aim. Her eyes demobilized me. If anything, I felt awkward, apologetic. Then she melted into the foliage—some four hundred pounds of primate gliding into the greenery. Hers was not a disappearance. It was a dematerialization, and the sudden calm after her going left me unable to do much more than giggle ridiculously like an adolescent.

One second becomes an hour. A memory evolves into a plateau. My gorilla soon assumed giant dimensions, but even after a year the story remained incomplete. In my mind I would start from the beginning, proceed from one instant to another, only to discover at the end that a component was lacking, as effectively in the story as in my understanding of gorillas. I had had merely a flash of the animal: one freeze-frame. Both of us had been startled, and when the smoke of the moment had cleared I knew little more of gorillas than someone who had read about them in an encyclopedia or seen them in a zoo. Mine was like a hunting story—one brief unnatural moment.

Three years later I returned to the Virunga volcanoes. I had enticed a friend from university to join me, and after I had raised the costs of my trip by working for two months in South Africa, he and I left for southwest Uganda.

When we reached Travellers' Rest, Walter Baumgartel was at pains to recognize me. He had grown slightly heavier, and his hair had changed from black to white without an intervening stage of silver. Where once he had been compulsively conversational, now he seemed dazed. There were many guests at the hotel, all of them refugees from the Congo. They had reached the hotel that morning, and some of the Belgian families were camped on the lawn, their pots and pans and boxes of diapers under groundsheets as protection from the rain. At dinner that night Baumgartel assumed his usual seat at the head of the largest table, but he said very little. He listened gravely to the refugees' accounts of the siege of Stanleyville. He shook his head morosely when he heard how nuns had been raped, housewives' eyes plucked out. He muttered only one remark about World War II and the Anschluss, and then he continued to shake his head with disgust. When dinner was finished, he abandoned us all at the table to retire to a corner where he listened to a wireless for more tales of cannibalism, just across the range of volcanoes. The crackling news, broadcast by the BBC World Service, seemed to lend even more strength to his private convictions, for he often nodded his head, sighed and once even slammed his brandy down onto the side table as if he had just arrived at a decision. The hotel walls were only just standing. The rot had penetrated everything and the staff were brazenly taking advantage of Walter Baumgartel. Now, absolutely nothing—neither the generator, the kitchen nor the mosquito nets—worked. But Baumgartel was no longer concerned about niceties. Not even the gorillas mattered. The next morning when Reuben arrived to collect us, Baumgartel dismissed us all as if we were irrelevant.

Reuben was now wearing boots, and as soon as we began climbing—this time up the volcano M'gahinga—I noticed his limp. The higher we climbed, the more he suffered. The laughing and buffoonery which had accompanied my first ascent was no more, and his breathing was strained and aching. I asked him once whether he wished to pause on the trail. From the way he glared I knew I had paid him an insult. He never replied and continued to climb the near-vertical slope, pedaling in the mud. We followed an elephant path that traveled straight up the fall line and at ten thousand feet we stopped beside a gorilla's bed, similar to the one we had seen three years before. This time, however, Reuben treated it with contempt: It was old, maybe even last year's. Coughing and fighting for breath, he stabbed his fingers at the dried shit and kicked all that remained with his boot. He picked up a few branches and broke them. No, he was not going to lie down in the bed. These gorillas had been here too long before. This was history.

We continued our climb, but it was clear from the way Reuben moved that he had no intention of finding gorillas, whether or not any remained on this volcano. Soon the light turned blue and Reuben swung his gnarled head in the direction from where we had come. He wanted us to believe that his limp was of little consequence, but as he slipped and fell along the muddy path returning to the hotel in the valley below, I thought that he would never again see another gorilla. Of all the Africans I had known, he was taking old age the worst. When he fell, he grew angry with himself, and even when he was making good progress his hands shook. We were still traveling when night overtook us. Now we could only follow the path by the sound of Reuben's voice. That business about black leopards eating the gorillas and scaring them from one border to the next, he said, was all nonsense, offered up to guests at the hotel. The real culprits were poachers—pygmies starving in the Congo. And who was to blame them? They pressed the gorillas from one side; Ugandan farmers, hacking down the primary forest, were pressing them on the other. Much of Reuben's monologue was punctuated by coughs. At the end, he added that there was no one left on these mountains to stop poachers, to stop farmers, to stop war. By now the air had grown cold, and our sweaters were steaming as we skated down the narrow path to the hotel. Reuben was repeating himself. "The gorillas," he chanted, "they've gone for good."

The mountain gorilla has had the bad sense to inhabit three politically unstable African countries—Zaire (formerly the Congo), Uganda and Rwanda. What has traditionally saved this subspecies from extinction has not been its size or fierceness, but its nearly impenetrable habitat. Shrouded by mountain mists, dense ferns, thick stands of bamboo, it possesses very little needed by us bipeds. Its meat is an acquired taste (so I hear), and the land it inhabited farmers would clear only if there was no other land available. So the gorilla managed to endure, more or less, until about a decade ago. In these last years, however, war and overpopulation have upset the old truths.

The Congo revolution, in particular, drew a veil of secrecy over its well-being. Shortly after we left Travellers' Rest, I learned that Walter Baumgartel returned to Austria, abandoning his hotel. A year later, Reuben was dead. From then on, few outsiders dared look for gorillas on the Virunga volcanoes. Within a year of the publication of George Schaller's gorilla monograph and his popular account, *The Year of the Gorilla*, close observations of the animal, such as his, were more or less impossible in both Uganda and Zaire. Conservation authorities reported that gorillas were being shot to feed both soldiers and rebels, and for nearly four years there were no sightings of them by outsiders.

There was one insider, however, who, during this period, had much to do with gorillas. Dr. Jacques Verschuren was then the head of the national park system in the Congo. While Diane Fossey, a towering occupational therapist from California, was getting all sorts of kudos for her coziness with the gorillas in Rwanda, Jacques Verschuren lost twenty-three of his game guards to poachers' bullets, while they attempted to protect the game. It was a quiet, unpublicized campaign, but those who were familiar with the Congo during those years had persistently told me of Verschuren's bravery and the selflessness of the national park employees working under him.

In 1971 I had occasion to meet Verschuren in Kinshasa, the capital of Zaire. He was now said to live permanently in Room 816 at the Intercontinental Hotel. I thought to myself as I walked to his room for our appointment that if Jacques Verschuren spoke English, smoked a pipe, wore knee socks and knew how to work the cocktail party set in New York and Los Angeles he surely could be in the public eye. (Gorillas, after all, were a natural for a fund-raising campaign.) But when Dr. Verschuren opened the door I realized just how private a man can be. He had none of the qualities ascribed to game wardens—certainly none of the flamboyance that would have brought to the attention of the West the very dramatic and romantic war he had just won.

Jacques Verschuren spoke only a few words of English. He was pale and sickly, and for the first few minutes of our meeting, he seemed excruciatingly timid. For a man devoted to the out-of-doors, he could not have selected a more confined environment for living. He kept the windows sealed, the air conditioner turned off and, even in the middle of the day, the curtains closed. The humid atmosphere was sweet with the smell of old banana, which was, he claimed, the sole item in his diet. I could see the depression on the bed covers where he had just been lying.

Dr. Verschuren seemed a hunted man. When he looked out the window he pulled the curtains back only a few inches. He explained that although he had an office at the Wildlife Ministry (since he now worked in the capacity of adviser to the new government), he rarely went there. Instead, he conducted his business over the telephone from this hotel room. For the last week, he had not even ventured into the corridor.

Dr. Verschuren came to life when we talked of the war. He boasted of the heroism of his men. He told me of the problems— lack of communication, no paychecks, spies in every camp—yet his men had never failed him. For him, war had clearly brought out the best in human nature. For a moment as he talked, his voice faltered and his eyes clouded. "Yes," he said, "that was heroism." He rose from where he had been sitting and walked again to the window, stealing a quick look at the parking lot, glaring with sunshine and heat. "Since the war," he explained, "the number of people working for the national parks has increased more than ten times. The game was saved during the war with a handful of men. Now we need ten times more men to save them during peacetime. The point of national parks therefore is to give your cousin a job, not to save animals. Now we save fewer animals. *La verité, monsieur.* These people don't care anymore about the game." Verschuren pointed at his stomach. "They care about this alone. And . . ." He drew me by the arm, urgently, so that my face was nearly pressed against the window. "Look, look: Mercedes-Benz—that's the other problem. Everybody in the national parks must have one. You don't work for the parks unless you do."

Verschuren drew back the curtains and slipped exhausted into a chair. "The man you must meet is Adrien Deschriever. One of the great ones still living. He is always thin and he does not own a Mercedes-Benz. Those gorillas you like so much exist today because of Monsieur Deschriever. You must meet him. But you must hurry, for one never knows in this country. Individuals and gorillas are not indispensable. . . ."

At the time, in 1971, no one was quite sure how many gorillas had survived the disorder of the last few years. Estimates ranged from a population of seventy in the Impenetrable Forest of Uganda, two hundred in Rwanda, and between two thousand and twenty thousand in Zaire. There was much more guesswork in Zaire than in any of the other countries for it is vast, unconnected by proper roads, covered by dense and often unexplored forests and swamps. Nobody to date had conducted a proper gorilla count. Nobody but Deschriever lived with them on intimate terms.

In Nairobi only a few people knew of Deschriever. One sa-fari guide admitted that he had been gorilla-stalking with him, but, determined to keep the man and his animals a secret to only his clients, he volunteered little else. Others were curious once I started asking questions about Deschriever. A new quarry, an-other eccentric were always of interest to Kenyan wildlife voy-eurs. Out of friendly crowds, strangers appeared eager to accom-pany me into the Congolese blue. Instead, I went to ABC in New York, told the producers about the gorillas, produced a Michelin map of Central Africa and pointed to the *B* in Bukavu. "Pockets of them everywhere," I muttered conspiratorially. "Man by the name of Deschriever knows them best. Sort of an oddity. Doesn't talk much. Said to be suspicious of strangers. Super shy. That sort of thing. No guarantee we'll see gorillas, mind you. High-risk film. Of course, if we do succeed, we'll be the first ever to get wild gorillas onto a television screen. See what I mean? It all depends on whether you're up to it."

The production survey was approved within the hour, and two weeks later four of us were driving from Entebbe, Uganda, southwest through Rwanda into Zaire. Bud Morgan, the pro-ducer, was an earnest, bald man who was never happy even with miracles. Also included was Liam Lynn, the comic balladeer of the hard-drinking white hunters of East Africa. Rob Glenn was a sculptor who had always dreamed of doing a study of moun-tain gorillas in the wild: for the network executives, the ideal human-interest story to punctuate footage of gorilla behavior. Rob was a good naturalist as well as an obessive rally driver. He drove fast, told graveyard jokes and identified small weaver birds all at the same time.

The journey from Entebbe took us three days. The roads were red, and at the end of each day we were red too. In Uganda, driving through farm country, there is the sense that any crop can be planted and harvested in the space of twenty-four hours. Bananas are always ripe, the tea stands head-high and the coffee smells of fine Italian expresso. In those days, nobody, it seemed, could be truly poor in Uganda. Children sprinted through fields, arms waving, to shout *"jambo"* at us as we passed. The little ones were well rounded and never without a smile—the fertile human crop in a fertile land. Good rains, neat fields, proffered hands— Uganda was then a very comfortable country. Within a few years, all was to change, of course, but to have known Uganda then is to feel sure now that the violence under Amin was never a product of the Ugandan temperament. Amin was from the north. Some say he was not even a Ugandan.

We passed not far from Travellers' Rest, by now derelict, and then crossed the border into Rwanda. As soon as we passed the frontier we might have been on another continent. The roads were jammed with foot travelers, the fields were cluttered with tin-roofed huts. To find an open, unpopulated savannah took me twenty-four hours of looking, and even then it was marred by haze from fires. With a giant and ravenous population, the land suffers from erosion, overgrazing and overburning. It seemed abraded and festering from one horizon to the next. The tall Watusi, beautifully coiffed, their skin copper-colored, appeared fey and unrealistic next to the small and avaricious Hutu, who make up the bulk of the population and who have, since the expiration of the Belgian mandate over the territory, retained political control. I never felt a camaraderie with the Rwandese as I had with the people of Uganda; all I could do was to play tricks on them— cruel jokes involving a realistic gorilla mask I had bought on my last visit to Broadway. In Rwanda I convinced myself that the tricks constituted a study, of great sociological import, to determine people's awareness of gorillas on our approach to real gorilla country. In truth, we just had a good laugh. On one occasion when I actually started brachiating, beating on my chest and scuttling gorillalike across a village square, I successfully cleared more than a hundred people out of the village. I could see little from inside the mask and I did not realize until after I had done a lot of chest-thumping just how successful I had been. I looked around and I realized everybody had fled. Removing my mask, I uttered a few words of apology. A hundred faces remained glued behind huts and storefronts. "Just a joke," I repeated as I clambered back into the Land Cruiser. Then they came for the car, waving fists, hurling abuse and stones.

As we drove out of the village, I was debating whether or not to continue my research when Rob and I spotted a very elderly woman on the road. We slowed to a halt as I pulled on the mask, and when she was abreast of us I caught her attention by beating on the side of the car with hairy "gorilla" gloves. By the way her back was stooped the old woman, I thought, must be over eighty, and on her head, she carried a huge stalk of green bananas. Her eyes to the ground, she probably would never have looked my way had I not barked at her. When she turned and saw that a gorilla, dressed in a safari jacket, was seated as passenger in a wonderfully modern Toyota Land Cruiser, she decided in an instant that she wanted nothing more to do with the twentieth century. Without a pause, the bananas flew straight up, as though launched from her head, while she hurtled off the road, over a ten-foot cliff, into a pyrethrum plantation where we followed her course for the next ten minutes by the sight of her head bobbing and weaving, heading toward the Indian Ocean, a thousand miles away.

We arrived in Bukavu that evening. The hotel where Adrien Deschriever promised to meet us had the unmistakable imprimatur of past elegance. In the meantime it seemed to have suffered a series of violent furniture moves. Portions of Regency beds were scattered about, but most chairs and tables were now of local manufacture. A vitrine that once had housed collections of French jewelry and Swiss watches now contained sixteen empty beer bottles. The manager explained that the hotel had been looted three times—first by rebels, once by the regular army and the last time by yet another group of rebels. The only article overlooked by the looters was in the manager's office. It was a Louis XVI Directoire desk, too large to fit through any doors. In any case, one could see immediately that it would not have suited a field commander's tent. Above my bed in my room there was an angry rainbow of machine-gun bullet holes whose presence spelled insomnia.

From the minute Adrien Deschriever walked into the dining room he looked tortured. He grimaced from the sound of the rock 'n' roll, he acted as if he even distrusted the chair he sat on and he treated us as if we were a conquering army. Adrien appeared about forty and there was nothing decorative about his looks. His hair was cut short for efficiency and left unwashed out of necessity. Like Verschuren, he had the pallor of a mushroom—not because he lived indoors but because he haunted the jungle. His clothes ranged in color from khaki to khaki. He mentioned his wife just once and he made it clear she preferred staying at home. Most of the time he stared at uneaten strawberries on his plate. Even talk of gorillas failed to animate him. During the two hours we sat together he voiced only one opinion—that his fellow whites in Bukavu were interested only in money. The remark, I believe, had been sparked by the sight of the white headwaiter accepting a tip from one of the guests. There was little to be added, so the dinner was conducted mostly in silence, and Bud Morgan grew more and more nervous that the star of his film was to be a man who was unable to talk.

The next morning when Adrien met us, there was a change. Although he still said very little, he was definitely in command. He looked at my Special Forces beret and obliquely asked me to remove it: "The rebels wear those berets. You'll be shot dead if soldiers see you." I delayed a fraction of a second before burying it at the bottom of my knapsack.

The Zaire government, for all its inefficiency and corruption under Joseph Desiré Sese Seko Mobutu, had at the time committed a greater percentage of real estate to national parks than had any other country of the world. A map of Zaire reveals a huge checkerboard of public lands held in trust for wildlife. That these parks were unmanageable and unmanaged was a matter of little concern. In Africa often the less management, the more the game prospers.

Kahuzi Biega National Park, protecting two small mountains and over six hundred square kilometers of forest, is probably managed better than any other park in Zaire, thanks to Adrien Deschriever. Nearly two hundred gorillas, possibly 10 percent of all those left in Zaire, are said to live here. Because there is a considerable human population inhabiting the contiguous country, there is probably more need here for human surveillance than in the other more desolate parks of Zaire.

Once our car has passed the gates of the park, the road becomes a dark hallway. Adrien's eyes, once so dull, now seem to shine with a sunlight of their own making, and I can see that each stately tree—thousands of them, their high branches our ceiling—is instantly recognizable to him. Twice he sticks his head out of the window of the car to orient himself by the smell of the forest, and the third time, he brakes to a halt. "Here," he says, inhaling deeply. The place is as distinctive to him as if it were marked by a signpost. We leave the car and follow him into the forest. Only hours later when I catch him looking distracted do I dare ask him why he has stopped at that particular spot. "Because," he replies, "there were gorillas on the wind. I smelled where they had crossed the road the day before."

Their trail is apparent only to Adrien and the pygmy game guard—broken branches, droppings smeared on leaves. Our footing is uncertain because of the fallen trunks of great trees concealing vines and barbs. For four hours we make damp and clumsy progress, with never a chance to stand upright without brushing against a branch or a liana. Never once in all that time do I detect a view. Finally, exactly at noon, Adrien waves his hand. "They are ahead," he announces flatly. He has stopped exactly where he made the revelation—in a narrow flute of sunlight. "We wait," he adds, crossing his arms and folding himself into the shrubbery, still in the bull's-eye of sun. The pygmy tracker, bowing to historic convention, withdraws a short distance and sits alone in self-imposed exile.

If the tracking has been painful, the waiting will be worse. Adrien accepts our ennui with characteristic fatalism. He makes no effort to silence Liam's roaring stories of great sexual exploits nor Rob's smoking of an Upmann cigar. Adrien might just as well be carved from one of the giant newtonia trees as he stares from his private sunshine into the tangle of ferns directly ahead of him, where the troop of twenty-two are said to be sleeping. Just once he acknowledges Liam's not so droll remarks about Mad Mike Hoare's resurgent popularity in Bukavu with a seditious clicking of his tongue, but otherwise he is indifferent. He accepts Liam's flippancy as most people do bad weather.

I am silent too, but for other reasons. I believe Adrien when he assures us we are within a one hundred feet of gorilla. I believe him, yet I cannot accept that the moment that died aborning some ten years ago will be brought to its rightful conclusion today. Adrien has already identified the gorilla troop ahead of us as the one led by Kazimir, a large male silverback gorilla. I question whether a man can be so certain of something just from sounds. Occasionally I hear what I take to be a rumbling stomach, a fart, a belch. With each new noise Adrien nods in affirmation. Such and such sound was made by the silverback, or by a youngster or by the oldest member of Kazimir's harem. If today is to be the climax of my childhood quest, then I am somehow not prepared for it. I sense no drama, just bloody-minded self-assurance.

Previously Adrien has explained that the worst encounter with a gorilla is the surprise one (such as mine on the Virunga volcanoes). If a group is familiar with humans they should not run. To them, he believes, we are a mere subspecies—crude, unsophisticated and thoroughly clumsy—to be pitied, if nothing else. Gorillas are not in awe of humans and they treat us as we might animals in a zoo.

Adrien has spent the last five years "habituating" (familiarizing) two groups of gorillas in Kahuzi Biega. The smaller troop, numbering eighteen, is still shy and difficult to approach. The other—the one now before us—has been more successfully habituated. Adrien insists that the gun he carries is not intended for use against gorillas. Rather it is to deter poaching. "Poachers," he said, affecting a look of such extreme ambivalence that only afterward did I realize it was Adrien's way of expressing contempt. "Poachers," he added with a spit. Such was the beginning of a short tale describing how three years before, while driving through the park in a Land Rover, poachers had taken a shot at him. The bullet missed him, but killed his brother. When Adrien's story was done, the look of resigned neutrality once again fiddled across his face.

Now, after two hours of waiting, Adrien stands up. He beckons to the pygmy to cut a path toward the sound of belches in the underbrush and within a few seconds the two of them are lost to view, only the slicing sound of the *panga* marking their route.

Unexpectedly, a few minutes later, Adrien returns, almost a smile on his face. "I nearly tripped over a sleeping female," he sings. "Very bad country for viewing gorillas." He nods his head for us to follow, saying that the gorillas are now on the move, and that we should track them until they reach more open country.

Within fifteen minutes we stop again, for Adrien believes we have overtaken the troop. Although he keeps telling us to talk in normal tones, I continue whispering, conditioned as I am to the convention of quiet on the stalk. Adrien sits on the rough ground, his back as stiff as if he were attending a Papal audience. The pygmy hacks away at the vegetation on the edge of our minute clearing, allowing us a better view. "We will make contact," Adrien says with absolute conviction. His hands are folded in quiet expectation. Now, the gorillas must choose their moment.

"Talk," Adrien insists, like a pushy host. I look at him, pale and placid. I check the others: Bud unimpressed, Rob determined to finish his Upmann cigar, Liam still whispering about a girl called Maggie. Suddenly I am scared. Everybody must be able to hear the beating of my heart over the hush of the jungle. I wonder if they sense how much we are at the mercy of these gorillas. No matter that Kazimir may be three times our weight or that he might possess ten times our strength. What matters is that the gorillas have the option of choice, timing, command. We humans are merely awaiting their pleasure. They can do anything they wish to us. I begin to shake, like I never shook on the Virunga volcanoes.

Adrien raises a finger, as if he has just discovered the truth. "Do you hear?" he asks. "It is the silverback . . ." (he pauses to struggle with the English word) ". . . tapping, no, beating at the ground." He listens some more. "They know . . . they know." He is looking at a high frond of fern, vigorously fanning, above all the rest. He cocks his head, pressing his ear against the wall of vegetation. "Cum, cum, cum, Kazimir," he says to the black tangle.

I pass the back of my hand across my mouth so the others will not hear my breathing. I am deafened by the gush and thud of blood in my neck. I imagine Kazimir everywhere: A shadow becomes a coiled arm, an oiled face forms from the wet bark of a tree. And then, I close my eyes. Suddenly I realize the waiting is over. A rank smell, half-skunk, half-underarm, settles over us. It is so powerful I open my eyes, only to see Rob grinning. Whatever we have been awaiting is happening.

At first there is one short bark. The bark becomes a shriek and the frond of fern above bounds from one tree to another. Branches snap and the cavernous roar becomes frantic. We are in the eye of a storm, unseen, but seeing, a force of insuperable but invisible power. Suddenly it stops. The jungle hushes. I search to see something—matted hair, eyes, a limb. Whatever created the chaos is now gone. We were, I fancy, being tested.

Slinging his rifle over his shoulder, Adrien nods to the pygmy to start cutting a path back to the car. "We have made contact," he announces without inflection. The gorillas have gone. Now, further contact with them must be cut short for yet another day.

Driving back to Bukavu, Adrien returns to the subject of poaching. "Read the official powers given to me by Mobutu," he says out of the blue. "When I catch a poacher I need not establish his legal guilt. Not necessary. If I suspect he is in the park for no good reason, then I call out to him to stop, once, twice, three times, and if he is still running when I call out the third time, then I have the right, not yet exercised, to shoot to kill." Here Adrien slaps his hands to dramatize the simplicity of execution. "There are few questions. No need even to know the man's name. 'Stop. Stop. Stop,' I yell. And then that is that. Simple." Again Adrien slaps his hands. "Just the other day my guards captured a poacher, and during the night the poacher tried to escape. My men stopped him with a knife between the ribs." Another slap of the hands. "My guard was thrown into prison for murder, but after a month we had him released, gave him a promotion and awarded him a medal. That's the way we work."

There is neither smugness nor cynicism when Adrien describes his absolute power. If anything, he wears a look of weary sadness. For him death is the inadmissible clincher of all bets, suspicions and beliefs. By carrying a gun he sees himself as the lawyer of wildlife, as the sole defender of animals in a court of bigots. Unarticulated but implicit is his belief that across the globe man has exceeded his authority. His story done, Adrien drives in silence, blinking only once between the park and Bukavu from the lights of an oncoming car.

Before I left Nairobi, someone who knew Adrien had spun a few legends about him for me. My informant was a man who sees only giants and dwarfs in life. For him, because all humans are on the brink of an apocalypse, the world must be divided between the heroes and the cads. Human motivation is tactile. "You must remember," he said, "that Adrien is married to an African woman, solidly built, barely literate and the mother of his many café-au-lait children. That she is the very antithesis of everything European is important. By taking her as his bride, you see, Adrien had, in effect, married Africa."

"But so do so many in French-speaking Africa. There, there is none of the stigma you have here in British Africa."

My friend was not listening. "That's only the beginning," he continued. "Adrien has been reduced to an essential form of life by the sheer necessity of having to deal with dog-eat-dog Africa. You see, he saw his own brother shot by poachers. Later he had to shoot his way out from his ruined farm when it was attacked by rebels. He's lived a life of war to such an extent he can no longer conceive of peace. Do you understand?" My friend did not wait for the answer.

"And then two years ago he fell in love. A sultry-eyed girl from California. His first white woman. She was working as an assistant to a German cameraman doing a film on gorillas. The cameraman left, the girl stayed on—just moved into Adrien's tent and that was that. From then on he dedicated himself to her. When she began her film about elephants he was there as her go-fer. He learned about cameras, carried her tripod, set up her tent. Quite a twosome, those two. She was in her mid-twenties, he nearly forty.

"You're probably wondering about the venerable Madame Deschriever back at the hut with the kids. Quite simply this: The moment she got wind of her husband's infidelity, she went straight to the witch doctor. Told him she wanted the girl rubbed out. Maybe they stuck pins into a doll or something. Not quite sure. But the witch doctor agreed to her instructions and assured her that the girl had only a few days to live.

"Sure enough. Just at that moment, the girl was with her elephants in Rwanda. She was filming them first being airlifted from some *shambas* to a national park, and then released from a big *boma* back into the wild. Smallest and last elephant of the day—couldn't have been more than four feet tall, just a little guy—he raced out of the *boma,* kind of crazed, and came straight for the girl. You see, her problem was that she was looking down a long lens. Didn't see how close the elephant was. And the moment she did—well, it was all over. That little bastard was pounding her. The girl had this damn battery belt attached to her camera and tripod and when she tried to escape there wasn't a thing she could do. Incredible, the power and weight of those elephants. Just killed her instantly.

"I guess Madame Deschriever was happy. Adrien was wrecked. He found a lonely spot in the park, with a magnificent view, and he buried the girl there. From then on he's been a little more sour, a little more contained. He's back with Madame now, but he's even more private than before. . . ."

In the morning of the second day of our search, Adrien does not utter one word for the first two hours. He mutters occasionally to the pygmy, whose face is deformed by childhood leprosy. This game guard is wearing a pair of girl's boots, abandoned, no doubt, by a grateful gorilla-watcher who had done her safari outfitting on Rodeo Drive. The pygmy looked better yesterday when he was barefoot. Dressed either way, he is the nimblest of us all, flowing through the forest, over logs, under knotted foliage as if he were a panther.

Our path takes us along the edge of a tea plantation contiguous to the park. Late yesterday, Adrien explains at last, the gorillas skirted the clearings and made their way toward a narrow wedge of forest that still juts into farmland. They should be just ahead, for on most days they do not travel far. Depending on whether or not it is raining they generally leave their nests two hours after dawn, traveling and feeding continuously until about midday when, once again, they take time out for a nap. At about four in the afternoon they resume their feeding orgy, advancing slowly until they are overtaken by night. Almost invariably the children and females sleep in the trees, while the males build nests for themselves on the ground. Theirs is, by most standards, a life of leisure, only threatened by leopards and man. By disposition gorillas are gentle, preferring to bluff than to fight. Even when two males are antagonists, they resort to combat only as a final measure. The power to kill, which they have in abundance, is one they prefer not to exercise.

We arrive at last night's bedroom. It is marked by considerable devastation. Branches are ripped from hagenia trees, with berries scattered across the ground, half-eaten. Two small trees, on the edge of the clearing, lie uprooted. The gorillas will never come this way again, sensing somehow, as many animals do, that their habitat must be allowed time to heal. Only in cases when man meddles have gorillas ever been known to abandon these time-honored wisdoms.

The trail cut for us by the pygmy is pygmy-size. We who are over six feet tall must scuttle like crabs, our field glasses and cameras, hung from necks, scooping up mud and banging one against the other. "*Siafu,*" Rob yells suddenly. "Safari ants." We bolt, high-stepping over the tunnel of skin-eating ants, and when the danger is past I pause to pluck leaves from my hair. Adrien is ahead, much more calm. A shaft of light now pokes me, first in one eye, then the other. If I squint I can see a cobweb, brushing against my nose; at the other extreme of focus I can follow a hypolimnious butterfly floating from branch to branch, five feet away. Out and in, back and forth, the jungle is an exercise in perspectives.

We follow Kazimir's family along the park boundary. Adrien is slightly unsettled, for he knows that when gorillas leave the protection of the jungle and the park, they risk a confrontation with farmers. Whenever they damage crops, Adrien must make reparations to the farmers, and already lines seem drawn between the two species of primates—the great apes and us. "Cousins," Adrien had once explained to me sadly.

When Adrien sees gorilla droppings, still steaming, he admits he is worried. Three months ago when the farms had not yet been cleared from the forest, the gorillas followed more or less this same route. Now the farmers have seriously encroached on the forest just outside the park. In all likelihood the gorillas do not know they are traveling into a promontory of thick cover which soon will leave them stranded with nowhere but open fields to cross. "They will be . . ." Adrien searches for the word.

"Frustrated."

"Yes. Frustrated. Sometimes they behave not well when they are out in the open. Last year a farmer threatened them and they attacked. He was not killed but he was injured." Adrien advances, shaking his head, as if this new plight of the gorillas might have been through his fault. From the east come the singsong cries of farmers, calling from field to field. For the first time, perhaps as a result, we talk in whispers.

When we halt again, I watch a fly. It circles Adrien's head and then settles on his cheek beneath the right eye. It wanders his face, poking his eye, spelunking a nostril, buffeted by his breath on a lip. For five minutes he lets it explore. Soon it is joined by others and half his face becomes obscured by flies. Only then does he act. His is a halfhearted measure—not a slap, but an abracadabra wave of his hand which makes five flies circle his face and attracts ten more. For a man of war, I meditate, Adrien surely has found a peace. In comparison, I feel venal. Just my presence here jeopardizes the jungle. I am unable to walk, it seems, without snapping a branch. I cannot contemplate my surroundings without the desire to steal something—a leaf, a fungus, a gorilla dropping, a story, a photograph. I need to leave this jungle with proof. Adrien, however, is different. He does not know how to tell a story, much less to reduce a gorilla to a still photograph. He neglects all his tenses but his present, becoming part of the jungle itself.

Somebody else—not Adrien—told me about the gorilla baby. It had been brought to him by farmers who had discovered it next to its mother, killed by poachers. By the time it reached park headquarters, the child was almost wasted. Adrien and his wife nursed it back to health. At first, the milk formula was a problem, but when they finally achieved the right recipe, the gorilla began to grow. In six months, Adrien decided, it would be independent enough to be reintroduced to the wild, perhaps into Kazimir's troop of twenty-two gorillas.

Every day Adrien trained it to behave as a gorilla. One day he brought it to the jungle, introducing it to its natural environment, and while there, quite by accident, Adrien ran into Kazimir's troop. Clutching the youngster to his chest he tried to slip away but he was spotted. Without warning, the six-hundred-pound gorilla lunged at Adrien, wrenched the orphan from Adrien's hands and then sprang back into the forest. Kazimir looked back only once, defiantly holding the tiny infant in one large arm. For the next two weeks Adrien pursued the kidnappers, knowing that the little gorilla was not equipped to survive the forest, and hoping, one supposes, for magic. At the end of the second week, the infant was no longer with Kazimir's troop. The rains had been heavy and every day the forest was cold and covered in mist. Adrien was never again to see the orphaned gorilla.

Now, after two hours of waiting, the flies have assumed almost complete control of Adrien's face. We know we are a hundred feet from the gorillas, but they have been remarkably quiet. Suddenly, I hear thudding. The silverback kidnapper, Kazimir, is pounding the ground and soon, sure enough, his rank odor envelops us. The most massive of all gorillas is now no distance and, as always, he remains invisible. He screams to show us just how near: no more than fifty feet, I estimate. For the next half hour he and his family belch, fart, hammer the ground, rattle lips and bark. Never once do we see them. I am wondering if my story has no ending, after all.

Impatient, I crawl along the edge of our small clearing to where I can peer through a tunnel piercing the undergrowth. At its end, some thirty feet away, a shaft of light illuminates a square yard of jungle. I had sensed I might see something, but the tunnel is empty. One cannot fail to be impressed how these massive creatures can tantalize you with their sound effects, yet remain so completely concealed. I crawl back to the others. I know I am being watched, yet I cannot find the eyes.

Almost immediately I return to the maw of that tunnel. Perhaps I am merely trying to occupy myself; perhaps I have an intuition. I look into the blackness, past the beam of sunlight, into the very throat of the jungle. Just where it is blackest of all, two yellow eyes, sunken into their own syrup, return my stare. The eyes are inflexible, unblinking, glowing out of blackness like moons. Soon, amid those shadows, I see two arms, as massive as legs, reaching to the ground. Midges form a halo over the oiled coat, and although no one identifies him by name, there is no doubt I am looking at Kazimir.

One by one, while the silverback guards their retreat, the others pass through the tunnel. For a few seconds they each have a chance to steal a look in our direction, but they hurry, under orders, it would seem, to pay us no attention. I count eighteen. (The other watchers later assured me I was wrong and that there were twenty-two in all.) The last gorilla to pass is a young male. For a moment he stands fully upright to stare at us, his head bobbing in and out of the sunlight, as if he believes the darkness can conceal him. His game could be one I played many years ago, just before I learned to read.

When they have all gone and the jungle again resumes its hum, I look around at my companions. Like me, I suspect they are not sure what to say or whether to say anything at all. Even Adrien is smiling.

My story begun ten years ago on the Virunga volcanoes may still not have an ending, but it now surely has more meaning. I have seen a gorilla face to face. And neither one of us had to run.

Bud at last breaks the spell to pull out his pad. He begins calculating film costs, days needed for production and size of film crew. All his previous fears have now been laid to rest. His eyes on the pad, he keeps repeating to himself, "Dynamite." His budget grows from page to page. "How much is the hotel?" he asks me. He is shaking his head with rare conviction. "I'm betting that in ten days we'll have it in the can." He explains to Adrien the meaning of "marquee value," and then he gives him his legal opinion about the use of the film for nonpaying audiences. "All those myths that King Kong got going—this film will settle the score. Let me tell you, it will be a spellbinder."

I doubt whether Adrien is trying to understand the jargon. He is listening for the last sounds of the gorillas' retreat. Soon he beckons us to follow him. Within a short distance the forest ends and we find ourselves perched on a small knoll overlooking a gorge and a glade. Adrien indicates for us to sit, and for an hour we wait, assured by him that the gorillas are likely to pass through this clearing, en route to their forest. If we are fortunate we shall see the whole troop together. Occasionally, through the wait, Bud sings out the cost of a soundman, the price of an air ticket, the overtime needed by an assistant editor. Soon he is done, just in time to see the worry in Adrien's eyes. Without saying a word, Adrien looks to the smoke haze in the west and then turns to glance over his shoulder. At last he talks: "I think the gorillas have gone the other way." He points behind us to the rise, concealing distant tea plantations. "They must have crossed that field. You see, at this hour of the day, they know that the farmers have gone home. They know they won't be bothered crossing the fields."

As if to acknowledge his words, there is a burst of barking from the direction of the tea field. At first the voice is deep and commanding, belonging perhaps to Kazimir, but then the others, less restrained than he, form a giant chorus. The symphony floats over hill, into ravine, through forest and the farther it travels, the longer it lasts, the louder it becomes. "They only scream like that," explains Adrien, "when they are back in the forest, when they feel safe. It is like victory."

We rise to our feet. The air has turned cool now, and if we do not hurry we will be caught by night. When we reach the bottom of the ravine, Adrien is the first to break the silence. He takes me aside and, pointing to where the gorillas had sounded their retreat, says, "They are the kings of these hills. And," he adds, "they know it."

For the first time, he laughed.

THE SEARCH
FOR ADAM'S
ANCESTORS

We all know that explorers and exploration belong to other times, not to ours. Burton and Speke, Thomson and Teleki surely left no heirs in our century, and anyone so uninformed as to call himself an explorer today must certainly be of the drugstore variety.

Before I was to become the first to navigate Ethiopia's Omo River in a rubber raft, I, however, thought differently. I was sure we could still be explorers in our time. I failed to see that the broad sweeps of geography—which had been the explorer's responsibility—had already been resolved. These days we know where the rivers run. Exploration today is often little more than

being "the first"—a precedent, broadly speaking, of little consequence. All that remained for us moderns, it seemed, was adven-
turous travel and a form of puffery that would surely have shamed
the Victorians. I nevertheless set out to raft the Omo from the
Abelti Bridge to its confluence with Lake Rudolf on the Kenyan
frontier, nearly four hundred miles away and almost five thousand feet lower. To do so I needed to be accompanied by twenty
Americans, mostly aging doctors (as a rule, the only profession
that can afford such travel these days). We needed to be nour-
ished by foil-packaged food, freeze-dried in Oregon. We needed
radio contact daily with a pilot in Addis Ababa. Everyone's tent
(mine being the only exception) was a perfect cocoon of protection against the regular evening cloudbursts. Yes, we had scorch-
ing heat by day, dripping cold at night, rapids as large as Quon-
set huts and the company of an extremely aggressive race of
crocodiles, but we were prepared—overprepared, in fact. Nobody even caught cold. Nobody could have. Most of us returned
home, at the end, as if from a cure. With all our doctors strung
between the rafts, our temperatures, stools, vision and water intake were constantly being monitored. We were astronauts without spaceships and at the end of our trip our success in being the
first palefaces to float the river from top to bottom, largely ig-
nored by the press, was recorded with a massive outpouring of
self-congratulation. Splits of champagne were waiting for us back
at the Addis Hilton, a Chihuahua was being groomed to be presented to the Emperor (he was still said to covet them) and various telexes were dispatched to learned scientific bodies just in
case someone cared. For the doctors, long inured to respectable
practices in places such as Louisville, Kentucky, this achievement
would not be lost on their patients. Pictures and citations would
line the walls of waiting rooms. This doctor, these records would
proclaim, was not just an authority on swollen glands but a living, thinking, walking, talking explorer.

Of course, since I too had sat in bilge water for twenty-two
days, I was an explorer as well. But although I was never convinced about myself, I still wanted to believe there was someone
else with the proper credentials. Anyone who could authentically
claim to be an explorer in Africa today had, I felt, a certain irrev-
ocable right to that Africa, much as someone in Wyoming claiming the earliest water rights might belong to the West. Explora-

tion was like tenure. I did not have it, but I certainly wanted to see what distinguished those who did.

I have been in this auditorium before. Perhaps it was ten years ago, and it was as packed as it is today. The audience has not aged. The old devoted ladies are still old, and the students are still students. But the speaker has changed. He speaks not as a revolutionary, but as part of the establishment, trying to rekindle a revolution. Moreover, the shape of his figure has changed—grown too comfortable, perhaps.

I first came to know Richard Leakey when he had a runner's build, hair bleached from long days in deserts and an abrasive manner that both startled and motivated those with lesser ambitions. He was then recognized mostly as his father's son. Clearly he was determined to be more. He rarely talked of the old man, determined, it would seem, to build his own legend.

If his father, Dr. Louis Seymour Bassett Leakey, suffered from any affliction, it was from being spontaneous, rash, irrepressible—characteristics most scientists train themselves to do without. He was best known for his discoveries in Tanzania's Olduvai Gorge. Years of devotion to the dream of proving Africa to be the cradle of humanity had paid off in 1959 when his wife, Mary (Richard's mother), came upon a portion of a fossil skull on the steep side of the gorge. At that time, Dr. Leakey was sick in his camp bed with malaria. He quickly recovered, pieced together as many fragments of the skull they could find, and announced to the National Geographic Society and the world that the "missing link" had at last been found. One year later, when Richard's brother, Jonathan, uncovered other fragments of a skull, Dr. Leakey amended his first statement. The first missing link was just *Australopithecus boisei*, "nutcracker man," "dear boy." This new one was *Homo habilis*, "handyman," the "missing link." Its features, although incomplete, were more refined, humanlike, and its brain was larger than the first's.

Nothing that followed in the elder Leakey's life ever matched those two moments of discovery, yet the world of popular heroes treated the white-haired gentleman as the Delphic oracle on all matters relating to prehistory: primates, archeology and even Mau Mau. The outspoken scientist, the flamboyant explorer, this true son of Kenya (he had been the first white child born in Ki-kuyu country) now became a world-class entertainer. Like his son after him, he had the knack of sounding informed on subjects unrelated to his own field. He became the darling of a set of lost people in southern California. He set out to plot a new human prehistory for America. He cultivated a band of young girls interested in primatology. He temporarily abandoned home, digs and health in favor of instant celebrity elsewhere. Richard, I believe, felt victimized by the old man. While the name Leakey could open many a door, it clearly was cause for some frustration in a son, longing to outrun his father in the same field.

My first meeting with Richard was in 1972 on a beach on the eastern shore of Lake Turkana, then called Rudolf. Young Leakey had already achieved a certain standing, thanks to an article in *National Geographic*. I did not know at the time whether his discoveries were of importance. I was, I recall, more lured by the self-assurance of the man than by his achievements.

My primary motive in meeting him was to obtain his participation in a film I was making for ABC about the lake. I was prepared for a difficult interview. He looked harshly, I was told, on all attempts to exploit the Leakey name.

The northeast shore of Lake Turkana, in those days, was a lonely lunar place. I remember that I had landed the plane on a rocky beach, walked to the site of our rendezvous, on the beach, and nearly sat on a sore-scaled viper that had burrowed beneath a log. To the southwest the shoreline vibrated in heat. No footprints, no plastic for a hundred miles, just the coughing of a forever wind, as if humanity was still on the drawing boards. Exactly at the appointed hour, 5:00 P.M., two stick figures materialized out of the light. Richard was with a graceful girl, Dr. Meave Epps, his second wife. Richard's stride was long and set, his legs seemingly unmuscled but balanced better than most for locomotion. His hair was tussocky, like sawgrass. "Here's trouble," I remember thinking.

But the meeting might just as well have taken place in an office for its correctness. I stood at attention. Richard's voice was clipped, utilitarian; he favored repetition of key words in soap-box drill. He liked my idea of the film since I would allow his monologue not to be interrupted by a narrator. He was not concerned about the script since he knew what he wanted to say.

Now he came to the point: money. His expedition was hardly flush. A fee was required. Were we good for it?

Once we had reached an acceptable price, he permitted a smile to turn the corners of his mouth. "Make sure your cameramen are quick. I hate to wait."

The meeting was over. Richard checked his watch, nodded good-bye and he and Meave receded into the north.

As I watched them, I remember thinking how persuasive Richard had been. ABC and I were publicity and money, and he needed both. I thought him then, as I think him now, on the verge of a political career.

Richard had reached Lake Turkana in the first place by a public relations sleight of hand. About four years before, he had been across the border in Ethiopia, leading a Kenyan team of anthropologists. He was useful to them, for he knew the bush and understood logistics. But while he talked persuasively about prehistory, he was much too green, in the eyes of the scientists, to be allowed any authority in fossil beds. After all, he had not even bothered to set foot in a university.

Richard was not going to be dismissed so easily. One day he commandeered the expedition helicopter to explore the lakeshore to the south—a place his father had once explored with no results. As the pilot flew him across the border into Kenya, the scrubland by the lake was uninterrupted lead, rippling in 110-degree heat. To the west the lake seemed, as usual, brimming with toxic chemicals, and to the east two lone pimples gave the only perspective to a carpet of sand, silt and clay that extended some two hundred miles until it met the Indian Ocean. Merely by casting his eyes from left to right, the twenty-three-year-old stood sentinel over a thousand square miles of the least-known country in Kenya.

"Put it down here," he shouted over the noise. The helicopter autorotated to the ground. Richard began walking, his eyes fastened to the ground. About two minutes after setting forth, and no more than seventy-five feet from the helicopter, Richard picked up a stone. It was more or less round, with each of its facets curiously sculpted. It fell into his hand as if it had always belonged there, and when he curled his fingers over it, a small corner protruded from the base. Clearly, this was the business end of a "chopper." The tool, Richard determined, had been made by a man, long ago, and it had been used perhaps to smash bones. Nearby, a fossilized pig jaw protruded from the ground. Richard identified it as having belonged to a species that had become extinct two million years before. If the stone tool was as old as the jaw—hardly a wild assumption since both artifacts were eroding from the same exposure—then Richard might be holding the oldest stone tool found anywhere in the world.

I like to think that Richard did as I would have done—a few cartwheels, a war whoop—but even then, twenty-three years old, he was economical with emotion. He remembers grinning for a moment or two before returning to the helicopter. He now knew he possessed the McGuffey that would launch him at cruising speed into his predestined career. He was already considering the future. No need to fuss with details (e.g., was the stone indeed man-made? was the pig jaw really associated? couldn't the stone tool have been manufactured yesterday?). Who really cared? Richard was now sure this country would yield vital hominid fossils. He was going to all ends to ensure the scientific establishment would not steal his thunder.

Still, Richard knew he needed the association of proper scientists to dignify any expedition he mounted. He had seen his own father's work become counterproductive through lack of team effort. Without even his father's credentials, Richard's achievements would be airily dismissed by the scientific community unless others were involved.

As soon as the Ethiopian expedition ended, Richard joined his father on his annual fund-raising pilgrimage to the National Geographic Society in Washington. Richard meekly sat through his father's meeting. Seconds before it was to end, he rose to his feet and made his pitch, passing the stone tool and the pig jaw around the room. "Lake Rudolf may someday become the richest hominid site in the world," he breezily claimed. One by one, the committee members, mostly elderly men, mused over the stone, listening to shards of the anthropologist's sales talk. At the end, even to Richard's surprise, they agreed to make a financial contribution to his expedition, but warned him that "if you find nothing, you are never to come begging at our door again."

Richard invited several promising young scientists on his expedition. In June 1968, with a few battered vehicles and a fiberglass cabin cruiser, they set off from Nairobi, bound for Lake

Rudolf, some 620 miles away. Then, there were no roads near the eastern lakeshore, just a track made by the Royal Engineers during World War II, now distinguished only by the occasional stone cairn. By the time the youngsters reached the lake, their spirits were at an all-time high. In the film showing them wetting their feet in the alkaline water for the first time, they all wear the smile of high achievers.

Lake Rudolf had been the goal of many past expeditions. Austrians, Count Samuel von Teleki von Szek and Ludwig Ritter von Hohnel, were probably the first whites to see the lake. They had marched for over a year from the East African coast and, at last, in 1888, the fabled lake was before them. Probably they had expected a more inviting place. They appropriately named it Rudolf after the love-crossed prince who would one day come to a nasty end with his mistress in the hunting lodge at Mayerling. One hundred sixty miles north to south, thirty miles east to west, it was vast and promising, but something seemed wrong. Von Hohnel wrote: "And when the sun rose higher, its rays were reflected from the smooth black surface of the rock, causing an almost intolerable glare, whilst a burning wind from the south whirled the sand in our faces, and almost blew the loads off the heads of our men . . . Although utterly exhausted we felt our spirits rise . . . rushed down shouting in the lake . . . and bitter disappointment: the water was brackish."

Its shores were more luxuriant than they are today, and on the skirts of the secondary vegetation there was considerable game, their numbers thinned long ago. At Allia Bay, where the count launched his prized canvas boat, hauled at great odds from Mombasa, a wounded elephant charged, crushed and sank it five minutes later. The lake's contemptuous attitude to small vessels would pose problems for almost all subsequent attempts at exploration.

Elephant hunter Arthur Neumann passed through this country some eight years later. He described his first impressions in language reminiscent of Jules Verne: "A violent gale blew unceasingly day and night. It seemed to come down like an avalanche from Mount Kulal, rushing into the deep basin of the lake sometimes in terrific gusts. At times it was difficult even to stand, and cooking and eating were conducted under disadvantages.

Nothing would stop on the table, the very tea was blown out of one's cup, while the black sand and small stones got into the food and filled one's bed at night."

Some forty years later arctic explorer Sir Vivien Fuchs's expedition lost two members to the lake when their small boat overturned between South Island and the mainland. During World War II the lake was backdrop to sporadic but not very strategic fighting between Italian and British forces. In the 1950s Robert Maytag, heir to an American washing machine fortune, amused himself with a large collecting expedition to the lake. His boat, specially designed and built in Canada, today sits like all others at the bottom of the lake. Probably the minuscule tribes along the lake—the El Molo and the Shankilla Molo—have the solution: They never venture far from shore, and they invest very little in their reed rafts.

During this golden age of exploration, the lake's fossil beds had remained concealed. Even the geology of the northeastern shore was never clearly plotted.

But in his first season at the lake, Richard found just enough to vindicate the National Geographic's gamble, so they allowed the "schoolboy expedition" to return the following year. Stubborn like his father, Richard may have reminded them of a family homily: "Look and look again until you find what you know must be there."

In 1969 Richard and his growing team of Ph.D. candidates experimented with camels as an alternative to Land Rovers. He was now with Meave, who was studying monkeys, having come to Kenya from Britain under Dr. Leakey's aegis. Meave and Richard both recall this season as the happiest and least complicated of their lives.

The expedition's first discovery was sheer chance, probably due more to the truculence of a camel than any human acuteness. For a few days, Richard and Meave had been scouting the country from camelback until finally Richard could stand it no longer. On the morning of July 27 he dismounted with an excruciating backache, deciding to stay afoot as long as he could. He and Meave described a large loop beginning and ending with the bivouacked camels and their syce; as they returned they chose to walk in a dry sand river instead of through the thorns and brush of the exposures. Almost exactly at eleven in the morning, Richard stopped abruptly and pointed excitedly ahead. Meave remembers thinking that he must have seen a snake or a lion so she took a step backward. "What is it?"

"It's an austral . . . austr . . . *Australopithecus,*" Richard blurted.

Resting on the sand, staring at them, was an almost complete hominid skull. Even from a distance it suggested *Zinjanthropus,* the skull uncovered by Richard's parents in 1959, but unlike Zinj there would be absolutely no need for reconstruction. Richard and Meave moved closer on all fours, cats after a mouse, worrying that if for one second they averted their eyes it might vanish. They circled it, moving in for the kill. At last Richard touched it. The skull remained intact. Its high browridge hung over the eye sockets. "I don't believe it," Meave repeated over and over again. "It's as though something had drawn us to it."

When Richard brought the skull back to base camp on the lakeshore, he found Mary, his mother, waiting. Of all the Leakeys, she is the most retiring, reveling in silent scientific enterprise. Her tall Katharine Hepburn figure topped by a colorful sun hat, a cigar often clenched between her teeth, it was she who had toiled at Olduvai when the reporters and photographers had gone home. Mary had also remained aloof to the father–son rivalry, encouraging, in fact, Richard's pluck.

Today, no arrival could have been better timed. She looked at Richard's discovery, remembering perhaps how she and Louis had had twenty-seven relatively lean years of exploration before their first discovery at Olduvai. Unlike that skull, Zinjanthropus, which required the piecing together of over four hundred pieces, this was complete, discovered in the second season of search. "It's beautiful, Richard. It's truly beautiful," she said, the one Leakey immune to jealousy.

Richard was becoming more and more self-confident. The National Geographic trustees were now delighted to help fund his expedition. Reporters were seeking him out and his lecture fees in America were mounting. The year following, he reassembled the 1967 team of gifted Kenyans, dubbed "the fossil gang," and in September they found another skull, which the museum registered as "732." It was only partially complete. While the previous year's discovery had been heavy-browed, thick-boned, this one suggested a race of beings small and delicate. Put side by side, the two skulls clearly seemed unrelated, but Alan Walker, the expedition's anatomist, and Richard suspected that they might have been simply the male and the female of one species. The function of the teeth seemed about the same in both fossils and the proportions of brain size to head size also ran parallel.

In the scientific world at this time, Richard was perceived as a kind of gunfighter. Everyone waited for him to make a slip. That he had no adequate schooling was considered a distinct deficiency, but he guarded himself from amateurishness with the utmost vigilance. He enjoyed his reputation as a difficult rogue, egocentric and arrogant. When told, one day, that so-and-so considered him his enemy, he seemed ready to explode with delight. The man, as he explained, was merely a "Kenyan Cowboy." But later, after someone reminded him that a certain Harvard scientist had walked out of one of his lectures, it was clear he felt wounded. As he explained to me one day, he had little time for friendships. He did, however, need supporters.

When I first met Richard I tried to press him for a portrait of the lives of the two beings his expedition had found. I could see that my question appeared to him as sheer fantasy. The veil of caution descended across his face. "What did these two people look like?" I asked him. Casts of the two skulls, the supposed male and female of the same species, lay before him on a table.

"People?" he asked quixotically. "Is it clear, in fact, they really were humans? What makes us human? What makes these creatures any less?"

A few years later, he appeared more comfortable in conceptualizing the lives of that male and female, some 1.7 million years ago. He imagined they stood no more than five feet high. They probably operated in troops, feeding on roots and berries, moving across the savannah, communicating with grunts, cooperating among themselves as baboons might today. Tools? They probably did not know how to fashion tools out of stone. They may have used natural objects, in the way a chimp does today— a twig to poke down a hole after ants, for example—but the deliberate process of using one stone to transform another into a predetermined shape, needed for a predetermined function, was beyond their technology. No doubt these creatures were far more advanced than any living ape today. Were we to come upon them by a streambed, they glaring at us, ready to run, we might feel a singular identity, dismissing them as mutant cousins, pleased to know perhaps that one million years ago they became extinct.

In 1972 Richard felt certain our true ancestor had eluded us. He needed to look further, perhaps matching the stone tool he had found years before with a brain capable of its technology. By now the fossil hunting had become more systematized. Geologists roamed the country trying to pinpoint an extinct volcano that spewed ash into the Pleistocene air and today has provided the expedition with a kind of chemical clock with which to date the fossils. Palynologists scuttled about on the lakeshore trying to fit together a mosaic of ancient landscapes. Archeologists looked for long-ago campfires. Invertebrate paleontologists cared mostly for mollusks, and other paleontologists looked for early man's neighbors—elephants, giant pigs and eccentric-looking giraffes. One geology student, fresh from Iowa State, found the company of two lions, padding behind him every day as he worked, most disquieting. While he did not know Richard Leakey well, he decided he ought to ask his advice. He explained the circumstances, telling his leader that he could no longer even enjoy eating his sandwiches at midday with those two sets of amber eyes glaring at him. He was sure they were awaiting their turn.

Richard pulled on his Oom Willem pipe, looking ten years more mature than he was at age thirty.

"Ignore them" was his solemn advice.

By 1969 base camp had been transformed from canvas to a structure made of thatch and stone. It was sited on a peninsula called Koobi Fora, windswept by evening and scrutinized in daylight by several crocodiles floating beside the beach. Sitting in the main building, used as a dining room, an office and a temporary fossil storeroom, one had the delicious sensation, particularly when the wind was mild (no more than fifty mph), that everything in the shade was air conditioned, while everything without, about to be fried. The lake dominated the view: the small cruiser, yawing in the deep swells of an afternoon blow, framed the volcanic knob of North Island, breaking the steady line of the Rift escarpment on the landmass far to the west.

Up from the camp, just beyond the hummock of hot sand, there was a large rectangular flat, outlined by white rocks, forming an airstrip. Richard had purposefully maintained it below twin-engine standards to discourage idle tourists from the temptation of taxing the expedition's slim resources of time and food. Land Rovers, a Ford Bronco and a Hafflinger Puch had now returned to vogue after Richard's brief flirtation with camels. No longer a will-o'-the-wisp routine, in the 1970s there were deadlines and meal hours, a line of leadership and a weekly supply flight. Overnight, it seemed, Richard had ceased being identified as Dr. Leakey's son. He was forever being interviewed for his own achievements. Since he served as the director of Kenya's National Museum, he could never spend more than five days at the lake at any one time. By 1973 he was almost always ashen and strained. He felt he had no choice but to work harder than anyone else, to hold down more jobs than most men could handle. Whenever I asked him why, he treated my question as if we were treading on holy ground. "It's all right for others to enjoy themselves, but I know what I must achieve and I have so little time in which to achieve it. I've no excuse not to work non-stop."

I had become captivated by his gospel whenever it dealt with bones and stones. By now Richard had proven his hunch correct: East Rudolf was indeed one of the richest hominid fossil sites in the world, to the extent that the introduction of livestock or tourists would have posed a formidable threat to their preservation. Kamoya Kimeu, Richard's deputy leader, was the head of the "fossil gang," composed mostly of wa-Kamba. Without much formal education he and his men could spot a hominid fossil and avert their eyes from remains of creatures already described in the textbooks. They traveled through this broken country like upland bird shooters, moving as one sweeping line. On their waists they carried sheath knives, to be used mostly as scrapers and shovels. Like Richard, many of them smoked pipes, affecting his pedagogic air, and like him too, they had learned to be thrifty with their emotions when discovering fossils. Once, in 1974, when I asked Bernard Ngenyeo, a member of the "fossil gang," to reenact for film the most important discovery made by the expedition, he performed five takes, each one identical, each one with the kind of jubilation appropriate to the discovery of a missing paper clip.

All Richard's grandstanding seemed vindicated in July 1972, when the "fossil gang" came upon a selection of bone fragments eroding from the ground some twenty-five miles northeast of base camp. Dr. Meave Leakey, recently the mother of their first child, performed the major reconstruction of the several hundred particles in just under three weeks. At the beginning Richard suspected the skull was going to be important, but not until Meave had finished did he decide it was far and away the bench mark of man's prehistory. Dr. Michael Day, an eminent British anatomist, was the first outsider to see the discovery, now named "1470." Emotionally, he went about as far as any scientist will dare go. "It was," he said, "one of the strangest skulls I'd ever seen, partly because its brain was so large and its upper jaw so small. Certainly one of the most interesting skulls that have ever come out of East Africa."

Dating the volcanic ash in the exposures on either side of the 1470 site indicated that the skull was between 2.4 and 2.8 million years old. As such it was the oldest known hominid. Later, when the potassium-argon dating method was reevaluated, Richard revised the skull's age to about two million years—thereby placing it in league with several others found elsewhere in Africa. Still, Richard argued that the skull was distinctive, the vital link to our earliest progress. This creature, he maintained, could have made that stone tool, could have possessed the genes that, little by little, led to the fellow who would one day split the atom.

Richard now preferred the philosophical implications of the search. If indeed the expedition was determined to find man, how could it be sure when he had been found? What, in effect, is man? And, once found, would his bones prove definitively that he was man, a near-man, and not merely a defunct cousin.

At first, Richard equivocated. "I don't think," he said, "you can separate man from beast, because I think we are all beasts; I think we're part and parcel of the same thing. I think what separates us is our behavior, a reflection of the adaptation of the body—the ability to manipulate with our hands, and the extraordinarily complicated development of the brain to provide for speech and for complex communication, and the coordination of the body to do certain functions. So I would say it's not the brain *per se* [that defines man], but the coordination of the brain and the body. I think it's a package, not a component."

Richard was determined to spend considerable time letting you guess what man really was. The problem was that Richard was no longer dealing with his field but in an area of philosophy filled mostly by conundrums. Now he could be vague, and no one would fault him. At last he admitted that man, at least from the eyes down, was probably the most unspecialized of all beings. The hands can do a number of tasks. The feet are mostly good at walking, less adept at climbing, and our tail has withered into oblivion. So much of man's evolution has gone into the development of the brain, making it his one specialized feature. With it, he can refine the rest of his body to perform the specialization of his choice. This happy association of mind and body led Richard to several further assertions: "Language is a prerequisite for the life that goes with technology. If you're going to make stone tools, and if you're going to come to live together . . . in campsites, sharing labor responsibilities and doing things together— which is the package that goes with mankind—then some form of language is essential."

Of course, most of man's distinctions, pinpointed by Richard and his friends as the very elements of our humanity, could simply not be proven from fossils. He had resolved that there were four characteristics prevailing for all of man's time: bipedalism, toolmaking, language and cooperation. The position of the foramen magnum on the cranium could, more or less, tell the paleontologist whether or not the creature stood upright, walking on two, not four limbs. The ability to talk also had a basis in the fossil evidence. Depending on the extent of a depression left on the interior left temple of the skull and once filled by Broca's area, an anatomist might conclude that a long-ago hominid communicated, more or less, as we do. On both counts 1470 qualified as man, but here fact ended and the guessing began. A large brain is no guarantee that its owner could make tools. Size variations among hominids can be wide, proving very little. While modern brains average around 1,400 cc, nothing can be implied by one that is larger or smaller. Anatole France's, we are told, was a mere 900 cc, while Oliver Cromwell's was 2,000 cc. To say at which brain size man began making tools would therefore be misleading. Hand bones might be more indicative of the ability to make tools, but these fossils are the rarest of all. Cooperation is equally difficult to ascertain. Long-ago campsites have been located at Rudolf. In some there is even a suggestion of a campfire. The only problem is the archeologists' inability to connect these campsites with their architects. Hominid fossils are rarely found in campsites—only evidence of their toolmaking. Was it 1470 who convened here, or was it someone else? Richard posed the question, often on the cool veranda at Koobi Fora, each time looking around with a sly smile to gauge the effect. If it was evening the answer to his question would often come from the lakeshore: the piping of the bats, the lament of the frogs in the reeds.

Even now, in 1974, I knew Richard was embarrassed to be called an explorer. Explorers deal with items—with the hard earth and the cold rivers. Richard wanted more. He could see himself changing perceptions, revolutionizing thought. Koobi Fora, after all, was just a place. The world, thumping its chest over Vietnam, Watergate and Nixon's resignation, needed a message of reassurance from the big heart of Africa. The message had to do with peace and brotherhood—dreams, admittedly, for us moderns, but, according to Richard, possible tenets of our ancestors. Richard clearly saw himself as a guru for a generation that had lost faith. So if it needed to believe in something, he would offer up early man.

Nor was Richard any longer the angular boy I had once met on the beach. He had filled out, his hair grown darker, his puckishness, the brazenness of his ambition almost smothered beneath team spirit and public relations. Nightly, once the filming was done, we launched into discussions of 1470 and his candidacy as a human being. It was splendid star talk, with pressure lamps hissing and the occasional slap of a crocodile's tail from the lakeshore. No one ever admitted that such talk about the way 1470 probably lived was a fruitless intellectual game. The scientists were working in an area where no substantive proof could ever be found. They did not seem particularly bothered by the hopelessness of it all since the pursuit of unattainable answers would keep them well occupied throughout their careers. For Richard, it was a springboard into a new vocation as a mind bender.

Richard, I decided, was at his best when talking in specifics, of bones and stones. One evening, watching the moon rise beyond the great dune, he recalled how he and his father used to scare vultures and marabou storks off lion kills. It was a routine the old man had refined as a way of transporting guests out of the twentieth century into the Pleistocene. Arms flying, crying shrilly, his father approached the carcass in his curious shuffling run. The lion huffed off into the bushes, the storks waddled away, leaving the dead antelope to the old man and his friends. Now Dr. Leakey, magnanimously sweeping his hand over the flesh, invited his guests to get at it. One can almost see him, resting under a bush, watching with bemusement as the outsiders attempted to remove the skin, as unbreakable as tin. Human teeth are quite useless in such instances.

Something besides the human hand is needed. By now the old man was on his feet, promising to solve his guests' dilemma. On the ground he found a stone. Expertly, he chipped it against another to form a cutting edge. "It's your knife," he said, and with one smart butcher's stroke along the stomach of the carcass, he laid open the meat to would-be human scavengers.

"With a stone," explained Richard, looking for inspiration at the black lake, "man embarks on a whole new range of behavior. He becomes a meat-eater, a predator, and before long he must struggle to decide what to do with the meat. Should he allow what he does not need to rot in the sun or should he carry it back to camp for the benefit of the others? The simple act of chipping a stone to make a knife is as significant as any of man's technology. It is the beginning—what distinguishes 1470 from that other fellow, the unsuccessful one. It's what makes man man. . . ."

I, of course, wanted to know what 1470 looked like, how its day was spent—specifics which raised eyebrows and circumlocutory answers from the expedition members. At last, with evidence on which no scientist was willing to risk his reputation, I pieced together a picture. Most authorities, for instance, believed "there was a good chance—nothing certain, of course," that the skull had once belonged to a woman. I thereafter thought of it only as a woman. She had died in her twenties. Most of her time, in between the childbearing, was spent watching for something to turn up, for signs of a fresh meal—vultures flying over a lion kill, a bird going to honey. I have seen the desert peoples of the Northern Frontier live in much the same way. A lone warrior squats under a bush during the worst heat of the day and when asked to explain his mission, he merely clicks his tongue. He has, in fact, been here for two days now, and to a Western mind that act of patience seems inhuman. So it must have been with 1470. Most days she survived on roots and berries. Favored spots for their collection became her landmarks. And collection was a communal event—women and adolescents were the workhorses of the band. Probably 1470 had no one home. Along with the others, she roamed far, carrying few belongings, marking each season (and her year might have contained many more than four) with a new campsite. Possibly the women and children conducted the short-distance foraging while the men went farther afield. By sunset there might have been some tacit understanding where to convene for the night. And night brought them together not merely for propagation but for company, maybe even for stories. They lay on the ground, bodies touching bodies, near a fire that, during the night, would be stoked by whoever was awake.

By first light they were ready for new tasks. I like to think that if the process of fossilization could also preserve soft material, it would have presented us with yet another aspect of man's humanity—the ability to fashion containers. No other creature but man can create receptacles to extend an individual's carrying capacity. I believe that if we could travel back in time we would discover that 1470 knew how to weave baskets, string together crude bags. With these, she and her fellows could gather numerous stones for their toolmaking factories, more meat or roots or berries or honey than one person could consume.

And whenever females were busy nursing, the troop would have reduced its range, the men assuming the lion's share of the food gathering. One can all too readily conclude that role structuring between sexes began in those primitive days when 1470 was abroad, yet here, once again, I take liberties with the scant evidence available from the stones and bones.

Dr. Leakey saw the 1470 skull just before he left Nairobi for an overseas lecture tour. He was enormously impressed, admitting publicly that "Richard has found more at Rudolf than I have done in forty years at Olduvai." A week later, Dr. Leakey was dead.

For many years Richard and his father had had little to do with one another. Richard had succeeded his father as director of the National Museum, and observers recall seeing the two pass each other in corridors without a word. The family had already had some epic silences (for nearly five years, for instance, Richard and his younger brother, Philip, never once exchanged a word), but this feud between father and son seemed the worst. Two giants in the same field were, in effect, working against each other. Richard, it seemed, felt his father had stopped focusing on the important issues, having become so besotted with matters far from home, projects that seemed to a son undignified of a father.

Then in 1971 Dr. Leakey fell from an auditorium stage in California. Thinking that he had a concussion, he was taken to the hospital where neurologists removed two blood clots from his brain. Evidently he had been suffering for quite some time. Once recovered from the operation, he seemed to friends more subdued, more stable, even reasonable, and Richard started visiting him at the family home outside of Nairobi. They talked of skulls and bones. The dialogue had, at last, reopened. And six months later, when Dr. Leakey died, Richard seemed, for the first time in years, content to be his father's son.

Discoveries were now being made regularly at the lake. In 1973, two more skulls suggested that the social mix 1.8 million years ago was not strictly composed of the crude australopithecines at one end and the 1470-type at the other, but that there had been in-between peoples. The skull that was named "1813" possessed a modest-sized brain with a set of teeth not altogether different from our own. A year later Rudolf offered up even more bounty. Once again the discoverer was Bernard Ngenyeo, a man hired originally as cook. In between preparations for lunch and dinner, he wandered off from the kitchen, returning an hour later with news of a strange pelvis. In fact it was the oldest pelvis found anywhere at the time, and it illustrated how that part of the human anatomy (nearly two million years ago) was surprisingly like our own today.

But the best news of all for Richard was when his team came upon a *Homo erectus* skull. This was the advanced humanlike species, more modern than 1470, not quite up to our own present-day standards. Until its discovery in Africa it had been best described as from Asia (e.g., Java Man, Peking Man), supporting a theory which claimed that, while we may have been born in Africa, we grew up in Asia. Now Richard could affirm, chauvinistically, that Africa had always been man's home. There were still other distinctions of the *Homo erectus* discovery that pleased

Richard. In the same sediment deposits, a robust australopithe-cine skull was also found—further evidence, he speculated, that as long ago as a million years several sorts of humanlike creatures might have coexisted.

Richard had his reasons for proof. At the end of 1974 Lake Rudolf's fossils had run into competition. Dr. Don Carl Johan-son, an American even younger than Richard, made a discovery that threatened to eclipse much of Lake Rudolf's uniqueness. On November 24 of that year Johanson and Tom Gray, a graduate student, had been collecting fossil animal bones that Gray had spotted during the previous year. This was the end of their sec-ond season in the Afar, a blistering-hot region in north central Ethiopia. On his way back to the Land Rover, Johanson hap-pened to glance over his shoulder. There lay an arm bone. From a distance it might have belonged to a monkey, but when the two young men approached for a closer look they could not see the characteristic bony flange. "It's hominid," Johanson blurted. All of a sudden, they realized they were surrounded by other skeletal remains—part of the skull, a complete lower jaw, a thigh bone, arm bones, ribs, vertebrae and on and on. At such a mo-ment, Richard might have allowed himself a quick intake of breath and one or two "remarkables," but Don Johanson, being American and considerably more animated, was incapable of self-control. They knew they had found the anthropologist's Holy Grail. They yelled, they danced, they hugged each other. When they drove back to camp, Johanson honked the horn for much of the way, yelling through the windows across the empty de-sert, "We found it! We found it!" They named the skeleton Lucy, after the Beatles' "Lucy in the Sky with Diamonds," which they had been playing over and over again in camp.

Once assembled, the skeleton measured a scant three and a half feet. From the shape of the pelvis the remains almost cer-tainly belonged to a female; her wisdom teeth, only recently emerged at the time of death, told Johanson she had died young, suffering, Johanson speculated, from arthritis. Lucy was dated at three and a half million years, older than anything found by Richard.

Richard quickly reduced Lucy to the genus of *Ramapithecus,* a very early humanlike primate, usually dated at between ten and fourteen million years and sketchily described by a handful of fossil teeth, jaws and a limb bone from Kenya, Hungary, Turkey, Greece, Pakistan and China. In Richard's chronology, Lucy would fill an awkward eight-million-year gap between the *Ramapithecus* remains at ten million years and the first known *Homo* skull, found presumably at Lake Rudolf. Her bones suggested to Richard that *Ramapithecus* had evolved slowly. "Lucy," he wrote, "in her dental characteristics was very similar to *Ramapithecus*—although Lucy is much younger. My impression is that Lucy might be a late survivor of *Ramapithecus*. A study of Lucy may well provide a lot of insight into the unlikely gait and local adaptation of *Ramapithecus*. My impression is that she was well adapted to her country: a small creature, extremely versatile both on the ground and in the trees; and while capable of upright stance, it wasn't developed the way it is in modern man. But while having this ability, it was also very agile in the trees; it retained a lot of climbing adaptations."

Richard's description was an extremely effective put-down. By characterizing her as a form of *Ramapithecus,* he was admitting she was interesting, but denying she had anything substantive to do with man's vaunted development where an almost complete skeleton such as hers could supply answers to truly important questions.

Of course, Johanson was enraged. He had now named Lucy *Australopithecus afarensis,* mainstream man, older and more humanlike than 1470, and at the crossroads of our development. Relations between the two scientists quickly deteriorated. Johanson, grasping for some of Leakey's luminosity, went into print and onto television to exacerbate the differences between them. He resigned from a foundation that Richard chairs, and in every possible way he drew up battle lines. Clearly the issue is over whose fossil material is most important. Richard, while proclaiming publicly that such recrimination hardly befits the dignity of the field, allows privately that a good fight does nobody any harm, apropos the sale of books and lecture seats.

Richard's hegemony was soon tested again, this time in a quieter way, by his own mother, the retiring Mary. In 1975 she was finally able to disengage herself from a ten-year work, compiling all her data on the stone tool cultures of Olduvai, to return to a region where Louis had been convinced they would one day find hominid fossils. She kept her promise to him in her first season there by finding a bonanza—fragments of a human jaw, dated at 3.4 million years. During the next season, the hunt led her to one of the eeriest of all early-man discoveries—a series of humanlike footprints, leading away from a waterhole. Until this time, footprints of our ancestors had been dated at eighty thousand years, in caves once occupied by Neanderthal man in Italy. Now, with some assurance, the date could be extended to three and a half million years. Judging by its gait, the maker of the prints was probably no more than four feet tall, completely upright when walking. Its feet were remarkably splayed, its gait slow, composed of short steps, no longer than the length of its foot. It seemed possible to Mary that, in fact, there were two sets of prints, one slightly smaller, overlaying the other. Mary is not given to speculation but it did seem possible to others who studied the prints that they had been made by a male and a female of the same species, and that the female had been following the male, almost always setting her feet in the tracks made by him. Mary waited two years before announcing her discovery, and even then she cautiously admitted she was only 75 percent sure that the prints were hominid.

One might have expected Richard to respond to Mary's discovery with bursting filial pride, but the Leakeys do otherwise. Almost all members of the family operate independently, treating each other with detachment, Richard referring to his parents by their Christian names, never as "my mother" or "my father." There has never been collective Leakey success. They try to be cordial, but somehow remain distant.

Richard's detractors—and there were many by now—were calling him "ruthless," "blind except to his own material," "preachy." There was no doubt that he was monomaniacally committed to his own area of study. As director of the National Museum, he had initiated the construction of a building next door, the Louis Leakey Memorial Institute. In one sense he treated it as a final measure of respect to his father's memory. But in its fullest design, it was intended to become the international center for research into the study of man's past. Richard expected it to house all the major hominid fossils of Africa and to serve as a kind of clearinghouse for all prehistorians passing through Africa. His was an ambitious plan, for it would place his Nairobi home at the academic bull's-eye of his narrow field. But like so many worldly dreams landscaped for Africa, it never succeeded as originally conceived. The funding was excruciatingly difficult to generate, forcing Richard at times to dig into his own pocket, and the Kenyan Richard had selected as director soon began to politicize the Institute. One tribe was pitted against another and many scientists were made to feel unwelcome, while personal friends of the director were given free rein.

Richard never once became disillusioned. His is a religion, not a job, and all dissent, all reverses, he judges as irrelevancies. He has now coauthored three books about prehistory, starred in a major BBC miniseries. While he, Meave and the two children could well use the royalties, Richard has chosen to return a large part of them to the study of prehistory. He generously offers his lecture honorariums to the American foundation he chairs, to aid research and to train African students. His personal behavior is consistent with the fundamentals of African socialism, ascribed to by Tanzania's Julius Nyerere.

Ten years after I first met Richard, I am in an auditorium listening to him speak. I can remember another lecture much like this one. Today the audience seems aged. The old ladies are still old and the students are still students, but the speaker has changed.

In his voice, strong and controlled for the last hour, I can now detect a slight unevenness, a strain: "More and more, people are beginning to realize that everybody aspires to a decent standard of living. And most people are sufficiently democratic to accept that that's fair. Now is it the lifestyle enjoyed by the majority of Kenyans—with a simple home, no electricity, no power sources other than natural fuels, firewood, charcoal, no motor vehicles, public transport, no running water? Or is a decent standard of living owning five television sets, three cars, three houses, a yacht and a vacation somewhere around the world whenever you want it? Those are, if you like, the two extremes. It is quite clear that everybody could survive at the standard of living that is typical of the Third World. I think that the resources are there at the moment. But if everyone tried to aspire at the Western end of the scale, it is quite clear there are too many people. You just could not produce the resources to maintain that system. So I think that what must happen is for both to shift. And you've got to meet in the middle."

Richard has changed more than most during the last decade of our friendship. Long hours, compulsive work habits and little sleep have aged him. Pouches hang under his eyes, and while once his voice was always strong, even late at night, today it seems to tire early. Frankly, Richard is lucky to be alive.

I dined with him one evening at his house outside Nairobi, and I thought he looked sick. He apologized for the salt-free diet his doctors had condemned him to. I noted too that he had given up his Oom Willem pipe. He appeared paler than I had ever seen him. Meave, moving between the kitchen and the dining room, was uncommonly strained. During a lull in the conversation, I recalled a talk I had had with Richard five years before. He had confided to me that he had been told by his doctors that he should not expect to live a full life. He mentioned this secret only to explain to me his determination to do so much in so few years. I had kept his confidence during the intervening period, watching always for telltale signs of deterioration.

Two days after the dinner, Richard fainted in his office at the museum. At the hospital he was found to be suffering from dangerously high blood pressure. His kidneys had, at last, failed. Since there is no dialysis machine in Kenya, Richard was immediately flown to London, where his system was cleaned. He was told that he could never travel any distance from his life-support system unless he could locate a kidney donor for a transplant. The only candidate, he learned, was his younger brother, Philip, the one to whom he had not said a word for so many years. Richard called Philip. The decision took only a few seconds: Philip agreed to give Richard one of his kidneys. "I suppose now," Philip claimed to have said, "I won't be able to hate your guts."

Philip was campaigning for a parliamentary seat in Kenya. He had previously failed in an electoral bid. This time he won, becoming the only white member of Parliament, his skin color somehow assuring his constituents that he was incorruptible. A few days later he flew to London, submitted to surgery at the same time as Richard, and successfully gave Richard the wherewithal to live a normal life, and to discover, one supposes, how to bury hatchets and become brothers.

Today Richard, not yet forty, is the graybeard of his profession. Young men, anxious for a future in his career, await the end of his lecture to identify themselves as candidates for summer work at Koobi Fora. Richard no longer perceives of himself as an explorer but as a patron of exploration, as the theoretician of his field. He crusades on behalf of pacifism, trying to prove over and over again that man began not as the aggressor, the warmonger, the bigot, the killer ape, but as a gentleman. He dismisses the evidence found by Raymond Dart in limestone caves in South Africa of "ape-men" with their craniums crudely smashed by blunt instruments. He rejects the logical theory that the fifteen *Homo erectus* skulls found in the cave at Choukoutien, thirty miles from Peking, had had their brains siphoned out piece by piece by fellow members of their species. In the strict sense it was not cannibalism, Richard claims, but a ritual. The eating of the brains of a fallen enemy was most likely performed to maintain "a bond of continuity" with the dead, the usurpation of the dead man's powers. Man had no need to be aggressive, Richard maintains. He managed by scavenging, by being an opportunist. "If there is any one thing that makes humans human," he says, "it is cooperation, *not* aggression. Warfare, for example, is simply a response by man to the environment he has created—and it is possible to create an environment in which warfare would have no place. And even warfare requires cooperation. The popularity of the concept of man as killer ape and macho male was needed to explain the terrible atrocities that occurred in World War Two. Even before that, there was a feeling in Western culture that Neanderthal man was primitive and brutish. Many people grew up with images drawn from comics of the caveman as the hairy brute with a club who used to beat fellow brutes on the head in the course of stealing women and dragging away victims. It's a dangerous perspective that leads to the conclusion that such behavior is inevitable. I would argue very strongly that violence and its acceptance are purely cultural."

My eyes wander. The audience squirms. Outside, a red light has turned green and the traffic roars. For a time I almost forgot Richard's early allure. Then he owned only one or two ties and treated a lecture as if it were his trial, working hard to manipulate the jury. He had found a stone and a pig jaw and he was going to prove to the world that our ancestors were older than previously believed, and that, best of all, they could be located by a young, undereducated Kenyan. He preferred not to discuss his father. If you wanted to know about him, there were, Richard implied, lots of books in libraries dealing with the subject. Richard was here to tell you of Lake Rudolf, of long nights on the desert floor, with the bellowing of camels nearby and the yip of a lone hyena far away. He was here to conjure for you how new treasures could appear each year, after each successive period of rain, how every May when he first set foot on those badlands, miles from help, he knew he could walk the same route of last year and expect to find a new assortment of fossils. Here Richard used to pause, his eyes rubbering around the room. "I leave next week. And I expect to be back here in this hall this same time next year. And if I don't return next year then you'll know I only found rocks."

Of course, at the time, I knew Richard would never only find rocks. He would come back, year after year, with new fossils, new insights into our vagrant past.

These days Richard returns to America with less treasure, more theory. His thoughts run to global schemes. He is not allowed as much time in his beloved badlands. He returns to America not once but sometimes three times a year, lured by something he cannot define. He is needed here, it seems, to lecture and to persuade, drawing yet one more inference from a roomful of bones, left only to interpret, as did so many retired explorers of the nineteenth century, the mysteries and bounty of Africa.

A MAN
AND HIS
DIAMONDS

When I was a sixteen-year-old schoolboy, I met a diamond prospector in Bechuanaland's desert. Even now, twenty years later, I can remember him introducing himself as Lamont. His eyes were a washed blue, his face smarting from sunburn and his neck, frame and bare legs so thin that I was sure he had suffered many privations.

It was customary in lonely places for the occupants of two cars, approaching one another, to stop, swap news and some form of liquid refreshment. Perhaps because Lamont was the first human being I had seen in two days, I can still recall that tepid beer, his looks and his talk of glimmering stones lying in the sand. Diamonds in the desert? I had much to ask this prospector, but he was pressed and our talk ran to heat, salt pans and broken half-shafts. These formalities over, he peered at his watch and waved good-bye.

Recently, in New York, I suddenly recalled my long-ago desert journey. I was lunching with Harry Oppenheimer, chairman of DeBeers Consolidated Mines. He knew of my interest in remote places and asked whether I had heard about the new diamond mines in the Kalahari.

Now these mines were part of Mr. Oppenheimer's empire, but that was not his point. Nor did he seem troubled by the prospect that they might greatly expand the world supply of diamonds, or that their discovery had dramatically transformed Bechuanaland (now Botswana) from one of the world's poorest nations to one of Africa's wealthiest. What he thought I would most like to hear was the curious story of the mines' discovery.

"And who found them?" I asked, rushing the story's conclusion.

"A chap who had been prospecting for us for about twelve years and had come up with absolutely nothing. I was ready to call it a day with Botswana."

"What was his name?" I broke in.

"Lamont. Gavin Lamont."

The best way to reach Botswana from the United States is by flying first to the Republic of South Africa and then retracing one's course for three hundred miles in a smaller aircraft, to Gaborone, the capital of this desert land. It is strange, I thought, how this black nation is inseparably linked to the outside world through Enemy-Number-One of the entire continent. Still, with as much land as France and with less people than one borough of New York, Botswana is somehow able to remain aloof—not just from the giant to the south but from all of Africa. For example, the Batswana not only talk about justice, freedom of speech and civil liberties, they also do something about these phantom principles. One need only check the jails to discover that there is not one political prisoner in the whole country. The government publishes the most widely read newspaper in the country, but it's remarkably devoid of pro-government rhetoric.

It is handed out free of charge to everyone in Botswana in the hope that this will make for a better-informed citizenry.

I stumbled onto these subtle African anomalies on my first day in Gaborone. I had come here to meet Louis Nchindo, the managing director of the DeBeers affiliate which operates the Botswana diamond mines. Gavin Lamont, I had been told, was now semiretired, living in South Africa, and no one was sure whether he would agree to talk to me. While awaiting his verdict, I chose to see the new diamond mines for myself and to find out as much as I could about Dr. Lamont at the scenes of his discoveries. Perhaps Nchindo would have some leads.

A handsome Motswana, faintly resembling Harry Belafonte, he sat in a large office located in Botswana's tallest skyscraper, all of five stories high. He led off by explaining that although the Botswana government and DeBeers are equal partners in the mines, DeBeers had made virtually all the capital investments, while the government's share of revenues was likely to exceed 70 percent of the total profits.

Louis described each of the three mines. First I'd visit Orapa, 370 kilometers northwest of the capital. The first mine discovered by Gavin Lamont, it is, in a sense, the father of Botswana's diamond bonanza. Nearby is its small stepchild mine, called Letlhakane. Some 350 kilometers to the south is Jwaneng (then under construction), Lamont's other great discovery.

Whereas the first two mines cost DeBeers around $40 million to build, the new one is budgeted at more than $400 million because sand to a depth of 160 feet has to be dug away before any mining can begin. "How many companies do you know of," asked Mr. Nchindo, "that would sink nearly half a billion dollars into a black nation?"

"I wonder," I said, diverting that subject, "how Gavin Lamont feels about all this?"

Mr. Nchindo shook his head. "Hard to say. I've only met him a few times—mostly at dedication ceremonies."

The most sensible way to reach Orapa is by air, and since the only planes are QueenAirs belonging to DeBeers or its parent company, Anglo-American of South Africa, the mine is virtually fortified against all curiosity seekers. Throughout the hour and a half flight I could spot no sign of life on the ground, only a dull throw rug of mopani trees, scrubby and shade-poor, whose leaves turn the color of copper for nine months each year. The most striking feature of the land is its almost total absence of features. If I had been Gavin Lamont I wonder if I would have known even where to begin.

The town of Orapa was a letdown for someone who had always associated diamonds with high intrigue. Were it to fall into disuse, it would never acquire, it seemed to me, the allure of a ghost town. Laid out with a city planner's precision, the streets are straight, the houses built to reflect seniority, or the lack of it. While the mine manager's had a tile roof, for instance, most everybody else had to make do with tin.

Jim Gibson, Lamont's assistant at the time of the discovery, met me at one of the clubs. His crisp white shorts, white socks and stiff formality suggested a military man, but as our chits mounted on the mahogany bar, his Scottish burr and a quirkish impulsiveness began to cut through the veneer. He had clearly enjoyed his early days in Botswana when there were not many conveniences.

When Jim came here in 1963 his boss was already a thirteen-year veteran of the Kalahari. The routine of prospecting, spelled out for him by Lamont, seemed numbingly boring. For six days each week he would have to walk an eleven-mile transect from a baseline—five miles out, one mile across, five miles back. At designated intervals he was to collect samples, and these were to be shipped to Johannesburg where the result would probably not be divulged.

"Gavin kept his geologists under a very tight rein," Jim explained. "He expected us to stay in the bush 99.9 percent of the time. We had only one weekend off a month, and during that time we were supposed to buy our supplies and then to hurry right back out into the bush." In addition, Jim was told to call Lamont on the radiotelephone at least twice a day. "It was as though we were children."

Finally, after three months, these frustrations began to dissipate. It was clear Jim was working for a geologist of superior qualifications. Gavin spotted anomalies of the bush through a curious intuition. "His powers of observation were uncanny," explained Jim. "If he was driving along a bush track, and a barbet whistled, or the vegetation suddenly changed, when a tree looked burnt—he noticed. I learned an enormous amount from him, and after we had been together for a while, he began to let his hair down, telling story after story about the Kalahari."

Jim worked with Gavin Lamont for three years before the big discovery. I asked him what happened on the day they first suspected the presence of diamonds. "I'm what you might call a canny Scot," he answered, "and Gavin's half-Scottish himself. We didn't throw our arms around each other and get blind drunk. I think we both inwardly knew we were onto something big. We each had a bottle of Scotch in our kit—it being winter—and that night we laced our coffee a little more liberally than we would normally."

Jim gathered that I knew little about diamond prospecting. So he began my education. Because diamonds are formed by a combination of heat and pressure, they are nothing more than carbon that has suffered a personality change—in effect, it has crystallized. Long after the tops of the volcanoes, responsible for all this stress, have been weathered out of sight, the diamonds remain concealed in their volcanic "pipes" beneath the surface. To find diamonds, however, one cannot blindly look for old volcanic activity or even for the substance of which the pipes are composed, called kimberlite or "blueground." In truth, this host rock is never even blue on the surface. More often it is yellow, or, in the case of Orapa, pink. So color is not a very helpful clue.

Instead, one looks for two other minerals that have undergone volcanic stress. These "indicators" are black ilmenites (titanium iron oxide) and red garnets, and for every one diamond in a pipe there may be as many as a hundred of those stones. But then Jim pointed out that finding garnets and ilmenites alone does not guarantee the presence of diamonds. In fact, for every two hundred mineral-rich pipes, only one may be diamond-bearing, and even then not every diamondiferous pipe is of economic importance. The odds, therefore, of one man finding a valuable diamond mine are distressingly remote.

After a day at Orapa I began to perceive that Gavin Lamont's name was known only to a few of the senior staff on the mine. Some knew that he had made the discovery, but not many outside the geological staff knew the details of that pursuit. On a nostalgic visit to the mine a few years before, Lamont and his wife had been presented with an oil painting depicting his role in the discovery of the mine. But whenever I mentioned his name to the junior staff members, most asked *me* to tell them his story.

A puff of smoke, the delayed boom of dynamite, cued me where kimberlite was now being mined in the pit. Everything is on a grand scale: A shovel the size of a brontosaurus dumps the stone on one of four mammoth trucks, each priced at half a million dollars. For every ten tons of waste only one carat of diamond will be recovered. The drivers, therefore, race their bulky cargoes to the treatment plant. They dump their loads onto conveyor belts, while they hurry back for more, knowing that the more they haul, the fatter their paychecks at the end of the month.

In the plant the stone is crushed and washed, centrifuged and parboiled until only small gravel remains to be sorted by X-ray selection. Then the concentrate will be sent to a small, unprepossessing blockhouse, where it will be examined for the first time by man. While everywhere else the air is charged with the roar of turbines, here there is a quiet monastic hush. Along two rows of partitioned workbenches Batswana sorters sit with bowed heads, scratching through neat piles of gravel. They work at great speed, flicking diamonds off to one corner of their tables, the waste to another, with light impartiality.

To my untrained eye, many of Orapa's diamonds still look like gravel. Many are black, as though the process of carbon crystallization is, as yet, incomplete. Lusterless, they will be put to industrial use as drill bits and abrasive instruments. Their value is a mere fraction of a gemstone. I asked Andrew Peter Brittz, the mine's manager, about the proportion of gemstones to industrials. A large, solemn man, he estimated that at Orapa only 20 percent of the recovered diamonds are of gemstone quality. Letlhakane, the small mine nearby, is, however, a different story. "Although it produces a mere 400,000 carats a year [compared to Orapa's 4,500,000], 55 percent of them are gems," explained Mr. Brittz. When I asked how much the total production was worth in dollars, his smile evaporated. Even if he did know, he was sworn to silence. DeBeers likes to keep its secrets, and especially here in Botswana, where the government is a major shareholder, any such revelation would not be in the national interest.

As I stood to go, Mr. Brittz brought up one aspect of Orapa that often goes unnoticed. For the last thirty years he had been moving from one mine to another, all of them in South Africa. Botswana was his first post in a black African country. He'd found the transition extraordinarily easy. "I would call it," he continued, "one of the most eye-opening and worthy experiences of my career." He leaned across his desk. "Think of it this way," he whispered conspiratorily. "I'm not alone. There must be over a hundred white South Africans at this mine right now. It may be the first time in their lives when they can sit at a club side by side with a black or take orders from a black man on the job." Mr. Brittz tapped his temple. "Orapa is for them a mental revolution. By the time they return south, their attitudes will have changed, and they, in turn, will affect the attitudes of other South Africans."

"And all thanks to Gavin Lamont."

Mr. Brittz had evidently never thought of crediting this social revolution to any one man. He paused. "Yes. Why not? It all began with Gavin Lamont."

I still had no word whether my Cape Town meeting with the elusive prospector would be possible. So I delayed to make one last visit to the DeBeers headquarters in Gaborone to see what became of the diamonds that each week were flown from Orapa in a heavily guarded airplane. Once in the building, I was escorted through two armored doors, past the eyes of closed-circuit television cameras, into a well-lit gallery where Mike Finney, the chief diamond sorter, met me. A tall man with an East End London accent, Mike escorted me down a row of newly trained Batswana sorters, sitting with bowed heads over their precious daily allotments. They were, he said, among the highest-paid artisans in the country, and by the time Jwaneng was producing, their numbers were expected to rise from forty to over a hundred, to handle the anticipated nine million carats a year.

Diamond sorting requires a memory for types. A working sample, much like a paint chart, contains three thousand different diamonds, which spans nearly every variety. Unlike a paint chart, however, the sample stays safely locked in a vault. When in doubt, a sorter can always refer to this precious assortment, but to be efficient, he should have most types committed to memory. There are at least seven colors to choose from, five major shapes, a multiplicity of sizes and a thousand surprises in the impurity department.

I knew that Mike had never lost his fascination with diamonds when he introduced me to his wife, another Londoner and one of his prize sorters. Even at work, she wore the diamond ring he had once given her—a handsome stone that seemed to splash and glare alternately, throwing brilliant sparkles of blue and white, under her desk lamp. I could not help comparing it to the 57.1 carat uncut diamond she removed from the vault to show me, just arrived from Orapa. The size of a lima bean, it seemed to my untrained eye remarkably commonplace. "The most valuable diamond from Botswana so far," she said reverentially. "Worth about a million pounds, I should think." Uncut, it looked no more exciting than a shard of sea glass. Nothing in its cool touch suggested that it was the hardest natural substance known to man; or that the cut diamond, inscribed with over eighty facets, would add allure to a woman's hand. "No diamond is like any other," Mike said, as though he were reciting a liturgical response. "Each one is as different as a fingerprint or a snowflake." He gently picked up the diamond, replaced it in a small canister and ceremoniously returned it to the vault.

Later I found out what became of the diamonds after they left the sorting room.

In New York I met with Nathan Akselrod, the chief rough-stone buyer for Harry Winston, one of the world's legendary names in the diamond trade. Mr. Akselrod, wearing a blue suit, a blue shirt, a blue tie and cuff links of blue-white diamonds, explained that through its Central Selling Organization in London, DeBeers virtually monopolizes the sale of over 80 percent of the world's diamonds. It is, in fact, the oldest known and most tightly controlled monopoly of any kind in the world today. DeBeers has decreed the holding of any uncut diamond by an unlicensed person to be a crime. The CSO can therefore keep tight rein over the wholesale market by adjusting the supply to consumer demand, thereby preventing wild fluctuations in price. If a diamond is to be "forever," according to the DeBeers rationale, its market value should be sustained by vigilance and enforced rarity.

Diamond dealers, like Harry Winston, are treated by the cartel as members of a privileged club, and membership is limited to about 250 key buyers. Only this elite gets "invited" to its sales, called "sites," which take place about ten times a year. Before arriving in London, the dealers submit their requirements to their brokers. A small order, for instance, would be "diamonds ranging from two to four carats for half a million dollars." Orders can run as high as $30 million. Even before a dealer arrives in London, he must have paid for the sight-unseen order by a certified check. Only then is he allowed to examine his purchase. Arriving at DeBeers's Charterhouse office, he is handed a shoebox with his name on it. Inside, a small cloth bag will contain his "goods." Basically, he has no control over the selection of its contents. If the diamonds do not meet with his approval, there is virtually nothing he can do if he wishes to remain in DeBeers's good graces. If he is foolish enough to renege on the order, it is virtually certain he will not be invited back to another site.

"Blackmail?" I asked Mr. Akselrod. "Perhaps," he replied, drawing on his cigar, "but DeBeers builds into each collection of diamonds a significant profit for the dealer. The only time we discuss the price," he added, "is when it comes to 'specials'— stones weighing over 14.80 carats." Because color, quality, imperfections and shape in stones of this size are matters of such personal taste, DeBeers will agree to bargain.

Until 1980 diamonds had increased in value at a rate exceeding most collectibles. In 1955, a flawless, perfectly white diamond of one carat cost about $1,500. In March 1980, that same stone would have brought $61,000. As a consequence, commodity investors had begun to enter the market and now there seemed to be two tiers of value—marginally imperfect stones that traditionally sold to young bridegrooms, and certified flawless diamonds that will be stashed away in neat plastic bags in bank vaults, waiting for a profit.

On Akselrod's desk, several stories above the window shoppers on Fifth Avenue, there were ten white packets of folded paper, each one containing several thousand carats of diamonds. He opened an envelope and pointed to a yellowish stone. "Sierra Leone," he intoned. Another diamond was from Siberia. "Lovely stones," he said, "but they're very dangerous to cut." He casually rummaged through another pile on his desk, like a man looking for a paper clip. One by one he picked up diamonds, chanting, "Brazil . . . Ivory Coast . . . Southwest Africa . . . Premier Mine, South Africa."

"But the Botswana stones," I interrupted. "Can you spot them as well?"

Mr. Akselrod thought for a second. "You know, there have been so few of them on the market up to now. Yes, I think I can, although I'm not as familiar with them as I am with others. That will change. If all goes as expected, Botswana will be the biggest diamond windfall in the Western world in twenty, maybe thirty years. They will be everywhere. . . ."

Gavin Lamont was still not answering his phone in Cape Town. While I waited in Johannesburg I met Dr. Louis Murray, the head of DeBeers's geology department. Dressed like a London stockbroker in a chalk-striped suit and a muted tie, he seemed very pleased to talk about the man who had once worked for him and whose keen powers of observation had led to Botswana's success story. He and Gavin Lamont had become close friends long before the diamonds were discovered. "We always gave Botswana fairly low priority," he explained, "because we thought it was covered almost exclusively by sand. Only after we were well into it did we find that the sand wasn't always that deep. All through those years when Gavin was prospecting, and nothing substantial was being found, we wavered between despondency and hope. I can remember being in favor of pulling out altogether. In the end it was Gavin who pleaded for yet another three-month extension that kept us going. That's when he discovered Orapa. . . ."

Gavin Lamont was a most exceptional geologist, he added, not just because of his technical expertise but for reasons of personality. "He is an acute observer, a good deductive thinker. And in the case of Jwaneng, the last mine he discovered, it was plain perseverance on his part. You cannot believe how difficult and soul-destroying it was, to stick it out with all that sand beneath your feet and so little to go on. To pinpoint anything, particularly something so innocuous as a kimberlite pipe in those millions of acres of sand, is downright extraordinary. The desert is a wide and lonely place."

At last Gavin Lamont answered his phone. He had been away on a short holiday and was now in the process of moving into a new home. He had never talked to anyone about the diamond discoveries, but, yes, with Louis Murray's approval, he would agree to see me. Our meeting was set for seven-thirty on Monday morning, so I caught a Sunday evening flight from Johannesburg.

Cape Town is the most beautiful of all of South Africa's cities—as lush a place as the Kalahari is dry. The sea is visible from almost everywhere, and the beaches, even on the city's edge, evoke an uncluttered turn-of-the-century mood, reminiscent, I thought, of long-ago Brighton. The cottages are brightly painted and the people who live here seem to have lots of time to talk to neighbors over white picket fences, or to casual acquaintances outside a post office or even to total strangers, sitting on benches, facing the South Atlantic.

The Lamonts do not live on the sea, but in a green Cape Peninsula valley that has plunged out of wine country and is on its way to the sea. Theirs is a suburban house with a neat driveway, a two-car garage and a few flowering shrubs. The sweeping view and the irregular landscaping add a touch of wildness to the setting. Still, this modest house hardly seemed the dwelling of a man who had discovered two diamond mines.

Gavin Lamont met me in the driveway. Did he remember me from that schoolboy journey of twenty years before? He politely screwed up his face to study mine, only to admit after a pause that he had never been good with faces. He had changed very little. His hair was now silvery, pressed down hard against his scalp, as if glued. His face and neck were still reed thin. His blue eyes had now faded and I wondered whether the Kalahari sun had bleached them. There was, however, nothing severe about him. As we relaxed in his sitting room his eyes darted from me to his wife, to the view of the rainy landscape with a boyish abandon; and his mouth was forever exploding in smiles, as though, for my benefit alone, he were discovering Orapa all over again. When he recalled events, he often corrected himself, explaining that he had never before needed to put them into any regular order. He apologized for being so elusive. "Geologists are always secretive," he explained. And having dispensed with the matter, he never once seemed to conceal anything from me.

Born in Kimberley when it was the diamond capital of the world, Gavin wasted little time in fulfilling his childhood dream of becoming a geologist. In 1947, at age twenty-six, he received his doctorate in geology from Cape Town University, and soon he joined the Geological Survey in what was then called Southern Rhodesia. Two years later he began work as a geologist for the Bechuanaland Protectorate (Botswana's previous name). Then one of the most remote outposts in all of Africa, there were so few whites in its 230,000 square miles of territory that Gavin actually knew them all by name.

Gavin's job was simple: to correct the maps. Those then in use were dated 1900 and some landmarks were a good fifteen miles out of place. Every time he and his team saw an outcrop of rock, he made a note, in the hope that it would lead to the discovery of a mineral deposit. But his superiors were convinced that, apart from a little coal, asbestos and copper, there was nothing of value in the country. So, while Gavin was busy relating vegetational frontiers to underlying changes in the sediment, those in head office seemed to dismiss him as conscientious but misguided. In 1955 Gavin was hired by DeBeers, which was then just beginning to prospect in Botswana.

Gavin's first boss at DeBeers was Arnold Waters. A first-rate geologist, Dr. Waters had one quirk. He believed that material privation was essential to the success of any field venture. His motive was not penny-saving. Rather, he seemed consumed by memories of his own early career during the Depression in Northern Rhodesia, where life's basics had always been in short supply. As a result, for the first ten years of Gavin's work with DeBeers, he was discouraged from having a refrigerator in his base camp—not because of the expense, but because it was an abuse of Dr. Waters's code. Nor was he allowed to touch fresh food except for that one day a month when he was allowed to go to town for supplies. "To bring your wife to a field camp was also a hanging sin," recalled Gavin. Consequently Toni Lamont and their young son frugally survived, first in a Johannesburg hotel, later in boardinghouses scattered through desert outposts. Jim Gibson, Gavin's former assistant, may have complained that his boss was a tough taskmaster, but it was clear that the Spartan life was an attitude inherited from head office. Their entire prospecting budget in those days, covering a team of two geologists, ten assistants, vehicles, fuel and equipment, was about $4,500 a month—small even by the standards of Africa.

"Everybody thinks prospecting is a glamorous job," Gavin complained. "But until you find your mine it's monotonous bloody work." For the first twelve years of Gavin's employment with DeBeers there was nothing even resembling a mine. Gavin's movements through the country were dictated from time to time by the moods of his aging four-wheel-drive Ford pickup, dubbed the Pig by Toni Lamont because it had few manners. By eliminating one expanse of country after another Gavin ultimately narrowed his search to the eastern central portion of Botswana. Several years before, another mining group, the Central African Selection Trust, had prospected here, and on the banks of the seasonally dry Motloutse River, a tributary of the Limpopo, it had discovered three small diamonds. The prospectors followed the river to its existing headwaters, but after three months they abandoned the search, surrendering to the hunch that the three diamonds had come from a basal conglomerate.

Gavin studied their report, now, in 1964, part of the public record. He concluded that they had misinterpreted the evidence. Concurrently, he had been reading a paper written by Alex Dutoit, the South African geologist credited with the theory of continental drift. When Dr. Dutoit first expounded this concept, it was regarded with considerable skepticism by his fellow geologists. He had hypothesized that originally all Southern Hemisphere continents were one, joined together in a massive landmass that he designated "Gondwanaland." Beginning in the Cretaceous period, integral structural plates underlying the earth's mantle began to bisect the continent, and ultimately it divided itself into massive crumbs, drifting farther and farther from each other. One was to become South America, another Africa, another Antarctica and still another India.

As other geologists dismissed his theory as fanciful, Dr. Dutoit proceeded to drop another bomb. This one he called *warp*. Long after the continents, as we now know them, had assumed their separate identities, crustal movements along the continents still continued to be felt. The earth, Dutoit asserted, is never static. Mountains are always being built, seas filled. The warps of twenty million years ago were merely small responses to all those previous tectonic rumbles. These warps built hills, opened basins and diverted the flow of rivers. In southern Africa one such warp,

Dr. Dutoit maintained, could be seen all the way from Bulawayo (in Zimbabwe/Rhodesia) to the southern part of Botswana.

Gavin admitted that he was enormously impressed by the warp theory. He wrote a paper for Dr. Waters contending that the flow of rivers such as the Motloutse had been much greater than at present. Having walked its entire length to the headwaters, where it petered out into black cotton *vlei,* he had seen evidence of a flow far more considerable than at present. "I was positive," Gavin said, "that this warp of twenty million years ago had been responsible for 'decapitating' the Motloutse—for severing it from its head. I spelled all this out in the paper to head office. When it was received in Johannesburg, I'm sure that no one thought too highly of it. My request was for permission to explore far to the west of the Motloutse's existing headwaters. Arnold Waters didn't even respond. He obviously must have felt the paper was written by someone who'd been in the bush too long."

Two years later, when DeBeers was considering whether or not to call off its wild-goose chase in Botswana, Gavin pleaded with his new boss, Louis Murray, for a three-month extension so he could prove once and for all whether his interpretation of Alex Dutoit's warp theory made any sense. More to assuage the prospector than because of any deep-seated optimism (according to Gavin), permission was granted.

Gavin concentrated on a chunk of land eighteen hundred square miles in size far to the west of the Motloutse. With time running out, there now was no leisure for the traditional eleven-mile slog from a transect line. Instead, he and Jim Gibson undertook a Panzer-type exploration of the country. With Jim in one vehicle, Gavin driving another, the two geologists traversed every hunter's track throughout this vast area, at regular intervals collecting soil samples. Ten days later when the two geologists reconvened in camp, they had hundreds of sediment-filled bags, and as soon as they began washing them and turning over the screens they found the minerals that had been so elusive during all those years. "There they were at last—those fickle ilmenites and garnets. As far as we were concerned this was indisputable proof that we had stumbled onto a pipe. Of course, we were still a long way from knowing whether it would contain diamonds."

At this point in our conversation, Gavin pulled his chair closer to mine, his eyes dancing. He seemed exhilarated to be able to tell the story that had been a matter of company record for so long. For a few months, he explained, the search had to be postponed because of other unfinished projects. Finally, in April 1967, it was resumed with Manfred Marx, another assistant.

"Almost as soon as he got to the site where we had originally located those indicator minerals, he called me on the radiotelephone to say that there were some fantastic counts coming out of that day's samples. I quickly got hold of an aerial map of the area and at the spot he had indicated I saw a huge formation. It was so huge, in fact, that I felt sure it was something other than a pipe. It looked more like an alluvial fan. But a pipe it was—I guess the second-largest pipe found anywhere in the world.

"Again, over the radiotelephone, I told Manfred to dig a small pit, and while that was happening, Jim Gibson and I got into a truck and drove to the site as fast as we could. We arrived forty-five minutes after Manfred had begun washing the material coming from the pit. Although it was merely surface material, it was richer than anything I'd ever seen before. We actually found a quarter-carat diamond in it. I called Louis Murray and he arrived very soon thereafter. It was then I realized its significance. We were very, very excited. . . ."

The mine was named Orapa after a nearby cattle post, and now, with other geologists arriving daily, Gavin moved on to follow up other hunches. Anyway, mine life was not necessarily for him. Almost as soon as the discovery was made, the country began changing fast, and new contract people were replacing many of the old-timers. Both Gavin and Toni Lamont felt most comfortable away from the bustle in some remote fastness of the bush.

At the official opening of Orapa in 1971, Toni Lamont was presented with a diamond brooch by Harry Oppenheimer, the chairman. "Sir Seretse Khama, Botswana's president, shook my hand," recalled Gavin. "He said, 'Now go find another mine.' " Gavin looked at me mischievously. "I guess he hadn't heard about Jwaneng."

Indeed, by 1971, Gavin Lamont had found another mine—

this time where he had once been told minerals could never be found. A hundred miles west of Gaborone, the relentless eleven-mile slogs had paid off. Garnets and ilmenites were found right on the desert floor, and when a deep test hole was sunk to reach the underlying sediments, 160 feet below, the results were even more promising than those at Orapa.

"You see, I believed that those indicator minerals could get to the surface. All because of termites. I'm sure you've seen their remarkable mounds in Zambia and in East Africa. Extraordinary bloody things. Well, I was sure they used to exist in the Kalahari when the climate was more temperate. Termites, you see, need water, so they dig down to great depths—three hundred feet beneath the surface would not be unusual. But termites aren't very good water miners. They bring back everything else—sand, rocks, and yes, ilmenites and garnets. So it was they who found Jwaneng. Scientists like to call the process bioturbation. Awful bloody word to describe something that should be so beautiful."

Gavin's excitement, as he waved his hand to describe the incredible logic of nature, was electric. He seemed delighted to be able to share the credit for a 4.5-million-carat-a-year mine with a colony of white ants. I studied his face once again. This thin, modest retiree hardly seemed the man who had changed the destiny of a country, created over three thousand new jobs, added nine million carats a year to the world's supply of diamonds.

His story was finished. He stood up to point out his wife's collection of cut-crystal decanters, and then, prompted perhaps by the sound of a boubou shrike stirring in the jacaranda outside, he decided to show me his small garden.

Yes, he would agree to being photographed, but it was clear to me he did not like all the attention. We walked through the trim garden. "Have you ever stopped to think what you personally have achieved?" I asked, waiting for him to look more relaxed.

His answer was quick, almost irritated.

"No. Absolutely not. I was lucky—that's all. I was doing a job. I just happened to look for elephants where there were elephants."

The look was perfect. I pressed the shutter.

$1' = 3"$
$4' = 1'$
$2" = \frac{1}{2}"$
$1" = \frac{1}{4}"$

Nose to base of tail $= 12\frac{3}{4}$

B = $2\frac{1}{2}$
C = $3\frac{1}{2}$
D = $13\frac{1}{2}$
E = $2\frac{1}{2}$
F = 2
G = 3
Back Leg
H = 3"
I = $2\frac{3}{4}$
J = $2\frac{1}{4}$
K = $2\frac{3}{4}$
L = $4\frac{1}{2}$
M = $6\frac{3}{4}$
N = 3

Last night, sitting by the tent, Alan Root explained to me that when he dies he intends his body to be left on an African savannah. He will be repaying old debts to vultures, hyenas and porcupines; they, in turn, will be scratching off obligations to the smaller creatures—the beetles, bot flies and termites. His end, in short, will be many beginnings.

Morbidly utilitarian, this is the nub of a philosophy that inspires one of the most joyful and talented men of the African bushland. Alan is generally considered the finest wildlife film maker south of the Sahara—a superlative that some would not

THE WATCHER
AND THE WATCHED

limit to Africa. They claim his films go right off the scales—laser beams in a field of bright lights. His *The Great Migration: Year of the Wildebeest* and *Mysterious Castles of Clay,* nominated for an Academy Award and winner of a Peabody Award, may well be the greatest wildlife films made anywhere.

Even in Kenya, where praise for compatriots is rare, Alan's is given without reservation. He is the success story of the bush. Much to the pleasure and anguish of his friends, he remains the absolute eccentric, the clown, the daredevil, the mimic, the misanthrope, the life of the party, the irrepressible idealist of nature, the steadfast bearer of petty grudges, the critic. His boyish face, crowned by a tangle of blond hair, is incapable of veiling his moods. Anger must run its course before a smile can break through and when this happens, the light explodes from his thick glasses and his entire body coordinates to the farce, doubling up, gyrating. When he mimics the sound of a warthog being savaged by a leopard, he becomes one, scurrying, bent double; and when he flies an airplane between two doum palm tress, he performs the feat within an inch of his life. He seems to have no other thought than of the moment's activity. He will die for a sequence in a film, a joke, a game of tennis. In short, Alan is so consumed by living that every day requires some proof that he has cheated death.

The stars of Alan Root's films have almost always been animals, in defiance of the network notion that animal films need human supporting players, especially blond scientists or Sandhurst-trained game wardens. In most of Alan's films it's as though the human race does not exist. As a result, Alan has never broken ratings records, not that he cares particularly. What pleases him above all else is that his films, unadorned with the usual commercial props, are still commercial. The statistics show that very few people who turn on an Alan Root "special" can ever turn it off. He hypnotizes because his language is spare and unpedantic, his stories controlled. His film technique avoids the usual pyrotechnics, yet many of his shots are so telling that film colleagues of his will often find themselves unable to resist a spontaneous round of applause.

Alan pretends to dismiss film technology—"I hate all the equipment . . . don't understand most of it. I certainly could not explain how film is developed." He avoids reading all reviews of his films, whether good or bad, and he refuses film awards. Modesty, however, does not come easily to Alan. Indeed, he accepts compliments with delight, yet he pretends to pay them little attention. "You are the greatest," a young admirer once told him. "I know," Alan replied. There was a pause. "Okay," he continued, "now what?"

Alan's history is curious because even at an early age he seemed to know what he wanted. According to his own account, nothing much happened in his life between 1936, the year of his birth in London, and 1943, when his parents brought him to Africa. Oh yes, there was the Battle of Britain and the odd bomb exploded near the Root family, but he was still in England and, as far as he remembers, he had not begun to live. His parents were from the East End of London and, like so many cockneys, they were better conditioned to life's ills than to its good fortunes. Alan's father was always on his guard for new opportunities, and in 1943, sensing that war-torn London would only become grimmer, he accepted the post of manager at a meatpacking factory in Kenya. The site of the plant was Athi River, twenty miles southeast of Nairobi.

Here at last there was no such color as London gray. A wide speckled plain surrounded Alan's house. To the east was Mount Lukenya, to the west the Kitengela River and to the south, on a clear day, the silver roof of Africa, Kilimanjaro.

His father knew virtually nothing about wildlife, so Alan was left to his own revelations. He began with boy-size animals, and with the help of local wa-Kamba tribesmen he built an aviary and learned how to trap birds, and then snakes. "I once shot two waxbills with my catapult," he recalls, "and I wept my eyes out for days." Two weeks later he had recovered from his tears and he was back collecting more specimens. "I don't know any good naturalist who didn't start off with a catapult. I think the 'killing stages' kids go through are pretty healthy . . . atavistic. It's when we keep doing it as adults—that's when it's rotten.

"The best I can say about my parents is that they were understanding." If Alan wanted to observe animals, they let him. When he started an exhibit at school, "Root's Reptiles," it was all right with them, and even when he returned after one of his bicycle expeditions with an account of pedaling into a pride of lions, they kept mum. You can't be mollycoddled in this world, they believed. Until recently Mrs. Root lived alone on the outskirts of Nairobi in a house that seemed held together with hairpins. If anything drew a smile to her face it was mention of Alan's renegade independence. " 'E really 'asn't changed much," she asserted with a big smile.

Of the few close friends Alan has had the closest was Nick Forbes-Watson. Son of a coffee grower from Thika, he and Alan spent nearly every weekend of their adolescence on wildlife quests.

The higher a bird's nest in a tree, the more valuable it seemed. On Sundays they returned home, battered from falls, their knapsacks filled with monitor lizards and sparrow hawk eggs. According to Alan, the two rarely talked because they knew each other so well. "I remember once we were sitting under a tree having lunch and we both heard a shrike call. Two beeps only. It was the male's note. He called again. And again. Neither of us said a word. And then, after a long delay, its mate finally answered. We both looked up. We didn't need to talk. I could see that Nick was as relieved as I."

Their undisciplined devotion to natural history was finally harnessed by Myles North. Wide-girthed, crimson from tropical sunshine, and forever dressed in white drill shorts and knee-length socks, Myles served as Thika's District Commissioner, the local representative of the Crown. Alan and Nick had stumbled upon him because of a reference in *Great Northern,* their favorite book. It concerned a group of English schoolboys who succeed in finding the rare Great Northern diver, and the dedication read: "To Myles W. North, my ornithological mentor." The boys made inquiries and found that the two Myles Norths were indeed one. They thereupon insinuated themselves into the ornithologist's life. "He was an old woman about collecting," Alan remembers today. "He made us skin, identify and label everything we found. Best of all, he turned me on to birdcalls. He was a master on the subject." The D.C.'s Morris van became the boys' command headquarters. As they took turns driving, Myles sat enthroned in the rear of the vehicle, his huge Ampex tape recorder and rotary converter cradled on his lap. Every half-mile they stopped the van and listened for birdcalls, and when a sound excited Myles the boys set off into the bush, carrying the parabolic reflector, microphone and yards of cable. Alan never considered these assignments with the elderly colonialist drudgery. "I think I'm better in the bush now because of him. I can recognize sounds. An alarm call, for instance, tells me a lot. On many occasions I've been alerted to the presence of a leopard by a bird."

Cisticola cinereola was Alan's first major victory. To the undiscriminating bird watcher it was simply an "L.B.J."—"little brown job." Though not particularly rare, the breeding habits of this grass warbler were unknown. Myles had recorded its song on one occasion, but had never found its nest. He played the recording over and over to Alan and challenged him to find it. For two days Alan wandered the bush near Voi, a railroad siding halfway between Nairobi and Mombasa. Finally on the third day he heard a male singing. The warbler was perched on a stem of grass, and in little plucky flights it led Alan to the female. Her bill was filled with nest lining. Since grass warblers have the curious habit of lining their nests after they have laid their eggs, it was not difficult to follow her and to find the eggs. When he heard the news, Myles was so ecstatic that he broke open a bottle of wine. "That was a big deal in those days," Alan remembers. "I was sixteen."

Predictably, Alan loathed school. His four years at Kenya's Prince of Wales were imprisonment, except for the many hours he spent exploring the bush around the school. "I was given at least three beatings a week," he recalls. "But it made little difference." One of the prefects, Mr. Foster, took particular exception to Alan. "He was often in charge of our table, and at the end of one meal, as he stood up to make an announcement, I slid a fork under the edge of his bowl of tapioca. When he pounded the table for quiet, his fist met the fork, and the pudding was rocketed onto his face. Foster never forgave me. He beat me for weeks."

On October 21, 1952, a state of emergency was declared throughout Kenya. The Kikuyu, in a frenzy of revenge aimed at Europeans and Kikuyu loyalists, began making clandestine attacks on remote farmsteads. Over the next five years about thirty whites and thousands of blacks were mutilated and killed.

Reacting as if this were another Battle of Britain, the European community had several infantry detachments dispatched from Britain and the entire white civilian population armed themselves. For four years no one sat down for dinner in Kenya without a revolver beside his plate.

Released from school, Alan was impressed into military service and sent off to the forests of the Aberdares, where several major Mau Mau gangs were at large. During his two years of military service, Alan learned much more about wildlife than about fugitives. In particular he spent many hours observing bongos, a rare antelope much talked about but little seen, and after his tour had ended he set out to trap one. For years zoos had been clamoring for a bongo, but the catching methods of the time, usually involving dogs and bloodcurdling chases, had almost always ended with dead bongos. Alan invented a humane self-triggering enclosure, and within a month, he had collected the first bongo then in captivity. It was sent to the Cleveland Zoo and soon Alan was swamped with orders for more. Apart from the money, Alan's rationale for continuing this enterprise was to establish a breeding pool of bongos in zoos so that the wild bongo population would never again be jeopardized by encroachment. For the next five years, animal catching became Alan's hobby. He collected more than thirty bongos—the breeding stock that today supplies nearly all the major zoos throughout the world. Just as he promised, one day he folded up the entire enterprise. "I'd caught," he explained, "all the bongos the world needed."

During his expeditions into the bush Alan had made an 8 mm film of snakes and charging rhinos. "It was just a home movie," he recalls, but it fell into the hands of John Pearson, an East African Airways pilot and would-be film maker who was so impressed by it that he summoned Alan to the Nairobi Museum and offered him £20 a month to film lily-trotters on Lake Naivasha. It seemed inconceivable to Alan that someone would actually pay him to sit beside beautiful Lake Naivasha. He accepted and a week later he was living in a shredded tent next to a school of hippos. He rose with the lily-trotters, fretted with their problems and watched the growth of their young.

In the late 1950s few wildlife film makers in East Africa could live without the patronage of Armand and Michaela Denis. Commercial wildlife filming, then in its infancy, had been more or less launched by the Denises' highly popular British series called *On Safari*. It offered measured dosages of armchair travel, glamour (the extravagantly coiffed Michaela), cuddly pets and wildlife homilies. No one in England could have realized that Armand and Michaela were not in fact the sole camera operators since the film credits noted only their names. In reality they employed up to six wildlife film makers, the entire roster of cameramen living in East Africa at the time.

As soon as Armand Denis saw the lily-trotter film he hired

Alan and assigned him straightaway to the Serengeti—then a re-mote expanse of grasslands where the concentrations of game were dizzying. With a sweep of the eye, one could take in several hundred thousand wildebeest, prides of lions often more than thirty strong, creation and extinction balanced against one another with eerie logic.

Alan was one of the first professional cameramen to film here; within a few weeks he had already exposed the first footage ever of a leopard hauling a carcass into a tree and of a zebra giving birth. "In many ways it was the easiest filming I'd ever done—merely a question of pointing the camera in the right direction."

Alan's work with the Denises was interrupted one day by a zebra-striped Dornier aircraft that circled the Serengeti headquarters and landed next to the game warden's house. The plane was piloted by Bernhard and Michael Grzimek, a father-and-son team, from Frankfurt, Germany. They wanted to record the movements of the herds of wildebeest and zebra over the course of a year, in hopes that the legal boundaries of the park would one day contain their migration. The first order of business was to hire a cameraman. Did the game warden happen to know one? Myles Turner, a man of fierce loyalties, made it clear that they could do no better than Alan Root, who happened to be filming nearby. Before Alan had even heard of the arrangement, Myles had successfully negotiated his contract.

The film they made with Alan was called *Serengeti Shall Not Die*. Of the few collaborations Alan has made, he can remember none so pleasant. He and Michael were much alike, not only in age, but in their approach to the game. They both were curious about the complex set of debts and promises that connect predators and prey; they both were consumed by the extravagance of life on these plains; and both of them were comics and daredevils.

The fun came to an end one day when Michael, flying alone, struck a vulture in midflight. With the ailerons and flaps jammed, the plane went into a dive. Michael was buried on the lip of the Ngorongoro Crater and the epitaph on his gravestone is simple: "Michael Grzimek—12.4.1934 to 10.1.1959. He gave all he possessed for the wild animals of Africa, including his life."

Nick Forbes-Watson had died tragically a few years before, Armand Denis would have only a handful of years to live, John Pearson would be shot by a trigger-happy game guard and so many of Alan's friends, particularly the game wardens of East Africa, would meet similar, usually violent ends. For Alan, death had begun to assume a place in life.

In 1961 Alan married Joan Thorpe, the daughter of a coffee planter and herself a safari guide. Alan had noticed her on several occasions but had never been able to cut through her shyness until one day he heard she was bringing up a small orphaned elephant. Elephants under six months are usually impossible to raise. Joan had been more successful than most people, and Alan, in his own words, "liked winners."

A master of the deadly pun, Alan recalls: "Before we were married, she wore a monocle and so did I. Together we made quite a spectacle." On the first night of their honeymoon, for instance, Joan was stung by a scorpion. They were camped next to the Tsavo River Bridge, where in 1898, the rail-laying crew had been terrorized by two man-eating lions. The Roots sat up until dawn, he comforting her, both listening to the howl of the passing trains and to a lion, perhaps a descendant of the man-eaters, roaring nearby. It was the beginning of an accident-prone but very happy partnership. "I don't know what I'd do without Joan," Alan admits today. "I'd probably have to marry three women at the same time."

A month after they were married Alan was invited to join Douglas Botting and Anthony Smith, two BBC producers, on a hydrogen balloon expedition across East Africa. When Alan asked Armand Denis for a leave of absence to help out the two Englishmen, Denis fired him on the spot. "It was a bit rough for Joan," Alan admits today. "She obviously thought she had backed a loser."

The balloon was called *Jambo,* and every launching led to an adventure. From the island of Zanzibar they crossed to the mainland and floated across much of Tanzania, with an unforgettable drift over Alan's beloved Serengeti. Their last ascent was an exhibition for a large crowd of aviation buffs at the Nairobi Airport. Egged on by the pretty girls, the balloonists unwisely lifted off in a high wind. To avoid an RAF squadron just ahead they had to throw out most of their ballast in the first few minutes of flight and by the time they were over the Ngong Hills they had little left and were virtually out of control. They hit the peaks three times and on the third impact Alan was pitched forward from the basket, his head smashing against a stone, then hauled back in as the balloon climbed to ten thousand feet. At this altitude the balloon leveled off and then started to descend, faster and faster. The three balloonists frantically heaved out the remaining ballast, then their lunch, the first-aid kit and finally their personal belongings. They were left with only the precious camera equipment, and just as Alan was throwing out film, battery, a telephoto lens, the basket smashed through a thorn tree and hit the ground. Alan looked around. No one was dead. The balloon ride had been a success.

Joan need not have worried that she had backed a loser. *Serengeti Shall Not Die* won an Academy Award, and within the small fraternity of East African film makers Alan had begun to gain a powerful reputation. In 1962 he was hired by a small British film company just embarked on a wildlife series called "Survival." Anglia Television, flushed with success after completion of a half-hour film on the animals of Hyde Park, had determined to go farther afield, this time into Uganda. Aubrey Buxton, the managing director, was camped with his wife on Lake Edward and had heard from the game warden that Alan Root was located somewhere on the far bank of the Rutshuru River. The bridge was down because of floods, and Buxton shouted across the river to Alan, offering him a job.

Except for one hiatus, Alan has been in league with Survival ever since. His first years of association call to mind a film-making sausage factory: a one-hour production on the Karamajong cattle raiders in northern Uganda, a half-hour film on Lake Rudolf, another on the plight of twenty thousand young flamingos encased in dried soda at Lake Magadi, gorillas in Rwanda, volcanoes in the Congo, sunbirds on Mount Kenya, white rhinos in Uganda. And just when the Roots seemed to be too confined by Africa, Buxton sent them to Australia, New Guinea, the Galapagos and South America. *Voyage to the Enchanted Isles,* Alan and

Joan's Galapagos film, narrated by Prince Philip, would be the first one-hour special Survival would sell in the United States and it would pave the way for future network sales.

When Alan and Joan returned to Africa they decided they wanted a home. Until now they had lived mostly in tents, and their growing collection of pets needed a base. Their friends insisted that a land purchase in Kenya now would be insane. The country had recently gained independence and the ex-leader of the Mau Mau movement, Jomo Kenyatta, had been elected the country's first president a few months after his release from prison. Settlers sure that bloodshed would follow independence were collecting their belongings and abandoning the farms and ranches they had once coaxed from the bush.

Joan and Alan wanted to live nowhere else but Africa. ("If Kenya packed up we'd move to Tanzania.") They bought an eighty-eight-acre farm from a despondent settler. Located on the shore of Lake Naivasha, just across from where Alan had made his first wildlife film, the house was (and is) a housewife's nightmare. The kitchen was sited far from the house, the interior rooms were dreary and the plumbing worked only on holidays—not that the Roots cared. They liked the house because it was framed by a large veranda for the birds, with plenty of space to build cages for other pets. Best of all, there was enough land for an airstrip.

Alan had just learned to fly. He soloed after eight hours of instruction, discovered he preferred flying without his instructor and decided not to return to Nairobi Airport. Henceforth he clocked a total of four hundred illegal hours in his Piper Colt before returning to complete the flying course. "I didn't have a clue what I was doing, particularly when I flew through clouds. Still, I figured it was a hell of an imposition forcing you to get a license just to protect you and your wife's life."

In the late sixties, Alan resigned from Survival to make his own films. Aubrey Buxton tried to discourage him by arguing that the history of one-man production houses was a story of failure. No cameraman could conceive, film, edit, complete and sell his own productions. Films were a corporate effort, after all, and Alan needed the manpower, facilities and connections of Survival.

The argument was lost on Alan. He set to work immediately on two simple notions. One was a story of a baobab tree, the other a study of a freshwater spring. Each ecosystem, on the surface deceptively plain, was composed of complex relationships—enemies that needed each other, kinsmen that ate each other. This world within a tree, or beneath the glass surface of a spring, would be shown to be stunning, wise and sometimes familiar.

Alan immediately presold his two ideas to the BBC, Survival's competition, for British distribution, but the "Beeb's" investment was only enough to cover the costs of the film stock. For the next two years the Roots bobbed in and out of debt, financing their lonely work with the sale of bongos to zoos.

For someone not so confident as Alan this kind of filming could have been numbingly boring. Days passed without exposing a foot of film, equipment broke miles from repair facilities and wildlife behavior that seemed certain to occur simply never happened. Alan and Joan seem immune to these kinds of frustrations. For days the two can live in almost total silence, conversations conducted either in whispers or arm codes. They let themselves be swallowed by the bush, their human presence overshadowed by a kind of animal intuition. Alan never committed the scenario to paper and for long periods of time, Joan admits, she was never sure where the film was going. But Alan's aim was deadly accurate. The Mzima Springs film took one year to work; the baobab required only five months.

The Mysterious Spring: Africa's Mzima is about the chain of life initiated by hippos. Their protein-rich waste feeds schools of labio fish, which in turn are preyed upon by the crocodiles—an alliance of needs between animals who otherwise share little in common. The film offered bit parts for spotted-necked otters, freshwater crabs, pythons, snake birds, finfoots, damsel flies, vervet monkeys and turtles, each living around the springs in a constant state of détente.

Alan tried filming the underwater sequences of the hippos and crocs through a cage but he found it much too cumbersome. By accident he discovered that swimming freely was not as dangerous as it seemed. "The first time I went in," Alan recalls, "I was washing my goggles in the shallows. That attracted the crocs and one came at me full-speed ahead. At that moment I fell into the water and I suppose my splash surprised it. I decided the danger to man was only when his body showed above the surface or when he stood in the shallows like other animals. So I swam right at the croc and it chickened out and turned tail." Alan's experiment yielded the most dramatic shots in the film— moon-walking hippos, and crocodiles spinning to pry flesh off the carcass of an impala. Often Alan was close enough to reach out and touch a hippo.

Of the two films, *Secrets of the African Baobab* is Alan's favorite. This remarkable "upside-down" tree can survive for as long as two thousand years, serving as a tenement for scores of different species, generation after generation.

One of the baobab's most interesting residents is the red-billed hornbill. For six weeks every year the female seals herself into a crevice to raise her family. Until the making of the film no one knew for sure what went on behind the mud masonry. Alan removed the back of a nest, replacing it with a wall of Plexiglas, a clear one when he was filming, opaque otherwise. Somehow the bird tolerated this disturbance. Undauntedly she laid five eggs, while her mate, doomed not to see her for the period of her confinement, fed her geckos, berries and frogs through a narrow slit in the hard mud. Prompted by the chirping of his just-hatched brood, the male's feeding pace soon became a frenzy. At last, when the chicks were too large for comfort, the female pecked her way out. As soon as she was gone the nestlings methodically replastered the hole, committed to the interior darkness until their biological clocks told them it was time to depart. Each left the nest at the exact interval it was hatched from the egg. The final scene of this extraordinary story was a subtle masterstroke of mood—the father bringing a damsel fly to the nest, only to discover that his children have flown away.

Alan's larger story soon becomes apparent: Baobabs, hornbills and geckos need each other. Individual deaths are nature's method of guaranteeing the survival of the whole. When a baobab is shredded into fiber by an elephant, or a hornbill egg devoured by a bushbaby, neither baobabs nor hornbills are doomed. In fact they prosper. "They go on. The whole flamboyant, chaotic spectacle actually works and works well, year after year," the commentary reads. "A seed once grown by a defunct baobab will, in several hundred years, be a giant of the plains. There will be no end to death, no final season."

Alan began editing the two films in the farmhouse at Naivasha, his only consultants apart from Joan being their pet colobus monkey and striped hyena. The work was completed in England at the BBC, and as soon as his British sale had been finalized, Alan flew to New York to sell the American rights, against everyone's advice. The Kenya bumpkin would fall easy prey to the New York and Hollywood sharks, he was cautioned. What actually happened revealed one of Alan's unexpected talents.

Alan states, "Most people who sell their films approach the producers with only an idea. That's how they get stung. The producers tell them to change their scripts and reduce their salaries. I, on the other hand, had a completed film." He was anything but an innocent when he got down to negotiations. After the first screening of his films in New York, a producer made him an offer over lunch in an elegant restaurant. "The figures were pretty mind-boggling," he remembers. "More money than I had ever seen in my lifetime. But I turned it down. It wouldn't have made much sense if I sold everything in my first day in New York. I'd have learned nothing." A few days later in Washington, the National Geographic made an even better offer. He also turned it down. (The president, Mel Payne, complained: "I don't understand why such a young man wants so much money.") In Hollywood Alan was wooed by David Wolper but he again refused to make a deal. At heart, the issue was not just money. Alan's preconditions to a sale were that no major changes to the film would be made. "One guy wanted to put in some shark footage to make Mzima look more dangerous. Somebody else was keen to have Joan and me playing with a lot of snakes, and a third guy wanted to get rid of all the dung in the Mzima film. I just said to them, 'No deal.' "

Alan wanted to consider all his options back in Africa. On his way home he stopped in England and said hello to his old employer, Aubrey Buxton. At the time, Buxton's company was looking for natural history specials to prime its newly created American sales force. Of all the people Alan had met during the last month he was still most comfortable with Aubrey. "I told him that if they could top all the other offers and promise not to butcher the stories, Survival could have the two films." Aubrey had no objections to the stories as they stood, and in the time-honored British midday salute, the two sealed the deal with a glass of Tio Pepe and a handshake.

Before returning home, Alan was invited by his ballooning friend, Anthony Smith, to test the latest toy in the field of wing-less aircraft. It was a hot-air balloon—far less dangerous and expensive than the hydrogen version he and Tony had flown over Africa. Alan made his first ascension from a village green in Hampshire: "As we lifted off I created a camera shot by cupping my hands around my eyes, limiting their field of vision as if they were a lens. I began by focusing on a daisy growing next to the basket. As we began our climb I could see people's legs, then all the village green. Pretty soon the entire village came into view and, after that, all of England. Before we landed I knew I needed a balloon for filming."

The difference between humdrum and interesting camera-work is often a matter of perspectives. Alan is always trying to find the novel angle, not just to be arresting, but to heighten the truth of the action. To film a herd of animals moving across a plain by holding the camera at eye level would have abused all the magical opportunities of Africa. Instead, Alan would bury the camera in their path to film their progress from a snake's point of view. In Alan's films, flowers are not just *in* bloom; they begin as petals and bloom before one's eyes. Similarly a bird's nest does not just appear; it is built on the screen, twig by twig, in a mere thirty seconds. The technology of this process is known as time-lapse photography, and it is a hallmark of Alan's films. Hot-air ballooning would add still another startling perspective to his Africa. It would also be the most hair-raising fun he had had in a long while.

Alan was to obtain the first hot-air balloon license ever issued in black Africa. His training period at Naivasha had not been all that easy: On several occasions he had performed "underwater" flying in the lake, once he had snagged around the telephone lines beside a road and on another occasion he had even "gift-wrapped" a thorn tree.

By now Alan was embarked on a new filming project—an ambitious story about the million wildebeest of the Serengeti. Every year nearly a quarter of a million are born and a quarter of a million die, and Alan, usually so preoccupied with miniature stories, was overwhelmed by the size of this sacrifice. How do you show such a herd on the screen? Naturally, with a balloon. An airplane is too fast and a helicopter too noisy. In the finished film the one balloon shot—it had been haunting Alan for so long—is so subtly edited that it nearly goes unnoticed: a half-million wildebeest grazing in the distance, and in the foreground, three vultures circling, watching for death. The shot lasts for only twenty seconds on the screen; it had cost the Roots a week of work.

The film was made in two and a half years. It would have taken far longer had it not been for Alan's secondhand Cessna 182. In the early mornings, he and Joan reconnoitered from the air and when they saw the herd, for example, about to cross a river, they would make an emergency landing as close as safety (Alan's idea of safety) permitted and then, clutching all their film gear, scramble on foot toward the bleating sounds of the herd. "It wasn't unusual to find that we were running alongside a few lions similarly attracted to the sound." One time when they returned from one such foot safari they discovered that the airplane had been speared by poachers. They patched the holes but failed to note that the battery cables had been damaged. "For weeks we did not know there were sparks flying in all directions from just behind our seats," remembers Joan.

"The Year of the Wildebeest"—"Brave Gnu World," as Alan liked to call it—appeared on CBS in May 1975 and was rerun by NBC in July 1976. Almost all of Alan's film colleagues consider it his finest film. Throughout, there is pounding energy, hammered onto the screen by the wildebeests' hooves, heightened by the terse, sometimes ironic script. By the film's end one is cowed by the wisdom of death. The spare language is often so good it draws attention to itself:

"The white-bearded gnu—an animal apparently designed by a committee and assembled from spare parts."

"Whenever there is a creature behaving strangely on the plains there are always other animals alert to wonder why."

"The wildebeest haven't changed in two million years. They haven't needed to; for, though they may choose some bizarre ways to die, they have found a fantastically successful way to live."

"There is a saying in Africa that somewhere there is a place where the grass meets the sky, and the name of that place is 'the end.' "

In Kenya, a country not noted for its verbal badinage, Alan's plays on words have become passwords to his life. His pet aardvark is named Million. Why? Because "Aardvark a million miles for one of your smiles!" On the front of his car the Range Rover lettering has been changed to read "Hang Over." When asked by a Walt Disney producer if he liked the name of their new film about bongos, *The Biggest Bongo in the World,* he was quite abusive. "Awful," he said. They challenged him to come up with a better one and in a second he solved their dilemma: "Last Bongo in Paris." On another occasion, he was drinking with his friend, Dr. Mary Leakey, who was pondering what to name her exhaustive monograph on the stone tool cultures of the Olduvai Gorge. Alan advised her to call it: "I Dig Dirty Old Men."

Ever since Alan had learned to fly a balloon, nothing gave him greater pleasure than offering his friends joyrides: a dawn departure from the lawn in front of the house to the strains of "Up, Up and Away," a climb into clouds, a descent onto the roof of a neighbor's house to wake its occupants with a few bars of "Born Free," out across the lake to surprise a sleeping herd of hippos, up again to search for plains game and to open a bottle of champagne, and a finger-barking landing in an onion field just as the rescue crew, driving a Land Rover, sped into sight.

These flights were so successful that Alan decided to go public with lighter-than-air travel. For years he and Richard Leakey had been partners in a photographic safari company, and when it was disbanded in 1976 because of personal differences, he formed another partnership with the leading hotelier of the country to take tourists across the Masai-Mara Game Reserve in his balloon. "The fun was getting Balloon Safaris going—convincing the local aviation authorities that it was okay to have regular charter flights to a destination never certain until you got there."

Looming above the business enterprise was an even greater

challenge. Kilimanjaro, at 19,340 feet, was the highest point in Africa; ergo, ballooning over the peak would represent the highest physical achievement in Africa, the ultimate seduction. Most people could have tossed aside this challenge but Alan presumably was taunted every time he saw the silver dome floating above late-afternoon clouds. By now he was a living reminder of other such dares. The index finger on his right hand was missing because of an indiscretion with a puff adder. A portion of his right buttock had been deeded to a leopard in the Serengeti, and most of the cartilage in his right knee was missing because he had once tried to set a Kenya record for motorcycle jumps. Now whenever he entered the Nairobi Hospital he was greeted as an old friend.

None of Alan's friends was terribly surprised to hear that he was preparing to be the first to balloon over the top of Kilimanjaro. Now that the wildebeest film was finished Alan had given himself four months before his next production. He gathered together some friends who were eager to serve as the ground crew and readied his balloon, *Lengai,* for the assault. From the lower slopes of the mountain, Alan calculated he would have to head away from the peak because of the winds, and then at about 24,000 feet, hope to catch an alternating wind that would carry him over the top. There the winds would be treacherous and the air nearly one-quarter its density at sea level.

The "shakedown" was spent test-flying the equipment, purchasing special gear and dickering with the meteorological service. One day the flight was off, another on, and much of Nairobi joined in speculating whether or not the madman would make it. In a society that warmly takes heart from others' misfortunes and rarely admits to heroes, Alan's apparent death wish had captured the imagination.

On the morning of March 25, 1976, the ground crew inflated the balloon on a farm to the west of the mountain. The clouds were down to the ground and nobody was laughing. Until the last moment there had been a question whether or not Joan could accompany Alan. It was generally agreed because of the load factor only one passenger could make the ascent. Joan had not said a word but it was clear that she would gladly have amputated an arm to meet the required weight. By now Alan was inside the basket firing the burner. He looked out at her. "You ready?" he asked, seconds before the balloon lifted off.

For the first half-hour of the flight Alan and Joan flew through dense cloud, never certain where they were bound. Just before they saw sunlight the flame on the burner blew out and for a frightening second Alan fumbled with matches to relight it.

Alan has coined an expression, "The Root Effect," to describe the illusion of the sides of the basket lowering, the higher the balloon climbs. At five thousand feet the basket's walls are at waist level, but at twenty thousand feet they seem little higher than one's ankles. Now as the balloon drifted over the top of Mawenzi Joan was behaving strangely. For a second Alan considered "The Root Effect." She was uncharacteristically snappy and clumsy. "What's the matter?" Alan asked. "Nothing," she shouted back. Suddenly he noticed the tube from her oxygen supply had gotten fouled. As fast as he could he reconnected it and soon she was her placid self.

Borne by a friendly monsoon, and with hardly a ripple, the basket sailed across the roof of Africa, its two occupants Phineas Foggs of a new sort. The altimeter registered 24,000 feet and directly below was the broken cone of Kilimanjaro. Old glaciers and the remains of last season's snows lay in pockets along the rims. Alan looked for climbers, but at nine on a March morning the mountain was deserted. The mountain and the sky made the balloon seem very small. When he and Joan had successfully flown over Kilimanjaro, they were forced to make a landing in then-hostile Tanzania. Minutes after their moment of triumph, both Roots were arrested as "astronaut spies."

Of all Alan's films, the one-hour special about his balloon exploits seems the most flawed, possibly because he was dealing with humans (particularly himself) instead of animals. The humor that abounds in his life seemed out of context in the film, and at times the commentary runs to unmitigated conceit: "Flying a balloon takes a bit of getting used to—but Alan Root is one of those naturally well-coordinated people who gets the hang of this sort of thing very quickly. . . ." On television *Balloon Safari* seemed an uneven pastiche, but when it is shown at the farmhouse on Lake Naivasha it is colorful and very funny. It seems to be an indulgence, an amusement for his friends. "Precisely," Alan admits today. "It's a home movie."

Survival was now clamoring for something bigger than ever before. "How about," one of the producers suggested, "taking all the best of Alan's films, shoot an interconnecting story about the Roots' weird life style and their damned balloon, and string the whole lot into a 35 mm film for movie houses across America?" A few months later the Roots were host to a film crew. And three weeks later the filming came to a tragic halt.

The crew had been at Mzima Springs for nearly two weeks, filming Alan and Joan underwater with the crocs and hippos. On one of the last days of the shoot, in murky waters, a second-ranked bull hippo charged. Joan was hit first. The impact was a colossal thud that Alan later likened to the blow of an "E-type marshmallow." The hippo's canines pierced her face mask within a millimeter of her right eye and she was thrown into the shallows, shaken but unscathed. Next, the hippo turned on Alan. It first took a bite from his bottom, missing flesh but making two gashes across his swim trunks. Then with Alan's right leg in its mouth, it shook him, like a pillow, its canines scissoring up and down. Soon the water was stilled. Feeling only a numbness in his leg, Alan reached down to see if he was okay. What was once his calf was now jelly. Martin Bell, the cameraman, put Alan in a hammerlock and swam him to shore before the crocs had time to investigate the blood. There he was bandaged by an Italian doctor, a member of a party of Italian tourists who had watched the attack as, surely, their Roman ancestors had once gawked at Christians in the Colosseum. "In less than three hours," Alan later wrote, "I was in the familiar homely surroundings of the casualty ward of the Nairobi Hospital."

Luckily, the hippo's canines had missed all tendons, nerves and arteries. Only the smaller of the two calf bones, the fibula, was broken. Still, the hole made through the soft part of his leg was large enough to pass a Coke bottle. Gangrene set in almost immediately, as the doctors frantically tried to match an antibiotic with the infection generated by all the organic material that had passed from the hippo's mouth into Alan's leg. In a newsletter to his friends he claimed he "became so odiferous that even some of my best friends told me. In fact, all my best friends told me. I had some spectacular fevers—boy! I have had the sheets changed before when I was sweating [presumably during his regular bouts with malaria], but never the mattress! And in between the sweats I needed an electric blanket to keep warm. Three days, seventeen pints of saline, eight pints of blood, many millions of units of intravenous penicillin and several cups of tea later I was declared okay and since then I have been on the mend." For a year afterward, particles of the hippo's meal fell from the wound, offering Alan consoling proof of his brotherhood with the would-be killer.

Nearly a year had been wasted. Hollywood had seduced both Survival and Alan and now the project was shelved. As soon as he could run, Alan, predictably, disappeared from view. He was at work on an idea that had been brewing ever since he was a child—the story of termite mounds, that bizarre architectural feature of almost all sub-Saharan Africa. Survival's American sales force was alarmed ("Selling a film about bugs—you gotta be kidding!"), but Alan paid little attention and in the autumn of 1977 the film was finished. In the face of continuing American distress he flew to New York and ad-libbed the narration as he rolled a rough cut of the film for would-be buyers at NBC. In a raw but effective narration, Alan characterized termites not just as "bugs" but creatures possessed of a curious collective wisdom. As soon as the lights went on at the end of the film, a completely captivated NBC purchased the film.

Castles of Clay is artistically as majestic as *The Year of the Wildebeest*; in addition it is suffused with mystery—worlds shrouded from man's view, lives within lives. One usually acerbic critic from the *Manchester Guardian* went beyond the usual praise: "My interest in the termite film is finite. Nevertheless I believe 'Castles of Clay' . . . is the finest natural history film ever seen. And, because even that seems qualified praise, I will put it among the finest films I have ever seen full stop."

Here is the quintessential Root film: Beneath an apparently inanimate object is concealed a command headquarters for a highly sophisticated form of life. One is tempted to conclude that beside termites, humans are as dull as river mud.

In preparation for the film, Alan had discarded most of the

existing literature on the subject. Eugene Marais's *Soul of the White Ant,* written some forty years ago and long held to be the final word on the subject, received an immediate Root broadside ("I don't need to be taught how to think by a South African, and anyway he's wrong"). Alan's only consultant was a Kenyan scientist who for the last three years had been cutting open termite mounds and examining the societies within. But many of the insights in the film are exclusively Alan's and, in several instances, the film breaks new ground with material unknown to science.

Alan had been warned repeatedly that opening the mound to film floodlights would immediately stimulate unnatural termite behavior. In effect, the insects would mount into defensive positions as if in a state of war. All these warnings Alan found to be true, so he improvised. He removed portions of the mound, brought them to a dark place in the farmhouse and allowed the termites to settle for a few days. Just as he had expected, they resumed normal behavior.

The source of all sentient life within the mound is the queen termite. "Four inches long, and as thick as a man's thumb, this grotesque creature looms over the workers that attend her. Beside their queen, the workers look like a ground crew handling a half-inflated airship." A vast egg-laying machine, every day she produces thirty thousand new termites. The workers feed her, remove her excrement, carry off her eggs and during this process, although she cannot move one inch without the assistance of thousands of bearers, she is able to rule her vast empire. Her system of communication is far more bizarre than the telephone: "The saliva of each termite contains a precise mixture of chemicals, a mixture that is determined by the condition of the mound and the 'needs' of the society. So the information is passed from mouth to mouth through the colony, and when the queen is fed she receives a chemical cocktail that gives her a detailed report on the state of her nation."

Sorcery does not end here. Consider how the termites feed themselves: They have their own gardens—mushroom gardens, to be exact. Air conditioning? Yes, they believe in that too. By opening and closing the ventilation chimneys on the top of the mound, and by descending through shafts 150 feet deep, they collect water to moisten the sides of their chambers, so that the interior temperature, year to year, night to day, varies no more than one degree from 85 degrees Fahrenheit.

Romance? That too. The alates, youngsters, one day destined to become kings and queens, are initiated into their commanding roles with a nuptial flight so unspeakably beautiful that, in the film, narration and music discreetly cease. Their diaphanous wings beating against blackness, they must fly, mate, shed their wings and survive a cruel night before they can inherit the responsibility of an empire. "These new creatures are princes and princesses who, like Cinderella, have one magical night before returning to darkness and drudgery."

When *Castles of Clay* had its debut on British and American television I was with Alan and Joan, a hundred miles from a telephone, camped on the banks of Kenya's Tana River, filming a pair of violet-backed sunbirds nesting, for protection, next to a wasp's nest. A new film was under way, a need that must yearly be satisfied if Alan is to restore to Africa what he has enjoyed from it.

There are those who say Alan could do more to raise money for the animals he loves so much. He disagrees. "I'm not good at standing up and shouting about conservation. Basically I don't believe in it—neither all the money nor all the good will in the world can save a species. They're all doomed, ultimately. Every species. I'm just good at making films about how it was."

It is a measure of Alan's artistry that, in the face of a dubious future for the only world he cares about, he is always able to retain the light touch. Hundreds of miles from the mailbox that was filling with congratulatory cables, I watched him and Joan transfixed by the violet-backed sunbird, whispering in monotones, like people at the ballet. Whenever the sunbird stood on its perch, its wings beating a hundred times faster than a heartbeat, Alan squeezed the shutter of his camera.

Last night, by the tent, Alan was explaining how in nature nothing is ever wasted—neither baobab trees, nor wildebeests nor termite mounds. Even humans, he believes, should have a purpose other than mere existence—one they may never yet have considered. Alan plans to realize his by leaving his body to the savannah. There it will be returned to Africa and used again and again.

And so now I study first Alan and then the sunbird. Maybe someday, I think, there will be another such beauty, brilliantly colored, its wings just a blur.

The watched and the watcher will have become one.

For those who enjoy conundrums here is a problem fit for a Go-
liath: 43 percent of the earth's land is either semiarid or desert.
In Africa alone every year nearly a million acres of once verdant
country is cannibalized by the Sahara. In Kenya, one of Africa's
greener nations, two-thirds of the land receives enough rain in a
year to fill only half a highball glass.

Those who have noted the population of this East African
nation treble in the last twenty-one years observe with alarm how
gigantic vistas, once waist-high in grass, have inexorably been
transformed into bald, dusty wastelands.

CASHING IN
ON GOD'S CATTLE

Causes for this creeping catastrophe vary. Some claim the process of desertification is natural, cyclical. Others blame man's worldwide interference in the atmosphere, even the cosmos. The majority contend that the fault is clearly nearsighted land management, pointing to the removal of the natural ground cover as the instrument of climactic change. And while opinions vary to the cause, there is an even wider assemblage of proposals for cures.

Dr. David Hopcraft, a rancher and ecologist, claims to have at least part of the solution. Hopcraft, now in his early forties, a third-generation Kenyan, wears bush shorts and sandals to his very popular dinner parties at his house outside of Nairobi. He has spent more than half his life proving that ranching wild animals rather than domestic stock is the best possible guarantee that Africa's dry lands will remain productive. The subject of game ranching is more often than not the conversational gambit of his evenings. Wild herbivores are selective feeders, he begins. They do not plunder the range as will cattle, sheep and goats. They shear off the tops of grass stems instead of pulling their root systems piecemeal from the ground. In addition, they tend not to trample and kill the natural ground cover on their way to and from waterholes simply because they can, in many instances, exploit the metabolic water stored in their grazing. Cattle, if introduced to raw bushland, can reduce it to a dust bowl in a mere two years. Without ground cover the atmosphere becomes drier, clouds thin, climates shift. Far better to let nature's technology guide you, Hopcraft advises. Without cattle the same land can be made rich, productive and far more profitable.

This tall, formidable-looking man with the soft voice recalls that he first began questioning the wisdom of cattle ranching when he was sixteen, managing a ranch for his aunt near Kenya's Lake Baringo. A brief and violent dust storm literally vacuumed one large pasture of all its grasses. His aunt was philosophic. For her the dust storm was part of a continuing trend. All the desert land to the north, she remembered, had also been prime grazing country until it too had suffered a similar apocalyptic change. Now it was good for nothing, neither for cattle nor game.

Evidently Hopcraft had been lucky enough to witness in microcosm what had been happening relentlessly across much of the dry north of Kenya. Domestic stock and routine African droughts had formed a kind of Bonnie and Clyde partnership. Cattle, after all, were relative newcomers to Equatorial Africa. *Bos taurus,* the slick European breeds, had arrived with the British at the turn of the century. Before them, *Bos indicus,* the humpbacked Boran cattle, had been herded into Africa from Asia by the Hamitic peoples during the last forty-five thousand years. Within the twentieth century the populations of these two exotics had exploded; where their appetites had taken them, desertification, it seemed, had followed.

These simple musings led the young Hopcraft first to London University, then to Kentucky for his bachelor of science degree in Animal Sciences and Agriculture, and later to Cornell for his master's. On each summer vacation in Africa he saw that destruction was occurring in geometric leaps. It was, in a sense, a personal problem, for David's family were among the most established European stock-raisers in the country, having originally collaborated with Lord Delamere by introducing many of the first exotic European breeds into East Africa. David's father's ranch, twenty thousand acres, an hour's drive southeast of Nairobi, was considered a model for other large landowners. David had been brought up in a ranching community that now suspected he was wasting his time; flirting, in fact, with revolution. Who was he to say that cattle were destructive, that their lifetime's work had been ill conceived?

Luckily, David Hopcraft can speak the cattleman's language persuasively and gently, and he knew the time-honored truth that nothing persuades better than facts. With a National Science Foundation grant he went to work on his Cornell Ph.D. thesis to prove conclusively that cattle were not as efficient meat-producers as the wild game.

His father was still unconvinced by David's line of reasoning, yet he was willing to let him fence off two identical enclosures, each with an area of 150 acres on the Kenplains Estate Ranch. One section would be reserved for cattle, and the other was to be stocked with gazelle, herbivores indigenous to the farm and ideally suited to the experiment since they were unable to vault over large fences. Now David's problems began. The "Tommies" living on the ranch eluded all attempts to be caught. Feeling slightly sophomoric, he approached a number of Kenya's professional animal trappers and was advised to drive two hundred miles north, to Rumuruti where the gazelle were not as "windy" of humans. In all, Hopcraft spent six months developing a system of capture. Wing traps were too expensive and chasing the gazelle in a "catch car" he found to be hazardous for the animals. In the end he settled on nighttime spotlighting as the only practical solution. A "light-bearer" would advance in front of the car, and when an animal was sighted and blinded, five or six men would hurtle through the open doors and hand-capture the quarry. On good nights when there was no moon, as many as twenty-five animals could be caught. Anxious to assemble as natural an age sampling as possible, Hopcraft used a butterfly net to catch the young animals. After a short quarantine, the gazelle, now distinctively christened with such names as "Good Grief," "Kink," "Pseudo" and "Rugger Posts," were trucked south to the ranch and the comparative studies begun.

Even Hopcraft was startled by the results. "At first I just couldn't believe them," he recalls. "The gazelle produced three and a half times more meat than the cattle." According to his findings, cattle grazed by the local peoples in Kenya produced about one pound of lean meat for each acre of dry land. On modern ranches cattle might produce as much as 3.9 pounds on the same amount of land. Gazelle, however, were by far the most effective meat producers: 14.6 pounds for one acre of land.

Hopcraft triple-checked his data and still the results were embarrassingly successful. The indigenous species, with millions of years of adaptation to the dry land, had, it seemed, evolved the perfect balance. For them droughts were not calamities but seasons of their life. Best of all, the vegetation they consumed went directly into meat production and was not wasted through the circuitous toil required of cattle.

For the Masai, those standard-bearers of Kenya's traditional stock raisers, wildlife is known collectively as "God's cattle." For Hopcraft the implication was very clear: Since the game is "God's cattle," man need never fall heir to its trusteeship. It is, in effect, well looked after without him. It requires no expensive bore-holes, no premixed dips, no imported innoculations, no water tanks, no nighttime paddocks for protection against thieves and predators, no vigilant herdsmen. After his six-year study Hopcraft estimated that 70 percent of the gross income of a typical well-managed cattle ranch is consumed by cattle overhead. On his model game ranch, gross income was more than three times higher and operating costs ate up a mere 20 percent of gross revenues. Amazingly, for each income unit per acre per year on a cattle ranch, a wildlife operation could produce up to eight times the profit.

Hopcraft's thesis was presented to Cornell in 1975, and he earned his degree of Doctor of Philosophy. His conclusion was that the meat produced by wild grazing ungulates is 95 to 99 percent lean, innocent of those saturated fats contained in beef. Presented neatly, "Tommie" chops and "Tommie" steaks promised Hopcraft's protein-starved continent an inexpensive and self-replenishing source of food, superior nutritionally to beef. "I had a bunch of American VIPs out to the ranch one day," Hopcraft recalls. "James Joseph, then the Undersecretary of the Interior, as well as the head of the Peace Corps. I treated them to a gazelle roast, and there wasn't one person who didn't go back for thirds."

Hopcraft admits that there are two sensitive areas which he generally avoids discussing. "First, the animal lovers are thrilled to hear that I am increasing the game population. At the same time, they don't particularly like to know that the gazelle are there to be culled. As a result I rarely mention slaughtering. Frankly, our methods are humane and clean. We decide first what portion of our game herd we wish to reduce and then we proceed at night with spotlights, shooting for the neck so the result is quick, clean, and the meat never tainted by an explosion of blood. I would never argue that our methods would appeal to so-called sportsmen. It won't, but that isn't the point either. Conservationists should take heart, above all, because we are guaranteeing the survival of several species by establishing a firm value for them. Previously they have been taken for granted, squeezed off land, killed mercilessly—all because they had no commercial value."

Hopcraft's other delicate area is philosophical. "I avoid the issue of ownership. Do I, as the rancher, own the game on my land? Or does it belong to the state, the king, the town council, the tribe or, simply, 'the people'? I have no answer. Therefore I don't ask the question. No doubt, the outcome would be snarled in legislation for the next several generations."

There is a despised tradition in Africa that so many foreign-born Ph.D. candidates have earned their degrees off African game and in the end their theses collect dust on foreign shelves never to be seen in Africa, never to benefit any creature or person other than the author. Not so in David Hopcraft's case, he is proud to note to his dinner guests. In 1975 his thesis returned permanently to Africa. Best of all, he saw it as the beginning. "If anyone was going to take a chance on the idea, it would have to be me. Ranchers can be stubborn. Their attitude is often 'what was good enough for Abraham is good enough for me.' But when I returned with my completed thesis I could see that every day more of Africa's dry land was being plundered, reduced to desert; more and more people were requiring more and more protein. And all the time I had what seemed to be a partial solution."

Around this time, David's father, recently converted to his son's ideas, died. David was now free to transform the family property in its entirety into a gazelle ranch, as long as outside money could be raised to erect a perimeter fence. He approached thirty foundations, most of them in the United States, with the proposal. In almost every instance the rejection was accompanied by the corollary that since the concept was so obvious, it had evidently never been attempted before because of its impracticality.

At last, the Lilly Foundation recognized game ranching's plausibility and soon the fencing was erected and the lengthy game-stocking process begun. In 1977 a population of seven hundred "Tommies" on the ranch was attained. Several years of good rainfall later, the numbers of gazelle have swelled to a total of five thousand. In a few years, Hopcraft believes, the ranch once stocked with twenty-two hundred head of cattle will sustain fifteen thousand gazelle, and as their numbers increase Hopcraft will systematically eliminate the cattle herd. The first crop of slaughtered gazelle he hopes will reach the abattoir soon. Their culling will begin on a limited basis—perhaps twelve the first month, slowly increasing in proportion to the natural increase of the herds.

David Hopcraft is not game ranching's only protagonist. Its simple wisdom has been discussed in Africa for more than thirty years. Two American biologists, Dr. Archie Mossman and Dr. Raymond Dasmann, had conducted an experiment on the Henderson Ranch in Zimbabwe in 1959. The results were compelling, but hard data still needed to be compiled. Deans of wildlife conservation, such as Sir Julian Huxley and F. Fraser Darling, begged others to pioneer this seductive field, but the only response was a rash of Hollywood films such as *Cowboy in Africa,* dramatizing the romance, but hardly advancing the science. In the late 1960s the African Wildlife Leadership Foundation, under the professional guidance of Dr. John King, domesticated a herd of oryx on the Galana Ranch in northern Kenya. Their object was similar to Hopcraft's—namely, to suggest an alternative to cattle in the dry lands of Africa—but their technique was considerably different. The oryx were to be herded in much the same manner as the local peoples traditionally managed their cattle. Perimeter fencing would therefore not be necessary, and the benefits of the experiment were intended to affect the livelihood of those people for whom the cost of such fencing would have been prohibitive. According to Robinson McIlvaine, the one-time director of A.W.L.F., the results of the Galana game ranching have been as interesting as Hopcraft's. It is his intention someday to import the technique to Botswana where, with large international funding, destitute Kalahari Bushmen will herd gemsbok, an oryx-type herbivore, and will benefit from the sale of the meat. Critics, however, point to the vast amount of funding required in both A.W.L.F.'s and Hopcraft's projects to dramatize the impossibility of the scheme in the hands of any one individual. Game ranching is essentially for millionaires or foundations.

Some ecologists add other doubts. Ian Parker, one of Africa's more unorthodox and acerbic wildlife consultants, says: "Destruction of land by any animal wild or domestic is usually brought about by man's mismanagement. There are cases in which wild animals under human influence have caused erosion every bit as spectacular and serious as that achieved with domestics. The supposition that, because man mismanages cattle, sheep and goats in Africa, he will not also mismanage any other animal entrusted to him is curious. . . . Game ranching is no substitute for domestic animals and all the arguments that have been put

193

up in this respect have been false. However, there is no reason why, as a specialized form of land use, it should not be profitable."

Conclusions vary widely on this now heated subject, in proportion to the wide spectrum of opinion that greets every novel wildlife idea in Africa. Dr. Leslie Brown, chief of the Kenya Agricultural Department from 1960 to 1963, and now a private consultant, disagrees with Parker. "Ecologically speaking, there is absolutely no doubt that wild animals are far less damaging to the environment than domesticated stock."

Few experiments in Africa have ever succeeded when initiated by the fainthearted. David Hopcraft enjoys hearing that others disapprove of his idea. He smiles secretively and affects a look of bemusement.

It is true that David Hopcraft has spent an inordinate amount of time on his experiment—some twenty years—and the results are today visible only in one place. Still, governments and public tastes are nearly immovable forces, and the work needed to permit the appearance of game meat on butchers' shelves probably exceeds the capacity of one human being. The fact that David Hopcraft need never do more than he has done so far is perhaps one reason why game ranching might never become more visible. Hopcraft can say he has achieved his original goal. That no one else wants to exploit a sensible idea is not his fault.

So game ranching and David Hopcraft remain more or less ineffective. But as with other innovations in Africa, failure is an invitation to dream. In the evenings when he and his wife, an American ex-model, sit in their many-windowed living room playing Scott Joplin on the piano or reading passages from P. G. Wodehouse aloud to their friends, they can see the faint glow, over knuckled plains, of the lights of Nairobi. Electricity and conference centers are fast becoming the hallmarks of progress throughout Africa, and for some there is comfort in witnessing the advancement of Africa from the Dark Continent to the Land of Lights.

On nights such as these David Hopcraft shares his public dream. He tells of the day that Africa's progress will no longer be measured by its appetite for foreign technology. He looks to a time when game ranching will be remembered as "the modern idea born and raised exclusively in Africa, an idea so effective that it will be exported abroad, that it will put food on the tables of Australia, Asia and the Americas." With such searing thoughts to occupy his guests while they study the view, he returns to the piano to bang out "Maple Leaf Rag."

All things considered, David Hopcraft can arrange the perfect African evening.

In his private game reserve he is known as "the boss." In the clubbish corridors of the Anglo American Corporation, his Oxbridge executives refer to him as the Chairman. His American son-in-law abbreviates his name to the sobriquet "HFO." Those who know him only as a legend think of him alternately as the King of Diamonds or the King of Gold.

With such a string of titles, one might almost expect the man to be imperious and unapproachable. Such is not the case with Harry Frederick Oppenheimer. As one of the richest and most powerful of South Africans, Harry (as he likes to be called

THE MAN
WHO WOULD CHANGE
SOUTH AFRICA

even by casual acquaintances) appears to be unaware of his aura. The talk about his being a billionaire he dismisses impatiently. He never seems to notice the awe which his opulence evokes among strangers. The fact that he stands over an empire ultimately employing half a million people daunts only others. His boundless acts of charity seem to be matters so private that whenever they are acknowledged publicly, he seems to recoil.

According to the popular caricature, South African tycoons come in only one size—treacherous, despotic and venally committed to the exploitation of blacks. But even Andrew Young, when he was the U.S. Permanent Representative to the U.N., took a breather from denunciations of white supremacists to describe the white capitalist Harry Oppenheimer publicly as "a kindred spirit, a man who was dedicated to justice in a land where injustice was perhaps most prevalent, a man who is sensitive and loving."

Harry Oppenheimer does not, as one easily forgets, stand very tall. He seems comfortable looking up to others, being shadowed by giants. His well-rounded physique suggests someone who has never had much interest in active sports. He himself only acknowledges doing a little swimming and taking an occasional long walk. Up until ten years ago he wore a mustache; it gave him the look of one of those dapper "punters" commonly seen at English racing meets, but now its absence is hardly noted. What distinguishes him is the energy of his face framed by conspicuously black eyebrows—the lines fanning out from his eyes whenever he laughs, the well-exposed teeth whenever he recognizes a friend, the cocked head, the gaze darting across the skies when he listens to others (which is often), or when he is dazzling his listeners with the conciseness of his thinking, the command of words, the art of expanding a petty idea, advanced by an interviewer, into a stirring philosophical concept. For someone with such a reputation for shyness, he makes much of being gregarious. Almost always surrounded by colleagues and friends, his occasional stammer, a difficulty with sibilants, and long disarming silences suggest a childhood handicap that now proves to be an effective antidote against small talk.

I think the only reason Harry Oppenheimer ever paid attention to me, some twenty years ago when we first met, was simply because he enjoyed the company of younger people. I was halfway between the ages of his son, Nicholas, and his daughter, Mary, yet not for many years would I become their friend. I do not mean to say that I was ever close to Harry in an important sense, but he did pay me the compliment of listening to my ill-formed views and allowing me to eavesdrop on his thoughts. I was a mere student, spending my summer vacation learning about mining and the Swazi labor force, and Mr. Oppenheimer made sure I saw everything he believed significant.

After that summer we kept in touch. On one occasion, he accepted my invitation to speak before the African Affairs Committee at Princeton University. Another time he invited me as his aide-de-camp on a trip through Rhodesia, Zambia and Tanzania. Other times, when our paths crossed in New York or London, we would meet for a meal, and generally, over coffee, he would make me promise to visit him and his wife, Bridget, in South Africa. "It has changed," he often said, trying to lure me. While I always knew there were many others he similarly singled out, I often wondered why he was so unflaggingly kind to me. My only explanation was my interest in Africa. He knew I was obsessed by everything that lay south of the Sahara; such passion for the land of his birth and of his dreams seemed to delight him.

Because Harry Oppenheimer baffles the typecasters, I have always sensed that for those who do not know him personally the anomalies of his life seem to spell tokenism, hypocrisy and cant. While shepherding a $10 billion mining, metallurgical and industrial empire, 80 percent of whose assets lie in white supremacist South Africa, he goes on record as a foe of apartheid and a champion of multiracialism. How can a man be such a super-capitalist and, at the same time, dine out on beliefs that seem to threaten his kind of capitalism? How can someone who has access to about a dozen corporate airplanes, who owns enormous chunks of real estate, who has an art collection numbering four Renoirs, a Bonnard, a Degas, a Chagall and several Picassos, with at least six homes scattered across the world in which to hang them, who has South Africa's finest string of racehorses, who owns a collection of Africana to rival that of any museum—how can such a man ever know what it is like to be poor and black and without a voice in South Africa?

Obviously, any answer to this question, no matter how compelling, is going to be inadequate for those doubters who are comfortable with the easy rhetoric. Harry Oppenheimer hardly helps ease their suspicions because he makes no apology for his wealth. His only public responsibility is to the shareholders of the Anglo American Corporation, DeBeers Consolidated Mines and a number of other companies of which he has been chairman; otherwise he views himself as a private man.

The empire that Sir Ernest and Harry Oppenheimer built is headquartered in Johannesburg on the site where the Gold Reefs first claim was pegged. Both its name—"44 Main Street"—and its concrete and Ficksburg freestone styling seem monolithic and unambitious, hardly the base of an operation that thrills to treasures beyond man's reach. Inside, hunting prints on the corridor walls and English antiques in the offices add to a sense of reserve. Opulent, yes, but not flashy. From these offices, Harry's executives command an empire that produces close to one-third of the free world's gold and markets 80 percent of its diamonds. In addition, it is the largest miner of coal in southern Africa, with enormous reserves, as well as the largest private manufacturer of steel and vanadium. Its timber holdings, the largest in South Africa, feed its very extensive paper-manufacturing interests, and it controls an industrial complex which manufactures most of South Africa's chemicals, a property development company, even an insurance and a computer service operation. Its domain extends throughout much of the free world. A major mining, finance and industrial house, based in London, is influenced from here. So too are investments in a Canadian base metal, oil, gas and chemical industry, the largest United States mineral and precious metal trading company, as well as giant exploration programs in Australia and the western Pacific. The number of companies in which the Anglo American Group has a significant interest changes from day to day, the total rarely less than two hundred.

With such awesome responsibilities, it is almost inconceivable to note that the Chairman still has time to smile, to say "That's very kind of you" for little courtesies, to read Shakespeare before giving a major address, to handwrite every single one of his personal letters and never, never to be even a minute late for an appointment.

Harry's father, the son of a small-town German cigar merchant, went first to London to make his fortune in the diamond business. Six years later, still impecunious, he was transferred to Kimberley, South Africa, to replace the diamond fields manager of his firm. The year was 1901, eight months after the death of Cecil Rhodes. Ernest Oppenheimer was shy, ambitious, and even at age twenty-two he had distinguished himself as a very knowledgeable "rough stone" expert. His starting salary—all his worldly income—was a not-so-lordly £500 a year.

Ernest's rise to a position "beyond the dreams of avarice" is still today one of the legends of South Africa. Like his son, he was an unlikely tycoon. Bookish, reserved, from the first he displayed uncommon business acumen and an ability to direct the bizarre, feuding personalities of Kimberley toward common goals. By 1917, along with his older brother in London, Ernest was in control of the diamond-trading firm which had originally sent him to South Africa. Almost immediately, he created an operation with a more ambitious goal, by enlisting the financial support of J. P. Morgan, to compete against the then disparate gold-mining operations on the Reef around Johannesburg. This company was to be called the Anglo American Corporation, to reflect that its initial investors were represented on both sides of the Atlantic. What distinguished this small mining house from all the others was the location of its administrative headquarters—on the spot, in South Africa. By 1919 (after a time when anti-German sentiment had risen to such violence in Kimberley that Oppenheimer's house had very nearly been burned to the ground) Anglo American had secured control of the alluvial diamond fields around the mouth of the Orange River in what had once been called German West Africa and today is known as Namibia. These diamond fields would one day become the highest-yielding gemstone area in the world. Throughout the 1920s Anglo American started buying shares of DeBeers Consolidated Mines—the firm once controlled by Cecil Rhodes—and by the time of the Wall Street crash Sir Ernest (he had been knighted in 1921) had consolidated his firm so effectively that it had become the leader of the diamond industry. During and after the Great Depression, when demand for diamonds more or less evaporated, Ernest demonstrated extraordinary restraint and foresight by resisting the temptation to sell any holdings, and by the mid-thirties he had effectively secured long-range stability for the diamond market by the creation of a London-based cartel, now known as the Central Selling Organization.

Harry, who was born in Kimberley in 1909, witnessed his father's rise from fairly modest beginnings to become a gentle giant in his industry. Never freebooting, parochial or especially acquisitive, the elder Oppenheimer exploited his power in hopes of bettering his community and advancing the mining industry.

For almost two decades Ernest was a Member of Parliament from Kimberley, and he used this seat to expound deeply felt beliefs about laissez-faire economics.

Harry was given all the formal education his father had been denied. Significantly, when he was at Christ College, Oxford, Harry read "Modern Greats," an honors course that limited itself rather grandly to philosophy, politics and economics. His was not the career-oriented education more in currency today and, in a sense, one could argue that his education prepared him for nothing, least of all technical fields like mining and metallurgy. It did, however, enrich his appetite for concepts, for logic; today his perspective on both history and the future suggests his inheritance from those Olympian academics.

Upon returning to South Africa in 1931, Harry immediately joined his father in business. Harry's older brother had died in a drowning accident and now, as only child and sole heir, there was no way for Harry, even had he wished, to extricate himself from the duty of apprenticing to his father's chairmanship. Sir Ernest was by no means an authoritarian figure, and years later Harry was to recall that "I, myself, as a boy and young man, was certainly outrageously spoiled and I really do not remember my father ever saying no to me. He would say it was impossible to spoil anyone who was, as he put it, 'naturally any good,' and if I was not 'naturally any good' it did not seem important to him whether I was spoiled or not. He imposed no positive discipline on me whatsoever, but the tacit underlying assumption that, for no other reason than that I was his son, I must be reasonably intelligent, hard-working and responsible amounted to pretty effective moral suasion."

Sir Ernest Oppenheimer believed that technical training was not nearly as valuable for his son as an understanding of "the stream of affairs." The older man "realized very well," Harry recalls, "that detailed knowledge of business methods and procedures was necessary down the line, but not, so he thought, in top positions. Major decisions were, he believed, best taken by some intuitive process, though he realized that these intuitions came only after you had worked hard to understand them. . . . What my father called intuition was really an ability to make up his mind quickly about the probabilities of a case and to act unhesitatingly on his judgment. He liked to say, 'If the wise man thinks too long, the fool does some thinking too.' "

Sir Ernest considered himself politically liberal, and although his son would one day redefine the meaning of that "South African liberalism," there was no doubt that the elder Oppenheimer was a decidedly humane individual. Some years after his death, Harry would say of his father: "By today's standards, he was not very liberal at all. He believed, for instance, that black people were less competent to run the country than white people. [But] he thought that white people were taking advantage of this fact and were treating black people badly as a result. . . . He had a good human feeling about black people, but, in looking back, I think he put too much weight on the state of black people as an average then and not on their potential. Mind you, though, I am sure what I have done since his death would have pleased him very much."

Even as a schoolboy, Harry had begun reflecting on racial inequities in the country, and it is clear that even then he was progressive. "I can remember debating race relations at school," he says, "but there did not seem to be much urgency on the part of others at the time. I thought we were very silly in those days when we talked about the race issue and all we were talking about were the problems of Afrikaans-speaking and English-speaking peoples. I was concerned even as a boy to point out that that was not the real race problem."

At the outbreak of war in 1939, Harry volunteered for military duty and was soon shipped to the western desert of Libya as an intelligence officer with the 4th South African Armoured Regiment. Some friends who had known him since childhood note that the war changed him considerably. The shyness and reserve, long his hallmark, were no longer as painful as they had once been. From close personal associations under trying, sometimes dangerous conditions, Harry's eye for the foibles and strengths of human nature was given its most intensive training.

Reflecting on the war today, Harry believes it did much to advance the cause of self-determination for nonwhites. There were not blacks, of course, in his regiment, but there were *coloureds* (the South African term for those of mixed race) and Malays, but the real effect of the war had to do with its grand purpose. "The idea that it was being fought," he says today, "to make the world safe for democracy and all that sort of stuff—which today sounds rather feeble—this caused people to think more about the rights of black people, not only their rights to decent treatment, but also their rights to determine their own destiny."

Upon his return to South Africa, Harry was married to the former Bridget McCall, and shortly afterward he was appointed managing director of Anglo American. Almost immediately Harry established his imprimatur on the conduct of business. The new Orange Free State goldfields were then being opened up, and Harry applied innovative standards in housing and social services to the design of the adjacent black communities such as Welkom. Simultaneously, Harry tried to redraft the laws governing migratory labor. To do so he had to wage battle with the then Minister of Native Affairs, Dr. H. F. Verwoerd (later to become Prime Minister and one of the key architects of the racist concept of "separate development"). Business conduct governing the treatment, compensation and movement of blacks was then rigidly policed by the government. Of all these statutes, Harry considered the one requiring all blacks to live apart from their families as a condition to employment the cruelest. But for all his lobbying, the only concession Harry could wrest was that a mere 3 percent of married blacks be allowed "in certain specified circumstances [to] reside with their families on the mines." It was a small consolation after months of effort, and it was to point out to Harry that even with all his economic power, his was a pitiful voice against the foghorn of public sentiment.

In 1948, Harry stood for a seat in Parliament, as a candidate for the then-ruling United Party (remarkably similar in policy at the time to its rival, the Nationalist Party, but distinct because it was composed mostly of English-speaking people). One can imagine the dapper and reserved Harry, his voice nearly plaintive, his language and wit elegant, standing up against crowds of Boer hecklers as he traveled around the small farming communities in his district. He would be the first member of his family to learn Afrikaans—an aptitude that would serve him well, years later, in appealing to Afrikaaners, the most entrenched foes of his liberalism.

Harry had entered politics convinced that his business life was inextricably woven into the forum of public matters. "I suppose it was the influence of my father," he recalls, "because I had always visualized my life as being a sort of second chapter in the same story. I felt I was carrying on the political side as well as the business side. Also, I think if you are running a large business, while you cannot take violent political views, you have simply got to concern yourself with politics: It is not realistic not to do so."

Harry won his seat in a Pyrrhic victory, for his United Party simultaneously lost office to the Nationalists, and for the nine years he served his party, he did so with the blunt sword of a backbencher. Early in his political career Harry announced that he would be loyal to party doctrine in all areas except that of race relations. Here he was at odds with the general caucus. Even in 1948, he was firmly opposed to economic, social, industrial and governmental segregation. At issue at the time was the loss of rights of the coloured and Indian communities. Harry was soon to become the loyal champion of this minority group. He spoke out about "grave injustices," of popular decisions reached from which "all confidence and all sense of purpose and all vision have been rigorously excluded." In the end, he was outshouted and outvoted.

The decision to retire from politics in 1957 was prompted by the death of his father. "Had I felt," Harry later wrote, "that I could have played a real part in Parliament, in other words, if I could have been in the government, I think I would have been very inclined to stay in politics and try to make other arrangements about business." What Harry was soon to discover was the even greater political influence at his command as a business leader.

Soon he began moving behind the scenes. In 1959 the most liberal-leaning members of the United Party broke away to form the Progressive Party (later known as the PFP, the Progressive Federal Party). The Liberal Party—those extreme left-wingers who advocated outright abdication of white power—was outlawed, and many of its outspoken supporters exiled. Such irrationality was too much even for the liberal Harry Oppenheimer. In an interview to the *Daily Express* at the time, he explained his moderation: "I hold liberal views—but in the old-fashioned sense, in that I object to black dictatorships just as much as I object to white ones. So many modern liberals seem to suffer from a sense of guilt over the Colonial past, and to think in a doctrinal way that to expiate that guilt they must support everything black—including the black dictatorships."

The Progressives, advancing the concept that all adults, regardless of race, be allowed a vote commensurate with their education, appealed to Harry, and soon he was lavishing his support on them, in the form of funds as well as counsel. The sitting room at Brenthurst, the Oppenheimer home, became the site of many policy debates, the scene observed coquettishly by Renoir's "Girl in a Straw Hat."

For the first fifteen years of its life, the Progressive Party lamely returned only one candidate, Mrs. Helen Suzman, to a seat in Parliament. Even then, that one lonely figure, propped by Harry's support, needled South African hard-liners. One Afrikaans-speaking Nationalist observed in 1962 that South Africa's most pressing problems were "the United Nations, the English press, the Liberal Party and Harry Oppenheimer." By the mid-1970s growing protest to apartheid, particularly from English-speaking suburban voters, swelled the PFP's seats to seven, and by 1980 that number had risen to twenty-eight. This still modest symbol of its political recognition is significant to Harry today. "What we were doing over the years," he says of the early sixties, "was, on the one hand, keeping an unpopular and, what seemed, unrealistic point of view, alive. That's altogether different today. I think that liberal causes are much more with the tide in South Africa. Things have changed immensely. . . ."

Harry concentrated much of his support on implementing the political rhetoric but during the 1960s and 1970s detractors claimed that Anglo American did little to advance blacks into management positions, to raise wages and to improve conditions. Today such arguments bear little weight. After the Soweto riots in 1976, Harry conceived of the Urban Foundation and immediately called upon South Africa's most prominent businessmen to sit on its board. In the first year he raised nearly $30 million. As a kind of small-scale Ford Foundation, it was able to build schools, improve slums and, most importantly, lobby successfully in Parliament to change the laws relating to black ownership of land. As a result, Soweto residents can now obtain ninety-nine-year leases, and with further lobbying they may one day be allowed freehold title to their property. Harry's personal contribution to this project is roughly a million dollars annually. One substantially staffed division of another foundation, known as The Chairman's Fund, is dubbed a "risk-financing" charity. It undertakes the funding of original projects—such as reading programs for rural children, teacher-education schemes and the creation of agricultural colleges—in the hope that other foundations will see their benefits and contribute to them on a large scale. One of Harry's most recent efforts involves $3.5 million in corporate funds committed to training a mere twelve blacks over a five-year period. At the end of their apprenticeship, Anglo American intends to offer them top management positions—until now, the exclusive stronghold of whites.

For all his public charity, there are many campaigns Harry undertakes privately. One such was a dinner I attended in a Johannesburg hotel. A month previously, Chief Buthelezi of the Zulu nation had complained to him that, as leader of the largest tribe in South Africa, he had rarely had the opportunity to address influential South African businessmen to diagram his own formula for business cooperation between the races. "I will see that that situation is corrected," Harry had said. Hence the dinner. Eighty of Johannesburg's most influential leaders are gathered. The convocation is deliberately off bounds to the press, and it is clear from Harry's self-effacing behavior at the head table that he wants the chief to be in the limelight, not himself. A hush falls. The chief stands at the podium and for the first four minutes of his speech he heaps praise upon Harry Oppenheimer. He talks of his "humanity," of his "simplicity," of his "humility" and, in the end, describes him as "this great son of South Africa." I look over to see how Harry is taking this eulogy. The smile has vanished from his face. Stony-jawed, he seems to be undergoing private torture.

Against all the praise, Harry receives his share of criticism. A prominent Afrikaans-speaking journalist sitting next to me at the dinner is, for instance, charmed by Harry's consistency and generosity, but, on the other hand, he feels the largesse is tainted. "It's all part of that English boarding school paternalism," he says, imitating a sort of Colonel Blimp accent: " 'You know, dear boy, I understand what these black chaps need. Let's give them a fair shake and all that, what?' But these English like dear old Harry have stayed insulated from blacks, and the blacks feel uneasy with them. It's all so philosophical and verbal. Not so with us Afrikaaners. You see, we're just as much a tribe as the blacks are. We're black in our own way. We grew up with them, we lived with them, we worked beside them. They have no illusions about us, nor we them. And in the long run, it will be us Afrikaaners who'll provide for the blacks; it's we who'll really make multiracialism work. . . ."

Harry seems as indifferent to criticism as he is to praise, and when at last I sit down to talk with him, the next afternoon on a shaded terrace at Brenthurst, I notice, first of all, how effectively he is able to exclude discussion of his achievements from our conversation. Almost as soon as I begin my questions, the private man submerges and the public person, jut-jawed, with eyes casting over the sloping garden for accuracy, takes control.

I may have had my worries, along with others, about Harry's loyalties. Liberalism, in the context of the very rich, often appears as substantial to me as a chocolate eclair. Of course, I knew about the "trickle theory"—the concept that allowed wealth at the top of the heap to follow the laws of gravity, precipitating ultimately upon "the lower classes." The rich, thereby, would get richer and the poor would trail along, in parallel fashion, their income and standards of living rising as long as the capitalists supplied growth to the economy. I could see how this theory might work neatly for house servants, but I would have found it laughable were it a fundamental in Harry's thinking.

The subject never arises. "I believe," he begins, "that this private enterprise system is what produces a higher standard of living for people in a material way but I also think it's the only economic system which is compatible with individual freedom, with freedom of choice. Therefore, when I say black people are badly treated and one wants to improve conditions for them, what I'm thinking about in the economic field is that they must be given the full chance to share on equal terms in what seems to me the benefits of this economic system. Where I think they've been badly treated is that, on the one hand, they're asked to back white people in supporting this economic system against communist or centralizing ideas and, on the other hand, they're excluded by all sorts of laws from the benefits of this system. It is not only a way of giving justice to black people, but it's also a way of improving markets, increasing productivity and making the economy, in concerns like ours, profit better. So I would be inclined to argue that seeking for justice and seeking to do the best for your shareholders call for the same type of action."

How about black trade unions, I inquire, knowing that many South African industrialists were opposing them. Wouldn't such organizations run counter to what's best for shareholders?

"No," Harry replies without pausing. "I believe very much in black trade unions. You see, in the past, if there were grievances, the first you would hear about them would be a riot. There was no one to negotiate with. Whenever there was a riot you'd go and say, 'Let us talk about these problems,' but there was never an elected leader. I believe this can only be put right by encouraging trade unionism among the black workers, in spite of the fact that I am very conscious there will be a great deal of trouble of a type we do not have now. I think that's part of the growing stage of an industrial state. I think trade unionism can be the machinery through which workers take part in the private enterprise system. I would love to see that sort of thing grow in South Africa."

We are overlooking a series of fountains and, far away, just before the skyline of Johannesburg claims the view, a larger-than-life bronze Venus peers at us through come-hither eyes. The rolled grass, topiary bushes and serpentine pathways are so overwhelming that one easily forgets this land was once the open veld. Consumed by beauty, so many whites living in South Africa, I think, are quick to eliminate all that they originally found so beautifully African. Everything about us—including the tea on the table—has been brought in from somewhere else. Even ideas, particularly those that threaten to set this country aflame as well as the ones that promise to put out the flames, are foreign imports. Still, Harry thinks of himself as African. His head is cocked, as though he is not sure he has said all that needs saying.

I ask him what he thinks of a recent statement made by Timothy Smith, director of the Interface Center for Corporate Responsibility, claiming that "an American company concerned with its public image would not want to be associated with the Anglo American Corporation."

Harry does not know Mr. Smith and, in any case, he thinks the concept muddled. He replies, "On the contrary. What happens when you invest more and more in South Africa is you allow black people to be trained and to do the same job as white people. This is necessary. It is the policy that will break down apartheid. The ideas advanced by the Reverend Leo Sullivan have, I feel, much greater influence. Instead of telling American companies in South Africa to get out, he tells these companies, 'Now you put things right in the country.'

"There was once a time when American companies in South Africa were really out of date, not because they were disinclined to make changes but because it used to be considered wrong for a foreign company to take actions that had a political implication. So there was rather a deliberate tendency on the part of American companies to resist black rights. Now American companies are taking a lead in improving conditions. This has, I believe, a very good effect."

Harry puts down his cup. The tea has grown cold. "You know, there is another benefit of private enterprise. It's no good for us so-called liberals to think that all we have to do is to improve black conditions. We must also change the thinking of the whites, and that may not be easy. For years, the Afrikaans-speaking people have had a tendency to go into the bureaucracy, to stay away from private industry. Now that's changing too, and as soon as you have Afrikaans-speaking supporters of government policy running large businesses, their thinking changes. The policy of not training black people, of not allowing them to do skilled work and thereby keeping their wages down—they discover that this does not fit in with a successful business. So these whites are beginning to change their thinking, even if they are merely shareholders of a company or running it themselves."

It is good to hear such optimism, I say, but there are so many people who do not share Harry's predictions. They are unable to see how change is even remotely possible under the current leadership in South Africa. Racial confrontation seems for them inevitable. Whatever promises Prime Minister Botha is making are neither enough, nor possible, nor, in the opinion of many, honest.

Harry interrupts: "I do not think his promises to upgrade black conditions was a ruse. He has invited criticism from his right wing and I would guess that he finds that sort of criticism far more disagreeable than he would find criticism that he is not doing enough from people like me. He is the leader of a party whose thinking for the last thirty years he is trying to undo. Something successfully sown for so long is difficult to unsow, and to bring it off he will have to split his party in half. I personally think he *will* have the courage to do just that. When I used to see him in politics, he made an impression on me of being extremely excitable, in the habit of losing his temper too often. I interpreted this behavior to mean he would take rather a hard line. I was wrong. He has indeed taken considerable political risks and I am rather full of hope. Inevitably, the head of such a party is going to take a step forward, then take a step back, which people like me are going to find very disappointing. But then I am optimistic enough to think he is going to take more steps forward than steps backward."

Harry walks me down to the bottom of the garden to show me the sumptuous Renoir nude. Dressed in a dark business suit and tie, he and the languorous lady seem an odd couple, and when he beams with a mischievous smile, almost imitating her brazenness, I think he realizes the irony. They are old friends, it seems, and now he turns his attention to our plans. Will I be ready for the flight on Friday? He hopes I shall like his recently acquired private game reserve, for it gives him such pleasure, although he has only had time to visit it twice in his life.

Friday: During the flight, as Harry inquires of each guest if he is comfortable, he overhears one of his young executives saying how worried he becomes every time the Chairman flies. "I always look on flying," Harry confides innocently, "as a kind of process in which I am being sent registered mail."

Toyotas are waiting at the private dirt airstrip near the camp. Harry hurls himself into the most uncomfortable seat and, as we make our way along the rough roads, he smiles with childish pleasure whenever an animal comes into view.

The next morning, as a fish eagle ululates from the stump of a tree near the stone lodge, the voice of one of the young executives can be heard reprimanding the camp manager: "That was an oversight yesterday. The Chairman is to be provided with a ladder whenever stepping out of the back of the Toyota. I was horrified when he jumped down. You all know he had a back problem last year. And there he was, absolutely oblivious to his situation."

The Chairman is also unaware that anyone could possibly

want to make such a fuss over him. He eats breakfast on the edge of the veranda, admiring an elephant that has come down to the river to drink, and telling us all about the giraffe he saw in his bathroom mirror this morning as he shaved. "I think it so extraordinary," he says, pouring himself some Earl Grey tea, "that as we look out from here we see a view of infinite pastoral charm, yet were we to walk into it we might just get eaten." He laughs, cocks his head in thought and then studiously looks from one guest to the next. He is thinking about something and no one dares look back at him directly lest they interrupt those thoughts. Is it business? Is it politics? At last he clears his throat. It was Darwin and *The Origin of Species.* "Does anybody," he asks, "understand how, by the laws of natural selection, a reptile could possibly grow feathers?" Nobody answers as his cocked head studies the knives dipped one by one into the jar of marmalade.

This weekend, like most, is for business, but it is conducted almost inconspicuously, not behind closed doors but in distant corners of the veranda, within sound of the stomach rumblings of the elephant. Voices are lowered. The Chairman is listening. He breaks in gently, halting the other's solicitous monologue. "Yes, of course," comes the reply, and now the Chairman's colleague does not know how to resume. As one of the junior executives was to say, "It is all very civilized. HFO is so astute that when a deal is presented to him and if there are fifty points, he will only go for the most sensitive one, the one that poses the contradictions."

For those guests not involved with the business of Anglo American there is no feeling of being left out. One evening we follow a ground-trembling roar to the airstrip, where at dusk a pride of four lionesses is padding down Runway 22. At its end, in the long grass, is a herd of impala, their heads raised, listening to one very vocal lion hidden in the distance beyond them—they not knowing that the real danger is in clear view, on the runway. "It's all so exciting," Harry exclaims, looking behind to make sure everyone is enjoying the adventure as much as he. He leans over to the resident naturalist to ask a question about the unfolding drama. Later, the naturalist was to confide: "Whenever the boss starts asking me questions I worry that he doesn't already know a little more about it than I do."

One of the junior executives—the same young man who had

issued a directive to the camp staff about the Chairman's back— is standing in the rear of the open vehicle and is clearly worried. Four full-grown lionesses are within two easy bounds of HFO. Without even a proper door for protection there is no doubt in the mind of the young man that these four lionesses have an appetite only for the chairman of the board of the Anglo American Corporation.

Admittedly, the lionesses have not figured on a Toyota following them down Runway 22. Clearly we are meddling. The lioness closest to us makes a halfhearted run in our direction, not to eat the Chairman, but rather to see us off. No sooner does the lioness begin her mock charge than the junior executive raises the heavy .458 to his shoulder, his thumb heavily jamming the safety as far forward as it will travel. The vehicle jolts into third gear and with the junior executive dangerously unbalanced in the rear, we make good our escape.

"Wasn't that awfully fun," the Chairman says, turning around, not knowing the real danger lay in the hands of his aide-de-camp.

In the evening when we assemble for an alfresco dinner in a reed stockade behind the lodge, the Chairman is expected to sit at the head of the long refectory table. He claims this prerogative reluctantly, for it is, he knows, an isolationist seat. The chairs on either side of him fill slowly, for the young wives are reluctant to look too pushy, while some of the other guests find the levels of conversation required as his dinner companion hard to sustain. All that separates this table from the stars is a small ionosphere.

Out of this silence, someone remembers a remark made by Harry's daughter at his seventieth birthday party—something about him one day writing a biography of Lord Byron. Was there any truth to it, the guest inquires? Harry impatiently brushes it aside, saying that he has no qualifications for the task. He merely owns a few Byron manuscripts (in fact, it is the most important Byron collection in private hands), ever since he was at Oxford. Harry pauses, remembering. "What I liked about Byron," he says, going to the heart of the question, "was the combination of romanticism and hardheadedness. While everybody else was helping the Greeks by buying them printing presses, Byron believed that what they needed most was to stop the Turks, so he went out to fight."

Again a pause while the clue sinks in. Somebody else pipes up about Kissinger's memoirs, thinking that the topic will provide Harry with conversational self-sufficiency. "A very, very important political document," Harry answers. "I found it impossible to put down. I also found it impossible to lift." Harry laughs and all too suddenly resumes his silence.

Circuitously, the conversation returns to South Africa and to Harry's days in Parliament. After the brooding silence, he is now ready to speak. The enigma then, as it is today, was the gap between the country's two white populations. "You know," he recalls, "when Vorster became our Prime Minister the only credential he had in foreign-policy making was the fact that he and his wife had once taken a package tour to the Argentine."

The remark is of course amusing, but Harry is after a larger point. He has begun to lose his shyness now, the words spilling out with pleasure; for his guests, all that is necessary is to sit back and enjoy the torrent. His head is cocked and he talks fast, often doubling back on a remark in a slightly different octave as though he is conducting a conversation with himself. "I used to drive down to Cape Town for the opening of Parliament in the old days. On the way I'd notice these farmhouses at either side of the road. Next to them would be a kraal with a few sheep inside. The tin roof of the farmhouse would be surrounded by a few dusty gum trees. And if you went inside the house, you would see that, apart from one large copy of the Bible, there was probably no other book. And here I was going to talk in Parliament to develop a foreign policy. I mean, really. Who was I talking to? And for what?"

Now all that is changing, Harry continues. "And anyway, all these whites living together in South Africa have nowhere else to go and just because they sometimes have differences of opinion and quarrel and just because they speak different languages, they belong irrevocably together and can never, never escape one another." The conversation has suddenly become serious.

"Isn't a revolution certain," I ask, pursuing my questions from the terrace at Brenthurst, "given the violent differences of hope between all the peoples of South Africa?"

"No," Harry says emphatically. "I am really quite hopeful there will never be a revolution. Of course, peace requires continuous change, starting now. I don't think there can be any stopping. There must be a real sharing of power between black and white within at least five years. But because Botha has stuck his neck out so far there can be no going back without an intolerable loss of face. Mind you, change won't be easy. I would be delighted but very surprised if we got away without riots, but riots are different from revolutions, and I think we can get away without revolutions. White South Africans, holding on to their exclusive privileges, are now conscious of a need for change. The real bitterness amongst the blacks lies with the young people in the towns. But even here, I believe, if they see changes for the better occurring regularly, they will accept the situation. I feel certain of it. I don't think any of this is going to be wonderfully easy, but I've always been reasonably optimistic and I feel more optimistic now than I have ever been for years. By putting itself on a slope so slippery, the government will be unable to stop . . .''

"But what if," I blunder in, "things just don't go quite as you imagine and there is indeed a revolution here in South Africa? Wouldn't it be foolish for you to stay?"

"Leave South Africa?" Harry bursts out. "Good gracious, no. It doesn't occur to me. Unless I'm chased out I'm going to stay here. You remind me that a while back when things were going badly a lot of people hived off. Well, I think that's silly. I think it's not very brave and I think it's bad judgment, too. It's worse than a crime. It's a mistake."

I now am convinced no critic will ever have much success sniping at Harry's bedrock beliefs. If within the next five years there is a revolution, then the future of the Anglo American Corporation, the future of Harry Oppenheimer, indeed the future of the free enterprise system in South Africa will be doomed. Harry's fate as well as that of his family's is irrevocably sealed to the success of multiracialism. No one can possibly lose more if it fails.

Tonight I am willing to gamble that Harry might risk all he has on a dream of Africa. The numbers mean very little now. I believe he sees money not for its security but for its power—not to buy people but to buy the future, not for personal acclaim but to thrill to the pleasure of preserving a belief. He sees Africa as a puzzle and of all the people I know no one tries harder to break its code. He has used logic, common sense, charity, wisdom, and he admits that out here none is truly successful.

For Harry, Africa remains the only real game. And this little wilderness represents for him that part of its soul he finds most alluring: danger, inscrutability and illogic. He hardly knows the bush, but he likes what it means. It is the most important ingredient in his mines, in his labor force, in his politics. It both puzzles him and amuses him. Even with all his power he knows he should not tinker with it.

So he cocks his head, smiles at the women and with a graciousness so rare in these parts, he invites us all onto the veranda for one last nighttime view.

DESERT DOCTOR

The doctor has apologized that there are no lion bites.

Whenever she flies through Kenya's northern desert she expects to treat one or two maulings. Today, in the mission hospital at North Horr, she notes instead the high incidence of mental illness. "Mama," she calls. The young woman lying on the cot does not respond. Coils of copper winding around her neck seem to divide her frozen body from the waxy composure of her face. The doctor lifts the patient's lids to examine her vacant eyes and then rolls her body roughly from side to side. The sleeping woman reacts only with a sigh. Except for one delicate hand, quivering as if from the pulse of a distant generator, she may as well be dead. Of course, it could be an act, the doctor reminds us. The distinction between mental illness and a physical disorder is often difficult to discern among people who cannot communicate.

I am most impressed by the trust. When conscious, this Gabbra woman had come to this hospital, agreeing to put her health and sanity into the hands of an absolute outsider—a woman trained at the Faculté de Médecine in Paris. In the mind of this barefoot patient, the traditional witch doctor was somehow not as trustworthy as this no-nonsense woman from another world. Throughout Africa, twentieth-century technology hurtles itself at the shamans of tribal belief, but nowhere is that encounter more clear-cut than when Dr. Anne Spoerry places her stethoscope on a chest, rutted and inflamed with ritual tribal cicatrices.

I confess, however, I am puzzled by Anne Spoerry. I have been hearing about her throughout Kenya for many years, and somehow the gossip does not offer a very satisfactory explanation for her motives in being an underpaid, underthanked physician to the tribal peoples of Kenya. It is said she has considerable private means of her own, thanks to a family textile business. It is also said she served gallantly in the French Underground during World War II, that she was imprisoned by the Germans, tortured, and forced to undergo an operation of incredible brutality. Her survival, they say, is one of the great testaments to human will. But Anne refuses to discuss these times with anybody, so such stories are only imaginings.

I guess she is in her young sixties. I know she has never married. For eleven months of every year she lives in Kenya and, as a member of the African Medical and Research Foundation (AMREF), she travels to remote parts of the country for three weeks out of every month, flying herself, caring for the sick. When she stays in Nairobi, she lives with friends. Otherwise she has a small farm in central Kenya, on the edge of the Rift Valley, and a house on the coast, in the style of a nineteenth-century Arab mansion. For one month of every year, she goes to France, to a resort that she owns with her architect brother, who designed it.

No doubt, an unusual woman. But the facts tell me little.

Why, for instance, is she the only member of her family to live in Africa? Why has she dedicated her life to caring for tribal people? Is she a do-gooder, propelled by that sense of guilt we poison ourselves with in the West?

Somewhat reluctantly, she has allowed me to accompany her on the last two days of her once-a-month tour of the Northern Frontier province. She complained she does not understand why she must be the center of such attention, and anyway, she will be too busy to talk. When I tried to explain, she brushed all my arguments aside. "Let's go," she said.

As she makes her way from cot to cot, I note that she stands a little over five feet. Everything about her appearance—from her brusquely cut hair to her khaki jacket and trousers, festooned with pockets—suggests utilitarianism; she might have been a child's nanny in another century. Although I find her punctual, a careful pilot, a meticulous note keeper, I also sense she enjoys being vague. Better, perhaps, to be thinking of two or three things simultaneously than plod through life at everyone else's pace. She allows her conversation to jump from subject to subject serendipitously, leaving thoughts strung together not by punctuation marks but by a clearing of the throat, a jingling of her keys deep in a pocket. An easily ignited temper is just as easily extinguished by a smile, seriousness suffused by humor, generosity made to look abrupt, as if it were a mistake. Most conspicuous of all, however, is her constant hurry.

The next patient is a man so old that he has lost count of the years. This morning he walked five miles to meet with the doctor, and now, as he lies on the rubber bed cover, I am convinced I am watching someone in the last hours of life. The skin is stretched so tight over his ribcage that it flickers with his heart. Coughing, he clings to the bed as if it were a boat in a heavy sea.

While examining him, Anne discovers that her stethoscope is broken. Another one is produced and that too is flung aside. "Either this man has no heartbeat or our technology has failed." She puts her hand on the old man's forearm for a second, decides there is nothing further to be done for him, then follows the sound of wailing into the examining room. A young woman is sitting on the floor. She is bare above the waist except for a whirlpool of copper coils at her neck, suspending a Maria Theresa taler. She sits on the floor, drumming her feet on the cement, engaged in a private concert, part hum, part grunt. Clearly she is insane. For the last few weeks, according to the nurse, she has ceased doing any of her chores in the village, spending her time instead distracted by some inner conversation. When Anne intrudes with a question she replies, "Cha cha . . . ata"—meaningless words in any language. She holds the thermometer in her mouth as if it were a cigarette.

"Is she supposed to get married and does not want to?" asks Anne.

The nurse shakes her head.

"What's wrong with her thumb?" Anne continues.

Dirty dressings are removed to reveal a small inconsequential cut.

Anne is clearly puzzled. She is not going to accept the explanation made by the girl's parents: that she has engaged in *hyana*—devil worship.

"A brain tumor?" she ponders out loud. She shakes her head, dismissing the possibility. "Not with that pulse." In quick succession Anne also discounts a brain ulcer, typhoid and snakebite. By now the girl is weaving, surely on the verge of a fall. Suddenly, while holding onto her shoulder with one hand, Anne gives her a push. "That's what I thought. You can feel her muscles tightening. She still knows enough not to let herself fall over." The girl, probably faking her condition for unknown reasons, wails once again. "Give her fifty milligrams of BD, then if she does not recover, send her down to the hospital in Marsabit."

Some of Anne's patients have been waiting to see her for twelve hours. They squat in the shade outside, suckling babies, shielding their eyes against the dust swirling across a grassless lawn. By tomorrow I will be used to such patience; today I think only of those for whom Anne will have no time. But by tomorrow I shall also have discovered that those who were rejected needed her attention least. Somehow she knows the sick.

On one of the chairs Anne deposits a basket of fruit and vegetables, just harvested over the weekend on her farm. She has finished her examinations and we have now gathered around a long table, covered in an old oilcloth. Anne's gift is very precious to the missionaries, for they have not eaten anything fresh in nearly a month. Equally, it has been a month since they saw an outsider. They regard Anne with wonder, intoxicated by the sound of another voice, by the torrent of her words, by the energy. She prods them to tell me their story, sure that it is far more interesting to me than hers. In so doing, one can sense that she has just restored a sense of earthly grandeur to their lives, reminding them perhaps that there is triumph in a lonely ordeal. "This is a town that should never be," the German diocesan priest begins, haltingly. "The people who settle here are Gabbra who have lost all their animals. These are the destitute ones. So we give them each fifteen goats and a few camels—but it will be years before they have a herd big enough to sustain them. In the meantime there are money-making jobs, like making table mats to be sold to the tourists in Nairobi. Little by little they should gain back their freedoms. Often they don't. We teach them to depend. I am not sure about that. You see, it is hard not to depend forever."

"Right," says Anne out of the rhetorical pause. She believes I have heard as much as I want. "We'll be flying in the dark if we don't leave now." She gathers up a packet of mail for posting in Nairobi ("That's all I am—the postman"). The lay priests drive us back to the Piper Lancer, shuddering in the fierce desert wind. She distributes an assortment of drugs and dressings out of the hold of the plane, kisses the missionaries on both cheeks, and long after her plane has taxied to the end of the strip, scattered the dust and the goats with a burst of power, and flown out of their lives for another month, they stand transfixed beside their car.

One week of every month Anne devotes to visiting the sick in the coastal province. Another is split between Rusinga Island on Lake Victoria and Masailand. This is her third week, and by tomorrow evening she will have inscribed references in her notebook to over 120 patients examined in the last four days of flying. The strips where she has landed sound like the refrain in an African mass—Laisamis, Loyengalani, Illaret, Moyale, Saborei, Maikona, Marsabit. At some, there were no missionaries at all, only patients who knew she was coming, waiting to be examined under a tree. Because many of Anne's stops are close to the unstable Ethiopian and Somali borders, rifle and spear wounds were not uncommon. At Moyale, the resident doctor and his wife were discovering that no one, not even doctors, were considered neutral during these hostilities. There, the *shifta* (bandit) emergency had deteriorated to such a degree that when Anne arrived the doctor admitted he and his wife were sleeping in their bathtub for safety, since their house was being ventilated by rifle fire.

Anne looks on war merely as an occupational hazard. This evening she is my guest for dinner at the fishing lodge at Loyengalani, on Lake Turkana, where we landed at sunset. The Mau Mau emergency, she admits, was not all that terrible. She did a lot of climbing and slipping on wet mountain trails; as a member of the Colonial countergangs, she fingerprinted the dead, cared for the wounded, and thought alternately like hunter and hunted. "You must have been twenty," I interject, "when the Germans overran Paris."

"No," she says hotly, "I'm not going to talk to you about those times. Yes, I watched those Panzer divisions move into Paris. Yes, the only way we could put up with it was with a bottle of cognac a day. And when there was no more point in being a nurse, I traveled south with all of France, along the roads, skirting the roadblocks. Yes, I was in the Underground for about a year, and then I was taken a prisoner. That's all I'll say. Those days have no bearing on me today, or on the Flying Doctors. Absolutely nothing. All I can tell you is that there should never never never be a third world war."

The conversation has ended, and Anne sips her beer, looking angrily across the veranda into the starless and windy night.

"I don't blame her for not wanting to talk about the war," Dr. Michael Wood had told me before I made the trip with Anne. He is the director general of the African Medical and Research Foundation, and Anne's boss. "She was one of the few who survived. There's no doubt she's seen the seamy side of life. Why have to relive it now? I can tell you one thing, though—she's been made tough by it. You know, to this day she bears no ill will toward the Germans. Amazing, I call it. You can't survive anywhere, particularly in Africa, if you are bitter."

Anne had only agreed to my accompanying her through the Northern Frontier if I were to interview some of her colleagues in AMREF before departing. "I don't want to be singled out," she had insisted. The foundation, she assured me, had moved beyond the airplane-and-bottle-of-antibiotics stage.

There was no question, however,, that AMREF, once called the Flying Doctors' Service, owes its existence to the airplane. Formed in 1957, it was the brainchild of three gifted reconstructive surgeons—two Englishmen, Drs. Michael Wood and Archie McIndoe, and an American, Tom Rees. They had all fallen under the spell of Africa and enjoyed flying airplanes, more as a hobby than as a vocation. Qualified doctors were, at the time, in short supply in East Africa—one for thirty thousand potential patients. The real roadblock to proper medical care was the remoteness of the rural population. The airplane was therefore the perfect solution, bringing care to where it was needed.

Almost as soon as the Flying Doctors' Service had begun operating the doctors struck on other solutions. A system of high-frequency radio transmitters, it was thought, could bring the expertise of a Nairobi medical headquarters to hundreds of remote bush clinics, at a fraction of the cost of airplanes. Today, the system has expanded beyond the doctors' wildest dreams. A battery of registered nurses now staffs a radio switchboard in contact with five hundred bush stations. Anything from spare parts for a hospital Land Rover to major surgery can be administered from here, and there is no doubt that the radios have saved many lives.

"You see," claims Anne, "the flying part is very tiny." She sits in her office, crowded with baskets of produce from her farm, preparing for her flight north. Her desk top is a clutter of Arab artifacts from the coast, lists of supplies and medical journals. "That's where you must spend all your time," she says, pointing out the window to a four-story modern office building that contrasts sharply with her antique quarters. I followed her advice and made my way from one office to the other, in an attempt to dispel the notion she was sure I had acquired that adventure and drama were AMREF's stock-in-trade.

"So much of our funding comes from large governmental agencies like AID," confirms Michael Wood. "They really aren't interested in the work that Anne and the other Flying Doctors do. They want to contribute to major revolutions in medical services." The burden of AMREF's work today, he continues, is in medical training. Paramedics look to the foundation (not necessarily to their own governments) to oversee their continuing education; to keep them abreast of new drugs, new techniques; and to sharpen their skills. AMREF is also a publishing house. On its first floor two large offset presses roar throughout the day, trying to keep up with the backlog of demand for medical instruction books. With annual contributions amounting to $5 million, AMREF has assumed a heavy burden of all rural health in Kenya, part of Tanzania and Uganda, and now it is being asked to extend its services into the Southern Sudan.

Those services are being expanded in some surprising ways. I spent much of my time with Dr. Norman Scotney, whose appeal for me lay in his unusual specialty. As a medical anthropologist, he is the Health Behavior Department. The need for such a discipline became clear not many years ago when it was found that health care services often ran counter to the traditional ways of life of rural people. Fresh food, clean water and hygiene may seem obvious concomitants of good health to us, but to some in East Africa they threaten a way of life. To a traditionalist, soap might be seen as a symbol of anarchy. "We must learn to temporize health care," says Scotney, "to work through existing tribal institutions and to make sure that while we bring a healthier way of life, we do so without upsetting other worlds. After all, most of the people we deal with are masters of survival. Take that instinct away and you'll end up with nothing." Scotney's department went to work, operating within the tribal structure, making sure that no one's authority was jeopardized. Under his direction, the tribal elders could become the spokesmen for modern health care. "The so-called hygiene revolution," says Scotney, "may have occurred in the West a hundred years ago. Here in Africa, it's happening now. Our job is to make sure it's painless."

Another startling departure in Western medicine, encouraged by AMREF, is a willingness to deal with "witch doctors." The gulf that once separated the folk healers from the Western medical tradition is being eroded. Scotney attributes this trans-

224

formation to the success of acupuncture outside of China. Suddenly serious attention has begun to focus on folk medicine. "Some of the best bone setters I've met," he insists, "have never known the inside of a hospital. What's wrong with that? Personally, whenever I appoint someone in a village as the rural health officer, I seek out the local witch doctor. If I find that he is more committed to helping people than aggrandizing himself, then what you can do with him is fantastic."

Anne was proud of Norman Scotney's work, exhilarated by the trailblazing surgery being performed on lepers by another of her colleagues, happy to show me the radio room or to talk about the rural health-training programs, but always, I thought, she retained a distance from the rest of AMREF. Her office was in the other building—the one with all the history—and her work, flying through Kenya, kept her remote.

If anyone could penetrate that remoteness, it was Dr. Michael Wood. With his bushy eyebrows rising and falling from the effect of searching for the perfect description, he rocked behind a desk cluttered with framed awards and royal tributes. He recalled the early days when the foundation was small and everyone flew a plane. He remembered surgery performed under the wing of a Piper or over the radiotelephone. Now, silver-haired and patrician, he saw his future challenges in overseas boardrooms where his job would be to dramatize the needs of a new Africa.

But Anne, Wood insisted, was not an anachronism. After all, in Australia the Flying Doctors' Service was nearly fifty years old and still going strong. No, Anne was needed desperately in Kenya. "I think when she goes we'll just have to learn to do things in a completely different way. Simple as that." We talked of her lack of bitterness, the goodness that blazed through the matter-of-factness. No, that was not the substance. There was something far more telling about Anne. "I know what it is, and, if I may be vain for a moment, I'll also lay claim to that same quality." Dr. Wood leaned across the desk. "It's almost too simple to explain. We just do the job. Others must evaluate, consider, weigh, before action. I call it paralysis by analysis. Modern people, it seems to me, are desperately analytical because they have no faith in what they are doing. It's easy, therefore, to talk yourself out of an act of courage. That, of course, is not Anne. She thinks by jumping in."

Tonight on the windy veranda at Lake Turkana, listening to the piping of bats during Anne's silence, I study her carefully. She is dressed in a colorful caftan in sharp contrast to the functional work clothes she wore during the day. But she herself remains functional. She arranges the orders for drinks, offers advice about the menu and delicately leads the conversation into areas she thinks I should understand. Whenever I prod her about her history, she dashes through the details, as though she is repeating her story for the fourth time. Why did she ever come to Africa, I persist?

"Why?" she responds, thinking my question the height of foolishness. "I've always wanted to, as long as I can remember." She casually notes that the books of Henri de Monfreid, the twentieth-century French buccaneer-adventurer, gave her the bug when she was young. Once she had qualified as a doctor, after the war, she rushed to Aden, where her brother, married to the daughter of an Adenese merchant, was then living. This British colony was, after all, halfway to Africa, and right at the center of de Monfreid country. In the spirit of his first book, *Les Secrets de la Mer Rouge,* she signed on as ship's doctor on a dhow carrying pilgrims to Jidda, the port of Mecca. A woman doctor was in great demand, not only because she was considered safe to examine an Arab's wives but also because the presence of a doctor on a pilgrim ship raised the legal capacity of these eighty-foot vessels from ten to eighty passengers. For a year Anne plied the Red Sea in this unorthodox service until she landed a trip to Ethiopia. Here the opportunities for a doctor seemed even more endless—a mere twenty-nine physicians were treating a population of thirty million. Soon, however, Anne had to bow to the realities: the feudal government did not believe another doctor was necessary. Most of the existing doctors, in fact, had not been paid for the last six months. Ethiopia was still in the Middle Ages. Unruffled, Anne flew south to Kenya on a two-week holiday. Here, at last, was the soul of de Monfreid country. The year was 1950 and Anne decided to settle.

She must be a romantic. "So what is it about Africa?" I ask to confirm.

She shakes her hands in the air. "It has something very gripping," she says at last, struggling even for these words. "Look down there," she says, changing the subject. The wind has suddenly stopped, although the low palms separating the guest cabins, called bandas, rustle and rasp like impatient ghosts. "Banda number six. There it is." Anne points into the inky darkness. "About Christmastime in 1963, I flew in here with Keith Mouseley, and there were Guy Poole, the lodge manager, Father Stallone, the missionary, and an Italian lorry driver—all dead. Pumped with bullets. Murdered by bandits." Anne is not telling this story for effect. She just happened to remember it. "We put the bodies in bags, and that was that." (Here she slaps her hands.) "Banda number six. I've stayed there since, after it was repainted and the bullet holes in the walls filled in. And there aren't any ghosts. My honor."

Little by little as our desert thirst is quenched, I piece together Anne's African story. For the first fourteen years of her stay she worked as a country doctor, employed by the Colonial government. In 1959, when she bought the thousand-acre mixed farm where she had lived as a tenant, overnight she added a new avocation to her life. "I saw my neighboring farmers doctoring people pretty well," she explains. "If they could doctor people without experience, I could certainly farm without experience." Anne's medical health office was eighty miles away and when she returned each evening, tired and aggravated, she would relax with her newly acquired farm problems.

After independence, she sold the big farm and bought another one—twenty-five well-watered acres—where she still lives today. This balance between land and people seems to be the combination she had always sought. In both, she can take pleasure in watching growth. In the French tradition, she keeps a small flock of geese. Otherwise, it has a British look: a Frisian and Guernsey dairy herd, a flock of sheep, a few patches of alfalfa and a small field of coffee. Anne looks on the farm as her retreat. Here she spends almost every weekend of the year, marveling at the harvests, listening out for an occasional eagle owl and in the evening making inroads into the jungle of travel books that grows in rude stacks, precariously perched on the side tables by her fireplace.

In 1963 Anne learned to fly "just for fun—to get my mind off the aggravations of working for the government." One year later she met Michael Wood and, to her surprise, he invited her to join the Flying Doctors. "I haven't regretted a thing," she says, recalling in one instant the intervening seventeen years. She suspects I want to hear about the near-misses—the time, for instance, she was caught in a whirlwind while landing at Labakat and came down so hard on the ground that she lost a wheel, or the other landing when she became mired in mud and had to wait a day for the isolated airstrip to dry before taking off. What about the pleasures, I ask her. She looks out beyond Banda number 6, trying to determine where to begin. "The pleasures," she says softly to herself. She makes up her mind in a flash. "The time I flew a pregnant woman to Nairobi Hospital, and one month later brought her back to her village with triplets. We sat them in the backseat of the plane, one dressed in blue, the other in pink, another in yellow." Anne's eyes crinkle in a smile, recalling the sight.

"Isn't birth control of concern to you?"

The smile dissolves. She returns her after-dinner coffee cup smartly to its saucer. "Handing out birth-control information doesn't do any good at all. And anyway, that's not my job. The bulk of Kenya will never be affected by such prodding. They'll have as many babies as they can." Anne's face is now beginning to soften a little. "Listen: I'm both a doctor and a farmer, and I've kept my eyes open. Personally, I believe we need better farmers more than we need less reproduction. When I see the forests being burned to make way for unproductive farms, when I see ranches being carved up to be made into one-acre plots that will support no one, when I see the Tana River flowing chocolate brown because farmers don't know how to stop erosion—that's when I really want to weep. The lifeblood of this country is in the earth and right now it's all flowing into the sea."

I have only one day left with Anne before she returns to Nairobi. This morning shortly after dawn, when I arrive at the mission clinic, she has already begun her examinations. Calling their names out on the windy porch, the hunchbacked Italian sister describes each patient's complaints. Anne diagnoses one as a corneal ulcer, another with suspected tuberculosis and a third who complains of "a bad tooth and a bad chest," who Anne dismisses immediately as frivolous. A pregnant woman says that her baby "is playing in my stomach." Medication is handed out to a man with amoebic colitis. As Anne leaves she solves the problem of an epidemic of intestinal problems by examining the well that supports both the El Molo village and the fishing lodge. "It's very simple," she says. "Everybody drinks from the same source, including camels and donkeys. Last time I was here there was a crocodile and her young in the pool. Either the pool will have to be cleaned out and a fence erected or everyone will have to start boiling their water."

"It's very simple," she had said. And so it is, but in Africa there are many simple truths which are never perceived, and solutions too simple for anyone to care. As Anne pilots her green-and-white Five Yankee Alfa Zulu Tango eastward, I begin to realize that she is effective because she has no grand design on anything. She knows what she can do best and, as Michael Wood confirmed, she does not dream. "It is simple," she might say. "Simple"—only because she refuses to embarrass "it" with complexities. No wonder she had been aggravated with life as a government bureaucrat.

Our last stop is at another diocesan mission called Maikona. It lies on the edge of a great sand dune, and all around are the remnants of last year's Gabbra encampments, called manyattas—circles on the ground that from the air resemble the scars of ringworm. Father Pelerino and Father Tablino, pale and thin veterans of Africa, glow when they see Anne, and once we are inside the examining room, they lead the procession of the sick. I, too, am becoming inured to the hurt and the ugliness. "Out. Out," Anne barks at the clamor. "I can only see one patient at a time." She pushes a towering warrior, closing the door on his back. "Now," she says, fixing her eyes on little Kabala. "What is the matter?"

Little Kabala is my undoing and, in a way, this tiny eight-year-old was to expose the real battle that Anne fights daily in Africa. With copper-colored skin, shimmering hair and a thin straight nose, she exemplifies all that is so beautiful in these desert people. "What a bonny little thing," Anne says. When the girl stands still she is as graceful as a ballerina. But when she moves she is a hideous cripple, balancing herself on only a small portion of her right foot, her torso twisted, her upper body flailing at the movement of her legs. Her mother, so weathered she could pass for a great-grandmother, seems immune to the sight of the contorted body even when Kabala removes her dress. Naked now, the girl tries a slow pirouette in front of Anne. One leg is at least three inches shorter than the other. The girl is placed on the examining table, and when told to straighten the exaggerated arch in her back, her eyes glisten with tears. She tries to follow instructions but it is no use. "Her hip is anchored in an awful position," Anne says finally. I suspect Anne already knows what her diagnosis must be, but she hesitates, buying time. Reluctantly she points to an open sore on one of her legs. "That's it," she says. "Osteomyelitis."

Later I was to learn that this disease is generally introduced by an exterior infection. It invades the bone and spreads, and in this case, it had cannibalized both the hips and even part of the spine. The crippling was sure to worsen. Ultimately it could kill Kabala. "Fancy surviving," Anne says, as charmed as I am by the little sprite who can switch from tears to a smile in less than a second.

There is only one course open for the girl, Anne decides. She must be X-rayed immediately in the Marsabit hospital, a hundred miles away. Then she must travel to Sololo where there is an excellent orthopedic surgeon. The operation will be in two stages: the first, to remove the infected bone, the second, to replace the missing bone with metal alloys. "She can also go to school in Sololo, and she will not be very far from home," Anne reasons. "Someday she might be almost normal."

Through an interpreter, the plan is submitted to the child's mother. Her only cost for the subsidized hospital care will be about two dollars. "I'll fly them both to Marsabit this afternoon," Anne adds, patting her hands, pleased that the solution is so obvious.

Only Anne and I, however, have found the solution simple. The child's mother is against airplane travel, Marsabit is too far, and anyway the child's father has not been consulted. When the interpreter mentions Sololo, the mother shakes her head with finality. She refuses to have her daughter operated on there or go to school there. "Why?" Anne asks. Because, the mother enunciates, Sololo is inhabited by the Boran, and the Gabbra have always despised them. There is no way she will allow her daughter any association, even for a few weeks, with the enemy. Kabala will not have the operation.

By now Anne is replacing her notebook and pen, preparing to see another patient. I cannot believe she will not intervene, for I know how fiercely she believes in the operation. Her expression is steel. "Ask me first," she says, anticipating my question, "why she wasn't brought in a year ago before her condition became chronic. Ask me why her parents didn't care enough until now, and then I'll tell you why I can't argue with the mother about going to Sololo."

"I know," I said, hating the words. "Because this is Africa."

"Right. Let's go."

Below the wing of the airplane, the scrubland is grayer than I can ever remember. Occasionally our shadow crosses a fluted strip of green, bordering a dry sand river. Only the lumbering shapes of camels give away the presence of man. Hard to believe, I think, anyone can survive here. Anne is smiling at the end of her four-day safari. I know, however, the smile has nothing to do with satisfaction. Last night she told me of the two happiest moments of her life. One was the day when she heard the bells ringing through France to celebrate the end of the war. The other was when an old woman stopped her on a footpath at the Kenya coast. The woman presented her with a basket of eggs. "Why?" asked Anne.

"Because you helped my daughter," the old woman explained. Anne recalled that a few months before she had flown a young girl, in the last hours of pregnancy, down to the hospital in Mombasa. The girl had lockjaw and ultimately both the girl and the baby had died. That girl must have been this woman's daughter. So why did the woman want to give Anne a gift?

The old villager pushed the basket into Anne's hands. "Because you tried."

I am beginning to suspect there are qualities no doctor should be without, qualities never taught in a medical school. They are acquired from an intimacy with "the seamy side of life," with suffering. And having been learned, they should be forgotten, buried in those regions of the heart and brain that trigger instinct, not memories.

The gray parchment land below has become a backdrop to that mysterious smile of Anne's. This morning at the Loyengalani mission, I recall, a woman pushed her way into the room, just before we left. Her teeth had been sharpened to points, and one of her breasts protruded from her cloak—a sure sign that only minutes before she had been nursing the child now perched on her back and fast asleep. She was a beggar like so many oth-

ers. The only difference was she had a child. I was sure Anne would throw her out. But on this occasion she listened. The mother said, "My child is sick."

"What kind of sickness?" asked Anne.

"He suffers from *njaa*—from hunger."

Anne looked carefully at the sleeping youngster, dressed only in an ostrich shell necklace. He looked to me as healthy as any El Molo child we had seen. "There is only one medicine for this disease of *njaa*," she explained to the mother. "And I happen to have it here." Anne reached into her wallet and presented the mother with two shillings.

Perhaps I am making more of this incident than is necessary, but it was the first time in my life I had ever seen a doctor pay a patient.

Recently a wildlife journal ran a short notice, rejoicing that the elephant population in Uganda's Ruwenzori National Park had risen to two hundred. For those who knew this lovely sanctuary of savannahs, rivers and a lake when it was called Queen Elizabeth National Park, this piece of news was hardly cause for celebration. Then it supported over three thousand elephants. Now not only have more than 90 percent of the elephants been slaughtered but all the rhinos are gone, the plains game heavily poached, the lodge looted, the roads mined and the whole structure of game protection, more or less, ransacked.

WARRIOR FOR
WILDLIFE

Admittedly rhinos and elephants all over Africa have been threatened by the sudden quintupling of the value of their horns and tusks. But in Uganda there was a particularly tragic side to the extermination of the game. Prior to Idi Amin's term in office, the Uganda National Parks were the most progesssive of all those in East Africa, having been the first to adopt Africanization programs, even before independence from the British. Uganda was also the first black nation to embark on game control programs, leading the way for other African nations to preserve their wildlife habitats by scientific culling. The result was a series of parks long considered the absolute jewels of East Africa. One writer in 1964 aptly described them as "the enormous zoo." He had seen elephants ferreting through dustbins at a lodge. Hippos were such a glut in one river that they had become serious hazards to navigation, and a program to reintroduce white rhinos to the west bank of the Nile had been, at that moment in history, an unparalleled success.

One wonders today if Idi Amin, now reduced to being the dictator of the two top floors of the Intercontinental Hotel in Riyadh, Saudi Arabia, ever stands on his balcony in a contemplative mood and considers the extent of the power he once wielded. Apart from having condoned the assassination of as many as 300,000 human beings, he can now lay claim to the slaughter of a million animals and to the virtual suspension of all tourism, once one of Uganda's most vital sources of foreign exchange. Anyone today worried about the earth's dwindling natural resources usually finds relief in the knowledge that the process is a slow one. But in Uganda it happened in less than seven years. Henry David Thoreau wrote that he "could kill time without injuring eternity." Idi Amin, it seems, tried to do both.

During those lawless days while I was in neighboring Kenya I occasionally heard from conservationists about a Ugandan Robin Hood of the animals. His name was Paul Ssali and he was the black warden of a remote park in the north of Uganda. While the looting was mounting in all of Uganda's other parks, poaching at Ssali's was almost negligible in comparison. His rangers were said to be the best trained in the whole of Uganda. With few supplies, obsolete equipment, infrequent pay, Paul Ssali and his men were able to fight off poachers as well as rebels from the neighboring Sudan, Idi Amin's reckless army and even, it was said, Idi Amin himself. Ssali ran his park like his own private fiefdom. He was, it seemed, a kind of lonely heretic in a state gone insane. He believed in strict discipline. He, a father of eight children, somehow refused to touch a penny of the easy money floating through the hands of the other bureaucrats. Even more peculiar, he was ready to die for wildlife. He valued animals' lives, so it seemed, above those of his own species—a common enough pose for an effete Westerner but a nearly unheard-of philosophy for a struggling African.

My conservationist friends in Nairobi tried to guess at his

motivation. The then head of the African Wildlife Leadership Foundation explained it in terms of a documentary film that had once been made about Ssali. The film had been released in America, played to a small audience and folded. In his isolation, some said, Ssali came to believe it was a box-office triumph. He was sure the world now knew of his lonely struggle. Although this theory seemed almost comically romantic, I confess I began to see Ssali as a kind of Conrad character—a black Kurtz living out his demonic destiny. Infrequently Ssali came to Nairobi to have his single-engine aircraft serviced. To my regret I always missed him. He was said to sleep in the uncomfortable rear seat of his plane at Wilson Airfield instead of at a hotel, and to eat cornmeal gruel with the airport mechanics rather than pay restaurant prices. He thereby saved enough money to buy eggs, bacon and Heinz's Ketchup to stock the lodge at his game reserve for the foreign visitors he was sure would arrive to view the game he had successfully preserved. Very few tourists, however, dared that journey during those tempestuous times.

In 1978 I heard that Ssali had been assigned to look after another game reserve as well and that within a year, threatened with assassination, he fled the parks and Uganda. While he was in exile, Uganda was invaded by Tanzanian troops, Amin's government collapsed and all attempts to restore peace to the country met with considerable resistance. Although Paul Ssali hurried back to this chaos, he was denied his old command. Today he was said to be merely a pilot for the National Park directors—a kind of overqualified chauffeur.

I now wanted to meet him more than ever. I wanted most of all to have him show me the Kidepo National Park, the scene of his great triumph. Perhaps there I might understand the dangers of preserving wildlife in a war zone and why Ssali had come to believe those animals were more important than his own life.

Paul Ssali meets me at the door of my East African Airways Fokker Friendship, just landed at Entebbe's International Airport. He is tall and built like a prizefighter one year out of training. His shirt is festooned with pictures of elephants. "I am Paul," he says, leaving off the surname as a child might. His handsome face is impassive, not a smile, not a scowl. As we breeze through customs he reserves a slight contempt for the officials, but otherwise he reveals no opinions. For the first twenty minutes he says not one word. He performs the preflight check on his Cessna 182, named Alpha Yankee Popeye, taxis past the wreck of a jet fighter to the end of the runway and then guns the engine. Even when we are airborne, and the sudden turbulence of the high-noon heat slaps and buckets us over Lake Victoria, he still chooses to watch me out of the corner of one eye.

Only the sight of his home, a modest mud-walled hut on the messy outskirts of Kampala, turns Paul Ssali to words. "Over there," he says, "just behind the bananas, is guerrilla country. We hear the gunfire every night." He is matter-of-fact.

"Do you worry about your wife and children when you are away for a few days?" I ask.

Paul shrugs his shoulders and says nothing.

A few minutes later Paul points to Lake Kyoga. "The hippos down there," he says each word with precision. "All butched." He lights his second cigarette of the flight and tells me that he once gave up smoking, but when he realized how close he "always lay to death" he decided that it little mattered. He is talking now with hardly a pause between words, as if he had been without company for several days, and this talk runs mostly to violence. He sings out the names of guns like old melodies—the Sudanese rebels' Russian AK-47s, the poachers' jerry-rigged Martini-Henrys, the park rangers' British Enfields. The national parks where he has served resound like Hastings, Armageddon and Waterloo.

The trip takes two hours. We cross the land of the Kara-mojong—tall naked herdsmen who were very nearly eliminated by a combination of drought and Idi Amin during the 1970s. Those few who survived have now become sedentary farmers and have started wearing clothes. We can see their amateurish attempts at growing corn in the shadows of great rocks. "The Nangeya Mountains," Paul intones as we make our descent. "And that is Lobalaneadi beyond, with Mount Lonyiri the highest." He recites these names with pleasure as though he were recalling his own children. "I have walked every single one of them with my rangers." His eyes scour the old land, haunted by dry sand rivers and now darkened by an electrical storm out of the Sudan. Two bolts of lightning strike almost simultaneously on the swath of clear-cut bush that is the border between Uganda and the Sudan. But Paul has noticed something else—small patches of cleared ground—and his face reverts to a scowl. "Already," he says, "I can see encroachment in my park."

Kidepo Valley National Park covers a mere five hundred square miles of land—small by the standards of most national parks in East Africa and the Sudan. A lush bowl in otherwise undistinguished bushland, it was declared a national park in 1962, in part to protect the game that was fleeing from the violent civil war in the neighboring Sudan. Elephants, in particular, are quick to recognize a *cordon sanitaire* free of rifle fire and they began to adjust time-trodden trails to the quirkiness of rebels. The other game—Jackson's hartebeest, greater and lesser kudu, rhino, ostrich, Bright's gazelle, giraffe and Grévy's zebra—proliferated beyond the lions and leopards, their natural predators. By the mid-1960s Kidepo had become an ark. It was also on its way to being a generous provider for the poachers, poised on its borders.

As a refuge, Kidepo was at first treated as a stepchild by the national parks system. Their crown jewels were in the west of the country—Murchison Falls (Kabalega Falls) and Queen Elizabeth (Ruwenzori) national parks. These were the parks tourists most wanted to see; hence the most senior members of the staff were posted there. Junior wardens tended to be sent to Kidepo "for a go" in preparation for more distinguished service elsewhere. Young Peter Pegg was sent to Kidepo in 1963, equipped with an old Land Rover, a radio and expertise in horse breeding. He did not even know Swahili, the lingua franca of East Africa. For three years he pleaded to his director for the use of an aircraft, claiming that the park was unmanageable without one. Finally, in 1966 he resigned to be replaced by Iain Ross, a Uganda-born farmer taxidermist. In a bureaucratic about-face, Ross was immediately supplied with an aircraft.

Iain Ross was partial to all things military. He had been a member of the cadet corps at the Duke of York School outside Nairobi and had served in the King's African Rifles in Northern Kenya. Shortly before he arrived at Kidepo, his all-consuming love for wilderness and game had found a champion in David Sheldrick, the warden of Kenya's largest national park and a military man. Strict discipline, long foot patrols and constant consultation of *The British Army Training Manual* were at the core of

Sheldrick's thinking. No sooner had Ross arrived at Kidepo than he translated these martial skills to the needs of this park. He dismantled all the ranger outposts established by his predecessors. In their place he created mobile foot patrols, operating out of one park headquarters. The beauty of such a field force was that its movements could never be accurately predicted by poachers. In permanent outposts, rangers had been sitting ducks. Now their routes were always different, their encampments movable. Of the six sections Ross created, no less than four were ever on patrol at any one time, while one was on night quarter-guard duty and the other on standby.

To deal with poachers, Sudanese soldiers and the increasing presence of Amin's militia, a warden had to be a general, a spy and a diplomat. Of all these there is no doubt that Ross was foremost a good military commander. He had the respect of his men, the fear of the enemy. He was inflexible with orders, unsentimental about human misery and decent in the finest traditions of the British imperialist. He evokes a memory of T. E. Lawrence: He enjoyed the pain of solitude and the company of a foreign race. When he left the park in 1973 he candidly admitted, "I think what I will miss most is the absolute sense of command."

I can sense Ross's ghost as we taxi toward the paint-flecked hangar where his airplane once resided. Over the door is his sign, rank with mock bluster, reading: KIDEPO VALLEY AIRWING. His house nearby has not survived so well. Where once bougainvillea and vegetables grew there is now bare earth. Chickens walk in and out of the kitchen, and the swimming pool is filled with dried acacia blossoms.

The lodge, a half-mile away, seems prepared for a great crowd. The bedrooms, each one a neatly scrubbed hut, are all stocked with clean linen. Paul and I are, however, the lodge's only guests, and I—so I am told—the first foreign tourist to visit the park in memory. In the lounge there is a corner bar and behind it, standing erect, a bartender. He wears a prewar Uganda Hotels uniform, and his inventory on the shelves behind him consists of a mere third bottle of Scotch and a quarter bottle of gin—all that is left of foreign spirits in northern Uganda.

The late-afternoon storm that heralded our arrival has turned south. We carry chairs and large bottles of unlabeled beer onto the veranda. The rocky outcrops that were once beneath us when we flew now tower over the distance, casting shadows across a giant washboard plain. The shape of the veranda mimics the bow of those hills—an arc in flagstone here, a half-moon of Mesozoic bedrock there. The air has turned fresh with evening, and when the wind blows, it brings with it a sweet smell of elephants. I can see them under the trees, black and glistening. They rumble and boom, moving west with the evening.

"It is here where Amin said, 'Bring me the gun,' " Paul announces.

"Start from the beginning," I insist.

Paul pauses for only a second. "I was dropped," he says, "at Namirembe Hospital fifteenth October, 1942, at seven-oh-three in the morning . . ."

I must confess I am still puzzled by Paul. I cannot see what led him to risk his life for animals. Conservation is, after all, a white man's sport. It is our sense of aesthetics that decrees some animals are to be looked at from Land Rovers and not to be eaten. But for an African to consider the hideousness of a world without animals is not even of academic interest. Neither he nor his ancestors have ever had the leisure or the conscience to consider anything beyond their own survival.

Admittedly, Paul, a member of Uganda's black middle class, was instilled with the virtues of achievement from an early age. His father was the first black medical assistant in Uganda, born to a Baganda family that was fairly well connected with their tribal king—the Kabaka. During World War II the elder Ssali served as a sergeant-major with the King's African Rifles in Kenya and Tunisia, bringing considerable distinction to the family, in a world which valued feats of arms.

Like many other African fathers, the elder Ssali spent every penny earned toward his children's education. Paul, however, was only an average student, interested mostly in things that roared and crawled outside the classroom. The Uganda Boys' Club opened his eyes to wildlife, on outings to national parks. He determined in his teens that he wanted to be a warden, but shortly after his sixteenth birthday his father was no longer able to afford Paul's school fees. As a result, Paul would never be qualified.

Paul believes he always wanted to help animals. He can remember as a teen-ager scouting with members of his tribe beyond the suburbs of Kampala: "The way they hunted was not proper. I used to take meat home but I never ate it because I was feeling sympathetic to the animal."

He worked at first for Pepsi-Cola's advertising department, gaining recognition throughout Uganda as a world-class goalie on its soccer team. After two years he joined the pathology department at Makerere University to help a professor hunt elephants for his study of the rate of fat accumulation around their hearts. A year later he joined the Uganda Wildlife Development Corporation as a trainee "white hunter," soon becoming Uganda's first black to rank as a full professional. But clients, particularly Americans, were wary about spending $10,000 on a hunt only to be led by "a native." Wasn't half the fun of such a vacation to be with a knee-socked ex-Colonial who could knock back gin slings around the campfire in the evening and regale his companions with tales of the "good old days"? Moreover, Paul's colleagues, the true white "white hunters," treated him with mild contempt. One, a South African by birth, flew into a rage one night when Paul had the "cheekiness" to tell him in front of clients how to bait for leopards. The South African took a swing at Paul. Paul reciprocated, and on the following morning Paul was asked to resign.

Paul next found work in the service of his king, the Kabaka, developing tourism and hunting in Buganda Province. On May 24, 1966, Prime Minister Milton Obote, fearing the king's popular appeal, had troops torch the palace and force the monarch into exile. When the battle was over, yet another of Paul's jobs had come to an end. Ironically, the leader Obote had chosen for this military operation was a loyal army captain by the name of Idi Amin. Five years later, Amin (by then promoted to major general) would assemble a handful of storm troopers and topple the government while his patron, the prime minister, was away at a conference in Singapore.

During those Obote five years, Paul served as a district vermin-control officer until finally, just as he hoped, his varied career dazzled the board of trustees of the Uganda National Parks.

At the end of 1971 he was at last hired—assigned to Kabalega Falls National Park as a junior warden.

In early 1972, Iain Ross, after six years as warden of Kidepo Valley National Park, realized that there was little future for expatriates in Uganda. Idi Amin had by now been in power for a year and, as Ross said, "the writing was on the wall." He tendered his resignation, promising to train a replacement for his job. As soon as Alfred Labongo was chosen as his successor, soldiers arrested this senior black warden on Amin's orders, for alleged connections with anti-Amin guerrillas. Labongo, who was at Kabalega Falls, was driven to the Nile to be shot. Seconds before his execution, he bounded from the car, dashed into reeds and escaped to Tanzania, where he remained during Amin's reign.

Paul Ssali was clearly not as qualified as Labongo, but he was the best the National Parks could offer Iain Ross at the time.

In the morning at breakfast on the veranda Paul enumerates the day's activities—the armory, the fort, the museum, the hospital. After a game drive, we shall fly in Popeye right up to the Sudanese border, and if there is a minute of daylight left, we shall visit the graveyard of rangers "who gave their lives to poachers' bullets."

The elephants have now gone, leaving only peeled bark to mark their trail. Helmeted guinea fowl peck in the grass near my sandals, and beyond them, waterbuck, indifferent to the clatter of my fork, stand motionless waiting to be dried by the sun.

In New York I had gone to the apartment of Eugene and Natalie Jones, the producers of a feature documentary film that had marked the transition from a white game warden to a black at Kidepo. It was released in 1974 alternately under the names *Two Men of Karamoja* and *The Wild and the Brave*. Before Gene began the screening he explained that he and his wife had been with Paul at Kidepo for nearly seven months. "He was just a little boy when I first met him—pouting, arrogant, willful and thoroughly impossible to work with." In fact, after a month Paul refused to be filmed anymore. "He felt he was being humiliated in front of his men." Jones reacted by threatening to intercede with Amin for Paul's cooperation. "It was a ruse, of course," explained Jones. "I was just as terrified of Amin as anyone." In the end Paul crumbled. The result, documented by the film, is extraordinarily candid. In one of its early moments, as Iain Ross, the white warden, and Paul Ssali, his black successor, walk, they engage in the following dialogue:

PAUL (abrasively): You should give me an opportunity to see how I work.

IAIN: Paul, it's my job to lecture you. I am supposed to be preparing you for the takeover.

PAUL (the veins on his neck now protruding): That is obvious, but if you keep lecturing me all the time it is useless. I expect that the director who sent me here had full knowledge of my abilities to do the work.

IAIN: Relax, Paul, you're getting your knickers in a knot again.

PAUL: Don't tell me to relax. I think you are talking bullshit and I don't want you to tell me about my knickers and all this blah blah blah. I know how Africans act. I am an African and I know more than you do.

IAIN: Paul, don't use that as a crutch to lean on all the time.

PAUL: Don't tell me how to deal with Africans.

IAIN: I was born out here, remember. I reckon I know African people pretty well too. So let's just stop right here.

PAUL: You are talking like a tape recorder.

IAIN (stopping in his tracks to face Paul): I must be old-fashioned. I know what I say goes against all the ideas of today—"doing your thing"—I think that that is wrong. I still believe very strongly in discipline and service. Many of the staff don't think I have any emotions. I firmly believe that if you want to be a good leader you can't allow your emotions to come into it.

PAUL: That's just what I said: there is a big difference between *you people* and *we people*.

Eugene Jones interrupted the film to say, "Half the time Paul thought he was another Sidney Poitier. And at the beginning he was certainly not up to performing Iain Ross's job."

On November 15, 1974, Iain Ross handed over the command of his park to Paul Ssali. In public school tradition, Ross

244

seems determined to remain stiff-lipped, as documented by the film. Yet, for a moment on the parade ground, his voice cracks: "This is my last ranger parade. We have had to build a park under the most difficult circumstances probably of any park in East Africa. We have had to build a park in the face of Turkana cattle raiders from Kenya, in the face of a civil war in the Sudan. We have had to fight Anya Nya rebels. Behind you on the parade ground are the graves of rangers who have been killed. I am the last of the British wardens to serve in Uganda. I was born and bred in Uganda, and although by law I am not a Ugandan, my heart is Ugandan. For me, all I can say is thank you . . . for the very hard work you have all done for me."

Iain's eyes blink, the sergeant major barks to his men to present arms and then, without a warning, the women spectators—nearly fifty ranger wives—begin to ululate. Nowhere but in Africa can a sound have such an effect. It is a lament heard at great funerals, a cry of victory when a conqueror marches into a capital. It is almost a birdsong, and when I asked Iain, whom I met in London years after the event, how he felt when he heard those women sing, he confessed, "I was almost caught. I very nearly burst into tears."

Rubbing a hand across his tussocky blond hair, Iain also remembered his departure from Kidepo the next morning: "I decided I would leave very early, at first light, before anybody else was about. I didn't want to say good-bye. So I was in my plane at the end of the grass strip just as the sun came up. As I gunned my engine, I looked down the runway. There, on either side, was every single man who had ever worked for me. Their hats were across their hearts. I don't believe they uttered a sound. They just stood there in silence."

Eugene Jones had more to add to Iain Ross's departure. "You know," he recalled, "there are some things that you as a film maker must never film. Moments before Iain boarded his plane, Paul rushed up to him, threw his arms around him and burst into tears. I just couldn't film it. It was much too private. So I just let it go—that big strong black man weeping his heart out on the white man's shoulder."

The fort where arms and ammunition are stored is high-walled and seemingly impregnable. As Paul and I walk through the great door into the courtyard, I see thirty men awaiting us, standing at attention. While Paul has not been their commander for two years, the sight of him makes them ramrod straight. Their heels click, they present arms and not one man coughs as the heavy dust rises to their throats. Paul reviews them, and after a few commands they retreat to an inner room and return bearing booty: wire snares, spears, bows and arrows, a half-dozen AK-47s and several tons of elephant remains. Clearly, the war against Kidepo has accelerated now that Paul Ssali is no longer its warden.

Even after nine years Iain Ross told me how delighted he still was with the selection of Paul Ssali as successor. "Paul," he said, "has a great attribute as a leader: He is arrogant. He *knows* he will do well. He is bright and quick—not brilliant, mind you, and not very well educated. But all this worked to his advantage. Most of all he is arrogant. I would say that Paul did a remarkable job under the circumstances and I'd say that his circumstances were far worse than mine. He was much likelier to get a bullet in his back than I was."

Today in Kidepo Paul wants me to know the dimensions of the job he had taken up, during that long-ago November. "When Iain left," Paul recalls, "there was a lot of weeping, not just because he was going but because people in the park did not feel I could maintain standards. They were weeping for themselves." Paul tried to outperform his predecessor. He bought a set of toy soldiers—crimson-uniformed Hessians and bandoliered Welsh Guardsmen—to illustrate to his men ambush procedures, extended file, single and arrow formation. Discipline became fierce. Accepted rules of behavior now were written down as laws. The files at Kidepo reveal a contagion of standing orders issued under Paul's wardenship. His SO/G/44, for instance, commands that "all pregnant women must attend the clinic. Failure to do so will result in such husband being fully responsible for transport and life of his wife." And, SO/R/56 admonishes: "Every ranger will report once a week to the dispensary and take two tablets of chloroquine as a prevention against malaria. . . . Any ranger who falls sick [from malaria] during the patrol will be regarded as disobedient."

"You see, as an African, Paul will always have a problem," Dr. Rob Malpas, the World Wildlife Fund representative in Uganda, had said to me. "While he comes from an unusual and very sophisticated tribe and while he has acquired certain characteristics that make him very good at commanding people, a European is, in principle, better qualified to operate a park. A European can say, 'Go and run five miles and then stand on your hands for an hour.' The order would be carried out to the letter and there'd be no bitterness later on. But Paul is an African. One tribe resents another, one man begrudges the authority of another, and no matter what Paul did, his motives would always be suspect. That's why when Paul was at Kidepo he was forever fighting an uphill battle and that's why his achievement there is so remarkable."

Paul was now all alone, experiencing for the first time the responsibility of supreme command. During all his time at Kidepo, his director visited only once. Radio communications with the head office were spotty. Mails were brought to the park by a "runner" who covered the sixty miles from the nearest post office, often through herds of elephants, prides of lions, on a bicycle. The payroll was regularly many months late.

Paul Ssali emerged with a flair for diplomacy. North of the park, on the international frontier, a battalion of Sudanese was stationed. With little food available in their own country, the soldiers were forever crossing into Kidepo to hunt. Stopping them by force would only lead to a political incident. Instead, Paul learned the commander's name and one evening he drove over the border with two bottles of beer. "It really worked," claimed Rob Malpas.

But diplomacy could not stop the Sudanese rebels, the Anya Nyas. The civil war was over, but there were many still at large. On one occasion Paul received a nearly illegible note reading: "Go from the Park if you want to be A Life, [Signed] Ida Olama Okooi." A week later, driving alone on a track in a remote area of the park, Paul's Land Rover high-centered on a log. He was stuck. As he tried to jerk it off, Anya Nya rebels, armed with AK-47s and spears, appeared out of the bush. Ssali had forgotten his rifle. He picked up the long starter handle from under his seat, pressed it to his shoulder and took aim at the commander of the rebels. They turned and ran.

Ever since the day in 1971 Idi Amin had dissolved Parliament and assumed all legislative and executive powers, he doomed his countrymen's lives to violence. In August 1972 Amin ordered the eviction of up to eighty thousand Asians living in Uganda. While their abandoned belongings were distributed among Amin's friends and followers, not even these, his trusted cronies, were safe. His ex-wife, Kay Adroa, was murdered and dismembered. One of his foreign ministers, Michael Ondoga, was found floating in the Nile. An autopsy revealed that Ondoga's liver had been removed—an operation, many Ugandans believe, that Amin personally performed, in order to eat the organ of his enemy. Virtually every civilian who became minister under Amin either fled the country or was murdered. Even the Anglican archbishop turned up dead. Whole tribes were halved in size by zealous killers in Amin's hit squad or at the hands of the State Research Bureau, a terror group composed mainly of Amin's fellow Nubian tribesmen. The standard charge made against every victim was: "Treason and spying for imperialists." In the seven years of Amin's rule it is estimated that between 100,000 and 300,000 Ugandans were thus condemned to death and murdered. One observer called it "the institutionalized brutality of a state gone insane."

For a national park warden during this period, there were no guarantees of personal security. Yet Iain Ross was not particularly alarmed by Amin on the two occasions they met. "He was," Ross recalls, "totally uneducated, not very clever, full of animal cunning, very big in stature and incredibly charming. You really could warm to him. He was very likable."

We have left the fort now and are driving in a Land Rover past the parade grounds where Iain Ross delivered his farewell address eight years ago. Today a group of new recruits is being drilled. "Too old," Paul observes. "They would never have made my grade."

Nearby Paul points out the assault course he built. It was the nub of his ranger military training program. The obstacles used to be thorns, pools of water, parallel bars. Now the bars are broken, the water has evaporated and the thorns have turned to compost. "The ruins," Paul says. And then, just in case I did not hear, he repeats himself: "The ruins."

The park garage houses eight Land Rovers. Paul excitedly indicates each one, ending with, "That's the one that was given to me by a Swedish tourist. You see," he explains, "the cook at the lodge was sick one day so I prepared breakfast for this tourist. He had never known a national park where the chief park warden is also cook so he offered to give the park anything we needed. I needed another Land Rover, and he wrote out a check on the spot."

Now none of the eight Land Rovers possesses a complete set of tires. The vehicles are perched on rocks, their hoods open, a carburetor missing here, a whole engine block removed there.

Only one Land Rover in the whole of Kidepo still operates. It is the one we drive.

Even when Paul is at the wheel, his flashing arms articulate words: "During Amin's time any warden could be a target anytime. It depends on how you dodge. Unless I was very careful, all my animals would be finished. There were majors, colonels, state research personnel—all of them involved in poaching. You had to make sure that if your rangers killed one or two of them in the bush, not a word of it should be said. If you were not quiet your whole ranger force would be wiped out.

"What people outside of Uganda didn't realize is that we were fighting Amin. Many wardens were arrested and taken to Makindi Prison simply because a poacher reported that they had been antigovernment. Full stop. Or that [a warden] was *planning* to escape to Tanzania. Full stop. Or that he was a follower of the Kabaka. Full stop. Just one suspicious word like that and a warden was finished. How many times did we say that if worse came to worst and Amin's men attacked us we would fight to the death?"

Paul explains that his first run-in with Amin was over a lost aircraft. One year after Paul had taken over the park, the Office of the President called on the radiotelephone asking whether a plane carrying several whites had landed. "Negative," replied Paul. The whites, Paul found out, were prominent Kenyans, Amin's personal arms dealers. The aircraft, having departed Arua, had never arrived at Kidepo, as scheduled. On the following day a helicopter landed near Paul's park office. Out stepped Idi Amin. Spotting Ssali, the President for Life threw his white hat on the ground and shouted, "You, chief game warden, you know where the aircraft is?"

When Paul denied any knowledge of the plane, he was arrested. Troops surrounded the park, as he waited in a makeshift prison for his execution. At last, on the following day, the truth emerged: The VIP aircraft had become lost, crossed the border into the Sudan and been forced to land at Juba. Amin left, Ssali was freed and the execution forgotten.

"You could be deceived by these people," Paul continues, the fingers of his right hand snapping compulsively. "Amin could come here and say this is a beautiful park and you have done a great job. He would leave and the next day you would be collected by his men and killed. Full stop. Only after two days and no troops had pitched up could you be certain you were safe."

Driving westward, Paul stops his narrative to note, "You know, there are many people who believe Kidepo is the most beautiful park in all East Africa."

On my left kigeria trees, their long sausagelike pods nearly brushing the ground, frame a lily pond. Even at speed, I spot two species of jacanas skimming the still water, their legs outstretched behind like clumps of asparagus. In the distance, between two hills to the south, there are more giraffe than trees and with every turn in the road there is a new rock formation, more elephants, a smell of decaying vegetation.

In 1967 a Swedish consortium began work on a luxury lodge on the edge of the park in a rocky massif called Katurum. Construction was still under way when Paul took over the park, and it continued for a few years while he was warden. Altogether nearly $3 million were invested in the lodge. Today, the site, 90 percent complete, has been abandoned. We can see it ahead, discreetly camouflaged within the rock. The caretaker, an ancient Dodoth Karamojong, cloaked in rags, salutes us as we enter the dusty lobby. He shows me all the fifty-six rooms, the bar carved out of natural rock, the swimming pool nearly complete, the elephant water hole, conveniently located in sight of the bar; and then he stands in the never-to-be dining room, and with a wild sweep of his arm, he indicates the view that was to attract tourists from as far away as China.

Paul is not so impressed. At every step of our tour he has pointed out the doors that were kicked in, the fixtures missing in every bathroom, the tiles ripped from the floors. "Amin's troops," he says dramatically. "Ten years to build this place; they destroyed it in two days."

When Paul was warden at Kidepo, there were as many as two hundred troops stationed near the lodge. "My rangers knew more about military training than they did," Paul claims, as we drive back from Katurum. "Whenever [soldiers in Amin's army] heard a shot fired they'd drop their guns and run. If they weren't drunk, they were suffering from hangovers."

Once, soldiers in the battalion stationed in Kidepo discovered one of their rifles missing. Immediately they accused a park ranger of having stolen it. When he denied knowledge of it, his ear was cut off and he was made to eat it. Paul, away on patrol at the time, only heard of the incident when he returned to find that three other rangers had been dragged behind a Land Rover on dirt roads, in an attempt to force confessions. Paul immediately instructed his sergeant major to open the armory and issue every ranger with a gun. The park rangers thereupon advanced on the army camp. Just before they opened fire, they saw a white shirt raised on a flagpole. A spokesman for the soldiers emerged to say that they had just found the culprit: their own captain. The captain was thereupon tortured and killed by his men. "It was terrible. It was terrible. It was terrible," says Paul.

Paul believes that Amin was attracted to Kidepo by its standards—the ones that had been effectively eroded under his sponsorship in other parks. He visited Kidepo three times during Paul's tenure. On the second of these visits, the President sat on the veranda of the little lodge. Waterbuck and guinea fowl were grazing a few feet from him. "Bring the guns," he barked at one of his aides. He rested the rifle on his shoulder and took aim at the largest waterbuck. Paul began his plea, whispering in his ear. He said that newspapers outside Uganda would give the President bad publicity if he shot game in the park. "They will think there is no meat in our country." If Amin shot here, Paul continued, he would be contravening international treaties, and conservationists from all over the world would be "after him." Paul couldn't stop: If the President, he said, was to shoot in front of the lodge, the animals would never again be so tame and tourists would not return to Uganda. "Is it not possible," Paul begged at the end, "that we can just go outside the park where I can show you some even better hunting?"

"Amin looked at me," remembers Paul, "and at this time I was almost weeping, and Bob Astles, his white thug, said, 'Yes, yes, Your Excellency, he is rrrrright, Your Excellency,' and then Amin said, 'Look, take this gun back.' Later he shot an animal outside the park, but never here. I don't know where I found the courage. Maybe I was young. I don't know. When I went and told my wife that I had advised Amin not to shoot, she said, 'Now it's all over. Have you made out your will? Tell me your last words.' But nothing ever happened. From that day on Amin never again tried to shoot in the park. He shot animals at Kabalega and Ruwenzori and his kills were announced on Radio Uganda, but he never shot at Kidepo."

Dr. Bernhard Grzimek, president of the Frankfurt Zoological Society, confirmed this story to me later. In a letter he said, "Somehow Amin was not offended . . ."

Rob Malpas in Nairobi also commented to me about it: "You couldn't begin to understand what it must have taken for one man to stand up to Amin. For him human beings weren't worth a damn."

Before the clouds have gathered in late afternoon Paul takes me for a flight in Popeye. The wind has freshened, but the big storms building in the Sudan are still far.

Although Paul is discouraged by the signs of poaching he sees from the air, Kidepo is still the most impressive conservation story in Uganda today. During the Amin years the elephant population elsewhere was nearly exterminated. In Ruwenzori Park, 3,000 elephants were reduced to a mere 153. At Kabalega

Falls, a recent aerial survey could only account for 172 of the 10,000 that roamed the park before Amin took office. At Kidepo, however, the figures were not nearly as dramatic. During the Amin years when Ross and Ssali ran the park the elephant population was only reduced by 20 percent. But during the two years that have elapsed since Paul ceased to run Kidepo, that 20 percent swelled to nearly 60 percent. Of the 1,200 elephants that once roamed Kidepo, today we can only count 450 from the air. "And of course," Paul adds, "all the rhino are butched."

Sometimes we fly so low we can see the red bill of an oxpecker climbing the neck of a giraffe. Once, when we bank a few feet from a hill, the stall warning sounds. Paul lowers the plane's nose, and soon we regain speed, whittling between two bifurcated doum palms like a MIG jet. The great sand rivers of Kidepo all point to the north, and although they are dry, today, they support a congeries of life: baboons hustling after nuts, vultures around a dead giraffe, two lionesses skulking out of a bush.

Paul seems to enjoy flying above these old haunts not for my benefit but for the memory. He knows every tree, every bend of sand, every emergency landing strip. Sometimes he calls out their names, other times I can see the muscles of his jaw working to keep them to himself. Even when the usual late-afternoon storm is upon us, the rain drumming its fingers against the windscreen, Paul still looks around for an excuse to remain airborne a few more minutes.

"The last time Amin came to Kidepo he decided to do a lot of publicity about me. After he had returned to Entebbe, every day for a week on Radio Uganda there were announcements saying how great a park Kidepo was and what a fine warden Paul Ssali was. And then Amin instructed me to go to Entebbe to collect a Mercedes 200.

"I'll tell you I was scared. You know how he is: He gives you all this praise and then he takes you to prison and you are heard from no more. Full stop. You know what it is like.

"I think it was because I never went to collect that Mercedes 200 that I am still alive today. I did not want to be in his pocket. All those who did are now either in prison or buried."

In 1978 Paul was promoted to the joint wardenship of Kabalega Falls National Park and Kidepo. The double responsibility amounted to an impossible job, the two parks being nearly three hundred miles apart. Worst of all, Paul regretted having to spend less and less time in his beloved Kidepo, where he felt he could do the most good.

"There were problems at Kabalega," Paul admits, now sitting in the lodge, watching the rain sluice off the thatch roof. "I am Buganda and the men under me at Kabalega were almost all Acholi. They resented me."

As soon as Paul left Kabalega his deputy at Kidepo began spreading discontent. In both parks he was alternately accused of being pro-Amin and anti-Amin. One rumor actually claimed Paul was Idi Amin's brother-in law. The fact that he wore epaulets when he flew his aircraft (a precaution when clearing officialdom at Entebbe Airport) convinced some people he was either attached to Amin's army or that he belonged to the State Research Bureau. Clearly, for Paul to be an impartial administrator during Amin's time was, or was at least thought to be, a contradiction in terms.

"It really made no sense," Rob Malpas had explained to me. "Paul looked after his men at both parks better than they had ever been looked after by a fellow Ugandan. He supported the loyal ones; they never went hungry. . . ."

Bernhard Grzimek added: "When Paul Ssali took over Kabalega Falls it was seriously endangered by poaching. By the use of strict measures he stopped it in a few months. Of course, in doing so he acquired a lot of enemies among both the surrounding tribes and members of his own staff whom he had fired because of corruption and inefficiency. . . . I have experienced three revolutions in Germany. Therefore I know that after a revolution people are always accusing each other of friendship with deposed politicians. This is exactly what happened to Paul Ssali in Uganda . . ."

By 1979 the government had lost control of the country. Coffee prices had plummeted, and now there was no economic cushion to soften the misery of the people. When Amin attacked Tanzania, Julius Nyerere reciprocated with a full-scale invasion of

Uganda. Amin's troops were now on the run, leaving a burned trail through the country, defining justice according to their own circumstances.

At Kabalega Falls National Park, Paul was sure the army would liberate the Land Rovers. As a precaution he drove each one into the forest, camouflaging it with branches. Noticing that these vehicles were missing, the army immediately accused Paul of having turned them over to anti-Amin guerrillas. On April 5, 1979, Paul learned that a secret meeting had been convened at Pakuba Lodge, attended by the army commandant. Its principle business had been to set a date for Ssali's arrest and execution, an order that had been issued by Amin himself.

To escape by aircraft would have been too logical. In fact, as Paul later discovered, the door of his Cessna had been rigged to a hand grenade, wired to detonate the moment he opened it. Instead, Paul chose an escape by land. Having loudly proclaimed that on April 7 he would need an army escort for special duties, he slipped away at six that morning aboard the local Toyota bus— he disguised as its driver, while the driver sat in the back masquerading as a passenger. At Karuma, where he had to stop, Paul told a suspicious adjutant that indeed he had just seen Ssali at Pakuba in the park.

"If they had caught me," Paul explains, "I know what they would have done: gone over me with the butts of their rifles, then cut off my lower parts and made me eat them. The one torture I most dreaded was when they drag you behind their Land Rovers at forty miles an hour until you watch your skin falling away from you. I wasn't that worried about death. I was lucky to be dying for the cause of game than for no cause at all. I was lucky because I had been able to educate most of my children. What I didn't like was that slow death. . . ."

At most roadblocks Paul exchanged positions with the driver while he ran a large loop on foot. On the third day of driving he reached his home in Kampala in time to watch the city under attack by the Tanzanians. For two days rockets and bombs exploded on either side of his small plot of maize. Paul received word that all his belongings at Kabalega, including his only print of *Two Men of Karamoja*, had been looted by the army. Thirty-seven members of his staff had been murdered and the retreating army of Idi Amin had opened fire on what was left of the game.

"I was sick," Paul remembers. "Throwing up and having to go to the toilet every other minute."

The next morning at dawn we take off from Kidepo, on our return to Entebbe. As a group of waterbuck on the grass strip scatters with the sound of the engine, Alpha Yankee Popeye slithers across mud and wet grass, plunges into a cloud of ground mist and, far too casually, becomes airborne. At last we are above the cloud, feeling the snappiness of the dawn air. Below us, the lodge, the staff quarters, the fort turn to miniatures, and mist lies in hollows like cotton wool. The tall grass is green beyond Africa's dreaming and the surrounding hills, belted by clouds, even greener. We circle and climb until, at nine thousand feet, Kidepo is only a buttonhole on an otherwise unadorned land. Paul sets a course of 200 degrees, and soon the cumulus clouds thin, the sun beats through the windscreen and Uganda turns gray. When he sets his eyes on the south, I can see Paul is already missing Kidepo.

Paul dismisses everything that happened to him after his escape from Kabalega—his life as a refugee in Kenya, the further attempts on his life when he returned to Uganda, the frustration of being a chauffeur for the sometimes inept trustees of the Uganda National Parks. One year is reduced to a thirty-second aside.

With one hand on the joystick, the last cigarette of his last pack hanging from his lips, he reaches into the backseat of the airplane for his briefcase. He is determined to show me something. At last the document is located, labeled the "African Wildlife Leadership Foundation" and signed "Kermit Roosevelt," it states that this award is its highest honor "for outstanding service to African wildlife." Paul Ssali's name is inscribed in Gothic lettering.

Paul understands this document more than he would ever understand a pat on the back. He looks at it carefully, still smoking his cigarette, and then with a finger he carefully describes each bold word. Throughout all this chaos in Uganda, with all its fast-order deaths and garbled leadership, this document is what blinds Paul Ssali to the hopelessness.

It is not enough for me to believe that Kidepo survived be-

256

cause this handsome, impatient man loved animals. Kidepo was *his* purpose in a nation that seemed to boast it had no purpose. Kidepo was the mission and the order once learned from a father who had succeeded in a white man's world. It was a pride in race, a vindication of Africa. This crumpled piece of onionskin is now, in a sense, a kind of middle-class African triumph.

Once on the ground at Entebbe, Paul parks his aircraft next to the Fokker Friendship that is to take me on its scheduled run to Kenya. He locks the door and extends his hand to say good-bye.

"Where would you really like to work?" I ask.

Paul points to the north from where we have come.

"But if that's not possible?"

"Then I'd start a ranger training school, and teach men all what I learned from Iain. Parks need men who are trained like soldiers and can fight for the game."

"Then why don't you start it?"

Paul smiles at me as if I am a child. "What did I tell you? No black man can run this country anymore. No black man can last in a national park. He will either do nothing or he will stay alive for only a few days. Full stop."

"Obviously whites can't come back to Uganda. There'd be screams of 'imperialism' up and down the whole of Africa."

Paul shrugs his shoulders. "Good-bye," he says, sticking out his hand.

"Paul," I suggest, "why don't you go to some other country until things cool down here? Some country like Tanzania or the Sudan. They need good game wardens."

Paul laughs for the first time today. "It would be as if my house needed painting, but I went instead to somebody else's with my paints and brush. Full stop."

There is a fable that periodically makes the rounds in Africa. "There was once," it goes, "a scorpion who wished to cross a river. Addressing a crocodile in midstream, he asked to be carried across on its back. 'Oh, no you don't,' the crocodile replied. 'I know what you'll do. As soon as I'm halfway across you'll sting me and I'll die.'

" 'Now why would I want to do that? If I stung you and you died, then I would drown, wouldn't I? Makes no sense.'

"The crocodile thought for a while and in the end agreed to ferry the scorpion to the other side. Halfway across, the scorpion stung the crocodile.

SUDAN SHOCK

"Floundering, gasping for breath, the crocodile croaked, 'Why in God's name did you do that?'

"The scorpion pondered a while and replied, just before he too drowned, 'Because it's Africa.' "

Often you hear people, smitten by Africa, say they are considering "one last safari." They would have you think that either they or Africa are growing old. A good safari may seem an embarrassment of riches—child's play, perhaps. Surely, it can never last.

I have made several last safaris, thinking despairingly that I must see Africa a final time before it all blows away on some evening wind, forever. Sometimes, I even grew homesick for Africa while I was still there. I can recall nights when pang after pang of longing, syncopated to the sparks from a green-wood fire, spoiled the child's air I was breathing. Hemingway had first talked about this African homesickness. He called the land a woman; his longing on the spot was the sadness felt at the moment of love's climax when one anticipates its sure end. I saw Africa as a promise never kept: I had searched for its heart and found only a geographic point.

I made a first and last safari to the southern Sudan because I believed it was all that remained of the old Africa. I was at that time discouraged by developments in Kenya, where the growth rate of the population was among the highest in the world. Where once I had driven for hours between Nanyuki and Rumuruti with only giraffe and elephant for surprises, today I saw advancing a new skyline of tin roofs and agricultural experiment stations. The southern Sudan had been deprived of all this glamour by virtue of a seventeen-year civil war, which had kept it secret from travelers and immune to progress. Usually when a country remains incommunicado for so long, its wildlife prospers. At one point, the southern Sudan, the size of France, Belgium, Holland and Switzerland combined, was said to contain the greatest biomass of game in all of Africa. One of my sources was a beautiful book called *The Cry of the Fish Eagle,* written by Peter Molloy in 1957. He said, "The Southern Sudan today is the last corner of unspoilt Africa, where wild life can be seen as it was in the beginning." Molloy talked of a place called the Boma Plateau, where white-eared kob mounted an annual migration more spectacular than on the Serengeti. He wrote of another place where an unarmed man could approach within twenty feet of the nearly extinct white rhino. Molloy told of great elephants ghosting out of Congo forests and of tall Dinka warriors who composed love songs to their cattle. His memoirs were, for me, a call to arms.

Since exploration is an expensive business, it seemed clear the most practical way of "opening up" (as we jokingly described our role) the southern Sudan was with paid safaris. Several hunters—Liam Lynn, John Sutton, Tony Archer—agreed to share certain fixed costs between them, to bring in their clients, and thereby to take part in the first exploration of this vast land in over seventeen years. Since I had stimulated the hunters, taken part in the first reconnaissance, I was now pressed into service to Liam Lynn as his assistant hunter.

My interest in hunting had been recent. Until the age of twenty-three, I had thought myself a conservationist, bored by hunting stories, impatient with many hunters, opposed to heavy guns, but several years before the Sudan safari Liam had talked me into three weeks on foot across Kenya's northern frontier. The animals we shot could be counted on the fingers of one hand, yet that hard walk along dry river courses had been a personal epiphany. I saw hunting as a lone venture, an excuse for thorns and burrs to get under your skin. The more strenuous, the better the hunt, whether or not it yielded a trophy, dinner or a rug. Through hunting I came to see the game as the game sees itself—predator/prey. And I came to perceive a sense of fulfillment in the stalk. I cannot be certain whether the instinct to hunt springs from an atavistic memory.

I find it difficult admitting a need to let an animal's blood. I can swear I am not alone: I am certain the hunt is part of the hardwiring of humanity. How we hunt is irrelevant—whether in business, in society or in the bush—so too whether we succeed in killing; all that counts is the expectation of success, the gamble, the uncertainty. So, at the age of twenty-three, after my first foot safari with Liam Lynn, I proclaimed myself conservationist, whispering in the same breath that I also enjoyed the hunt.

Liam helped me work out this contradiction in terms, for he was ashamed of nothing. He was now in his mid-forties, wavy blond hair going gray, a handsome face verging on puffiness, beginning to feel the effects of an unrestrained life. While he had always enjoyed a reputation as one of Kenya's most successful hunters, he had not achieved it by being more energetic than others or by outdistancing them as a naturalist. His talent was in language and luck. He was a master at the repartee, the turn of phrase, the brassy compliment, the mordant put-down. He returned time and again from his safari with charmed clients and great trophies. He insisted his hunting success derived from his logical mind, his defiance of accepted methodology. "Silver candlesticks," he often boasted. "What other hunter offers silver candlesticks in the mess tent?"

True, he did take outrageous risks and he never came to grief. He built a successful business out of virtually nothing. He was never short of "brides" (ranked by him publicly with a number as if they were in a holding pattern over a major airport), and whenever he appeared finally to have encountered a losing streak, some wonderful windfall always came his way. No, Liam was very lucky and very generous.

Liam was unquestionably the only white hunter in Kenya from Northern Ireland, and he exploited this distinction not just as a point of honor—say, a Cyrano nose—but as the nub of almost every human issue. A parking ticket in Nairobi was held up as an example of Kikuyu bigotry against Ulstermen. The orange tie worn by the headwaiter at the New Stanley Hotel once became an issue. An elephant worth shooting was invariably nicknamed "Ian Paisley." Yet, for all this Irishness, Liam rarely sought out the company of his countrymen; rather, he preferred outlining to his many English friends their genetic inferiority. And the funnier his friends found his outlandish taunts, the more Liam drank. He drank so well, with such abandon, that even those who disapproved of alcohol were never offended by it. He claimed he drank because of women. He also claimed he had to drink because he was Irish. He insisted he only drank while in Nairobi. But sometimes in the bush, he felt compelled to drink to mourn the "troubles" at home.

Now Liam was beginning to show signs of slowing down. His short list of twelve "brides" had been whittled to three. Worst of all, he was tiring of the hunt and the clients. Kenya's bureaucracy was no longer a laughing matter; now it had become meddlesome for a liberated spirit like Liam. He had come to believe other hunters were copying his style and that good hunts now required more work than they were worth. The Sudan promised him the free life he remembered in Kenya when he first arrived in 1954. "It'll be," he liked to muse, "a place where men are men and women wide-open spaces."

I saw the southern Sudan as the promised Africa. It seemed still a place where Emin Pasha, Sir Samuel Baker, Captain C. H. Stigand, "Karamojo" Bell and Peter Molloy would today feel at home. My past safaris had all been too much of a good thing and now was the right time to put an end to this surreal, childlike life and turn to sensible projects. One "last" safari, one rigorous, more venturesome than all the others, was necessary as a final salute to Africa. Best of all, the Sudan seemed to be at the very heart of Africa, not so much in Conrad's language of "darkness" but as a bright alluring soul.

Liam started appropriating deposits from prospective clients, promising them the "real" Africa. With the windfall in cash, he bought the second Range Rover ever seen in Kenya ("Just wait until they see me in Juba, purring through the streets like a big fat rajah"), tuned his small open Land Rover ("Diki Diki") and his Bedford lorry ("Big Buster"), bought twenty cases of Tusker beer and then invited everyone to the veranda of Nairobi's Norfolk Hotel for a last round.

"Sunshine [his name for me] has just signed on as my gentleman's gentleman," he announced.

"Your assistant, Moonshine [my name for him]," I corrected.

I kept a journal during this two-month safari, and to reread it is to see how Liam changed, and to comprehend, at least through my eyes, the shape and feel and effect of that Africa I had so yearned to find.

It begins on January 13, when, in a convoy of several hunters, assistant hunters, African staff, clients, lorries, Land Rovers and Toyotas, we drove north through Kenya, bound for a rarely used border post, Lokichoggio. Thence we would head westward on a track of our own making for about one hundred miles until we reached a Sudanese village, Kapoeta, and from there on a sort of road to Torit and Juba, the administrative capital of the southern Sudan, sited on the west bank of the Nile, where we arrived late on the afternoon of January 20.

During this week of tough travel, Liam's mood infected us all. While waiting for the lorries to catch up with us one day, crossing the Marich Pass, he lay by a brook, examining the blue sky, and mused: "I may stay in the Sudan for the rest of my life. You've heard of Clive of India, Lawrence of Arabia, Gordon of Khartoum. Well, I'll be Liam of the Sudan. They may even wish to change my name to Dr. Dolittle or Dr. Schweitzer—it makes no difference . . ."

JANUARY 15: Shortly after our arrival in Lodwar [still in Kenya], Liam discovered Father Kevin O'Garahy from the island of

Aran. He plied the gentle missionary with warm beer and after an hour made him swear eternal allegiance to the IRA and death to all Orangemen . . .

JANUARY 17: We have left behind all man-made tracks today and are following a compass course that brings us from one sand river to another. The land is flat, wildlife scarce and the native people tall, combative and completely naked. The last lugger [sand river] of the day: While winching the non-four-wheel-drive lorry across, the hook straightens out, the heavy cable snakes through the air, lashing at my leg just below the knee. After spilling a few pints of blood, the flow is halted and the wound cleaned out. Liam claims that antibiotics are totally unnecessary [he had forgotten to bring them]. "Stick with me, Sunshine," he says, "and you'll be okay." His serendipitous smile has a medicinal effect [although for the next month and a half, I could never run very fast because of the infection]. "I'd like to propose a toast," Liam says, looking across the great plain where we had stopped the convoy for a moment. He had brought along a bottle of champagne, and suspecting that we are more or less on the frontier between Kenya and the Sudan, he had called for a celebration: "One small step for mankind," he announces bravely. "One giant step for Liam Lynn."

The Sudan indeed was as exciting as we had hoped. We encountered people who had never seen a white since they were children—Topoisa spearmen, dressed only in a strand of beads. Along the Nile we found Dinka, sometimes six and a half feet tall, herding goats, and dressed only in beaded vests from which they never emerged even to wash. In the Sudd, a swampland to the north of Juba, we lived alongside the Shilluk, the Nuer, the Anuak, the Fashile and Liri, occupying beehive huts along the Nile and standing guard over one of the rarest of all African antelope, the Mrs. Grey's lechwe, dark elegant shadows on the horizon, their long hair insulating them from damp, dry, cold, heat and the ever-present clouds of mosquitoes and flies. The game in the southern Sudan was not exactly waiting for us by the roadside. We had no real guide except Molloy's book, so we had to stab the mouse-eared map with pins and declare: "We haven't been here yet. Let's give it a try." My journal is peppered with names, lifted from that map—names that became occasional destinations and quite often yielded little more than frustration: the Badengellu Swamps, "lone sacred Tamarind Tree," Bor, Wau, Terakeka, the Imatong Hills, the Boma Plateau, Fanyikang, Chief Karpeta's Village. The names read as if they came from the most romantic of all Baedekers.

The country we traversed was almost all flat. Occasionally to the south, abutting the frontier with Uganda, there were ranges of rock massifs, escarpments, but overall, the country seemed to be on the order of an ancient floodplain, bearing a sometimes red, sometimes gray pallor. Dust clouds called *haboobs*, reaching well above the serviceable ceilings of light aircraft, often swept over us for a week at a time, and during this period, the sun grew hazy and turned the color of an old egg yolk. When finally the blue sky reappeared, the ground, the trees, every blade of grass for miles—even the wildlife (including ourselves)—was colored pastel red.

The Sudan was therefore beautiful only after one had grown accustomed to it, and the beauty summarized palpable pleasures—an evening breeze, a morning clearness, a glint of water, a sea of game.

JANUARY 23: Red-billed hornbills dip and soar in pairs across our path, African fire finches catch my eye flitting from one bush to another, and once I am able to recognize a red-cheeked cordon bleu. Oh my gosh, I cannot believe that I am able to spot these Sudanese varieties, based solely on what I picked up in Kenya. And here come the doves—laughing doves and the emerald-spotted wood dove—and then, yes, my old pal the namaqua (could be all the way from South Africa). And around the camp, morning, noon and evening, old Ruppell's long-tailed starling (not to be confused with the superb), bothering us for crumbs. This is paradise . . .

The central geographic feature of the country is, of course, the Nile. It bisects the country, posing problems of communication. Throughout its entire length, for instance, there was not one bridge, leaving the only crossing to an antiquated ferry at Juba. Most days, the ferry was *hors de combat* because of a faulty generator, a broken propeller or the black mood of the usually sullen captain. Several times I waited half a day on the east bank, within sight of Juba, aching for a drink of fresh water, but unable to have one until the captain aroused himself from his afternoon siesta. The Nile was the aorta of all the country. All supplies, notably petrol, spare parts and beer, came from Khartoum via the Nile to either Malakal or Juba. If the riverboats were not operating (often the case since they had not been given a thorough overhaul since the mid-1950s), Juba went hungry.

The Nile was, at least for me, the very soul of the Sudan. Not a sinister African river, festooned with lianas and yawing with crocs and hippos, it was wider than any river I had ever seen in Africa. The current raced (at some ten miles an hour) on its way out of Uganda, bound across aeons of desert until it dissolved into the Mediterranean. I liked to think of it as a linear oasis where every animal, great and small, human and nonhuman, came and went. You could set calendars and clocks to the cycles of animal thirst, just by sitting in a hide on the Nile. Sometimes the river refused to take a river shape, as in the Sudd, where it spread across many thousands of miles never quite describing a true riverbank, making travel almost impossible. Other times the river descended through gorges, reminding me of a tributary of the Colorado. We never liked to stray too far from the Nile.

JANUARY 22: Seconds after the false dawn several pairs of glossy ibis make their way to the river's edge, screaming raucously; the fish eagles take up perches on stumps near the river, crying like herring gulls back in New England. Chunks of *sylvania* (sometimes called Sudd, these are hand-size islands of grass that never cease breaking loose from the shore) are always floating by . . .

JANUARY 23: A great stern-wheeler churns its way upstream toward Juba. We can see the silhouette of the captain standing in front of his kerosene lamp. Mark Twain would have glowed with the sight of this antique churning in and out of our lives, beating against the current. Pity there is no steam calliope aboard. Much later, whoops and cries come from

across the river: Crocodile hunters must have made a
kill . . .

MARCH 6: . . . We arrive back in camp in time to see the piapiacs
[birds looking a bit like long-tailed starlings] coasting in for
their evening drink. Just then the *camp* hippo snorts in the
gushing stream near my tent. All is well . . .

If you looked very hard, you might be able to uncover a
certain grandeur that had once been Juba, the capital of the
southern Sudan, the chief trading post, commercial and communications center. There was, of course, a large cathedral,
roofed, as you might suspect, with corrugated tin. There was
also a row of residences, still bearing the unmistakable Colonial
imprint—heavy stone, commanding porticos, sweeping drive-
ways, the remains of great shade trees. What was peculiar about
these houses—peculiar, in fact, about all of Juba—was the strange
monochrome texture of house, gardens, trees. Lawns had become extinct during the revolution. A trace of green would have
made Juba a lush paradise, but throughout the entire town, not
one blade of grass had survived the thin cattle who were allowed
to graze everywhere. even around the ex-governor's house. Only
the red dirt remained and this had tainted all the town's wood-
work and stonework; if you walked a block in sandals, it also
colored your feet. Even in the Juba public gardens there was no
grass (in fact, there were no gardens); this small area was surrounded by barbed wire and padlocked to keep the public at bay.
Over the wire you could see a papier-mâché statue of an Arab,
wearing a fez, and a near-naked African, shaking hands.
"The most interesting way to enter Juba, I discovered, was
standing up in an open car, to have one's nose assaulted by the
rainbow of smells," I wrote on January 21.

Being the old melting pot, Juba is a place where Shilluk,
Dinka, Murli, Topoisa, Mondari and now Arab do their
cooking and plumbing. The first "suburb" may be spiced
with woodsmoke and shit, the second, pigs and charcoal;
while "downtown" Juba is a little more upbeat: curry pow-
der, fine dust, diesel and homemade beer. . . . The most
impressive monument is to Sir Samuel Baker and Gessi, the

two earliest white men to venture into this world. It is a tribute to this country that it still stands. Anywhere else in Africa, it would have been scrapped . . . I pass two Sudanese army lorries (the army is mostly Arab), one bristling with heavily armed men, the other overloaded with dead hartebeest, oribi and reedbuck: quite a sight for the main street of a nation's provincial capital . . . There's a six-hour wait at the town's only petrol pump, and the precious stuff sells at over $4 a gallon . . . The only bookstore in town—the Catholic bookstore—sells mostly pornography. . . .

The mattresses on the beds of the town's only hotel smell of decades of incontinent bodies . . . At the hotel there is no beer for sale, as the government is stockpiling it for the Independence Day celebrations. Also the ice has run out. Flies settle on the rims of warm orange squash glasses, and the hotel staff stand behind closed doors, angry if anyone should ask them for service . . . The Regional Administration Building is the only skyscraper. It is two stories high . . . and the balcony on the second floor, always crowded with petitioners, looks on the verge of toppling . . . I have noticed one or two Mercedes-Benzes bouncing through the streets (there are still no tarred roads in all the country). I suppose they must be owned by government officials, as is the case in every African country . . . We are told that the Greek Club is the best place in town for dinner, with a menu consisting of two items—tough steak and Nile perch . . .

For Liam, it was love at first sight. Of course, he was discouraged to discover there were no supplies in the shops. That meant he would have to buy candles for his silver candelabra in Nairobi and have them delivered by air. Still, there were some advantages. The southern Sudan game license, drafted some twenty years before, had not been amended since the revolution. It was cheap and allowed the hunter to kill three elephants, countless buffalo, lion, leopard and any number of plains game. Better still, the game department often came to him for advice, since he was the first full-time professional hunter to come to the southern Sudan in years. Advice was one of his specialties. He had massive ideas, most of which were conceived at the Greek

Club, where, after a few weeks in the Sudan, he had become a notable. "Ah, Mr. Lynn," the owner would cry, seeing his white Range Rover parked under one of the nearby tamarind trees. "What can we do for you tonight?" And Liam was always extremely courteous, tipping his Special Forces beret to the photograph of King Constantine, mounted high on a wall, as he stretched his large frame into one of the metal chairs and routinely checked the menu with its two lonely items. In a very short time Liam had become the most famous person in Juba. With his gleaming Range Rover and clover-green bush shorts, he was, to the Sudanese, capitalism glorified. Greeks and Arabs were forever taking him aside at the Greek Club with yet another scheme for mutual advancement. And whenever Liam entered into any of these arrangements, he was always careful to let others invest their money and he his charm.

The safari business, however, was different. It was hard work and it was becoming—although Liam would not have then admitted it—philosophically disturbing. There were many issues of life, bigger than the safari business, that had begun to distress Liam. He was merely forty-two, but he seemed, somehow, to be slipping into old age. I was never aware of this until we escorted our first clients through the Sudan. Tom Kearney (an invented name) ran a successful business in the Midwest. He had lots of children, lots of money (so he said), and "he had beat the odds" by surviving a double bypass heart operation. His son Randy (also invented) had just returned from Vietnam. For the first few days of the safari, the only word I heard Randy utter was "Sure." He was even silent with his father who, I suspected, had intended this trip to be a kind of reconciliation. My journal describes the outcome:

JANUARY 29: While Liam repairs the lorry, I take the Kearneys out hunting. This is the price I pay to remain in the Sudan. I discover they are little interested in the extraordinary natural history around here—just the shooting . . .

Our first stalk is a standoff, the second brings us into range of the reedbuck. "Never shoot until you are sure you can kill the animal," I advise Randy. He thereupon wounds the animal and it plunges away. We follow it and after half an hour we are once again within range to shoot again. The buck has now joined a small herd of females. I ask Randy if he is sure he knows which is the buck. He nods and the bullet brings down an immature female. I'm livid and embarrassed at the same time . . .

Enroute to Peter Molloy's fabled Boma Plateau:

FEBRUARY 2: I am rushing to write my notes before the sun fades on this dim veranda that was the pride of some forgotten District Commissioner many years ago. We have reached Pibor Post, over a hundred miles from the Nile, every inch of which I feel has been fairly well earned . . . For eighteen miles we were moderately impressed by the road, then the country flattened and emptied of all life, the grass growing high until not a breath of wind could reach us, and we couldn't see more than a few feet to either side. No road repairs, we learned, have been made here since 1955. The black cotton mud was granite, scoured with wide-wheel-base tracks of heavy lorries. For ten out of twelve months, this road is off-limits. The Diki Diki is forever boiling over. We stop every mile or so to fill it with our now diminishing supply of water. Little game, no people, no landmarks. Down with all kites [a sort of African hawk], forever soaring overhead! Later, I am amazed to see crested plovers on an open stretch of plain, not distant from a huddle of Egyptian vultures. In five hours of driving, the only game: one Mongalla gazelle, bounding off at a great distance. With no shade, no water, I wonder how he could have survived at all . . .

Finally arrived in Pibor Post:

The Sudanese Commissioner asked if we would be good enough to sit on stools in front of his house in the village square for the benefit of the children who had never before seen white people. They touch our bare arms to see if the color will wash off . . .

FEBRUARY 3: Every few miles we must stop to clean stalks and seeds off Diki Diki's radiator screen, and then sit under shadeless trees to wait for the boiling to stop . . . The track is pitted with concealed pig holes. Am continually clenching my teeth against long wallowing drops and smashing bumps, also against Kearney, playing Boy Scout with his unsolicited advice. He never lifts a finger and makes every one of our problems a major effort in self-control. He rambles on for three hours, insisting the hose we use for siphoning water is the one originally intended for petrol. He is wrong. Liam shrugs his shoulders and tries not to listen. . . . The Range Rover's petrol tank springs a leak and we lose nearly twenty gallons. Clearly we cannot get to the Boma Plateau, and we will have to change our plans. . . . Liam sits on the rear bumper and says: "I wish I'd never heard about the Sudan. I'm going to Juba, sell all my equipment and start again in South America."

While Liam goes ahead in the other car, I jerry-rig a patch on the leak, take Tom Kearney out on foot after a white-eared kob, which he brings down in two shots.

Later that evening we rip off great slabs of tough steak with our hands; there's no telling how far we might go as predators. Sleep is a pleasure—relief from Kearney's boasting of his shot.

More boil-overs and two punctures in Diki Diki. Liam, having gone ahead, returns in excitement.

FEBRUARY 4: "Like the Serengeti," he says. He has just seen huge herds of game, plains filled with maneless zebra, giraffe, white-eared kob, tiang, oribi, Mongalla gazelle. High hills far to east. So much for Liam's black mood of yesterday. The only trouble is we do not have enough petrol to carry on. We wait for the cool of afternoon. Kites swoop toward our dried meat, getting closer and closer each time . . . The heat lies about us like a blanket. Hard to bear this schedule in the Sudan—from noon until four we must disappear under shade and avoid all physical effort. And without chairs or tables it is difficult to write or sketch.

In late afternoon, I shoot a magnificent white-eared kob which turns out to have one broken horn. I feel quite sick with my senseless shooting.

Later in camp, I mutter to Liam: "There's never an end to it. You just get trigger happy and anybody can shoot well. How can you take part in this dumb sport, Liam? Taking chumps out one after another so they can get their rocks off killing a bunch of meat? What do you say to yourself at the end of each safari? Another job well done?" I am irate and can barely recognize my own words. Must be the heat.

Liam replies, "Now you know what I mean when I refer to the producers and the nonproducers. Perhaps you'll understand why I sometimes drink." The Kearneys somehow cannot follow our conversation. I sit up at dark, to make us all some soup and listen to the croak of a tree frog.

FEBRUARY 5: I dreamed of mountains in winter last night, and woke up thirsty. Hunger is tolerable, but this thirst is impossible. . . . A beautiful waterbuck presents itself and Randy decides to pot it. He lets off two shots, and the waterbuck barely notices, merely lifting his head from a good graze. Then Randy's father grunts to say he will show the kid. He tracks the waterbuck for ten paces and then lets off a round of bullets. This time the animal does not even raise his head.

Back at the car, Kearney explains: "I didn't want to show Randy up. You see, it would've embarrassed him if I'd shot the animal. A father's got to think of these things."

Liam is right, I think, when he sometimes tells me he'd rather be a men's room attendant than a professional hunter.

The Kearneys decide to abort this leg of the trip and return to base camp: a revolting decision, but we hardly have enough petrol to continue. . . . The good water we notice is vanishing, as Murli cattle have invaded our pool. The warriors sit in our camp, propped against their Martini-Henrys, loaded with homemade ammunition stolen from

Ethiopian raiders. They stare at everything we do, squatting with their scrotums hanging onto thorns . . . "This is no candy-ass safari," Kearney repeats over and over. His bravado drones in a melancholy way, as woolly-neck storks perch for the night in a nearby acacia tree. . . . Returning in the Range Rover, Kearney as usual does all the talking, first about Randy: "Christ, he's got broad shoulders," and then about his son-in-law back in the Midwest who has been trying unsuccessfully to make Kearney's daughter pregnant: "I suppose they'll have to adopt; he only shoots blanks." We reach the police post after some twenty miles, then proceed until we can keep our eyes open no longer. It is now midnight. Liam reports: "I've been keeping myself awake by thinking about my best lays." The night is cold and not far away we can see the fires of the Murli. We light our own, and Liam, now too tired to sleep, tells me once again his life story: "I was one of the Bevin Boys: At the age of twenty-one I was offered the choice of either serving in the army or going down a coal mine. Since I hated the British army, I went down a coal face in Yorkshire for some three months. In November it was fucking cold in Britain, and I knew I couldn't go back to Ireland because my father was a tyrant. I had no money and I was trying to sort out what to do. I had read J. A. Hunter's *Hunter*—which made me very impatient with my life. One morning I read in the newspaper a notice asking for volunteers in the African Colonial Police. I pitched up to be interviewed by an old police superintendent from Kenya. He told me there were ten thousand applicants for five hundred places, and then asked whether I'd treat an African any less fairly than I'd treat a white. I quoted Bobby Burns: 'A man's a man for a' that.' I don't know if I agree today.

" 'If you were accepted,' the old boy asked me, 'when would you be prepared to leave?'

" 'In a week,' I replied. They gave me thirty pounds to buy a solar topee and a frying pan. I cashed the check and went on the piss, and on 26 December, 1953, I stepped off the train in Nairobi. It was during Mau Mau. They gave me a .38 Smith and Wesson revolver, and I was sent down to

Gilgil for training in Syndicate number 27 for six weeks. An ex-colonel was my syndicate's sergeant major. He started us off by making us do our 'right quick step.' All the others had served in the military and knew what it was. Not I. So they put me in the middle of the line where nobody could see me. We had enormous esprit de corps. Mercenaries— that's what we were. I was posted up to the Masai country, which was then a semihot Mau Mau area. Best of all, I became fast friends with the game warden they called T-B— Major Lynn Temple-Borham. He was the most English gentleman I ever met, yet he had a sense of humor, a sense of decency that is rare to see in his countrymen. He also could drink me under the table. 'What we need,' he said to me, 'is a commando force. Would you join us?' Of course I would (you never said no to T-B).

"Several months later, one night when I left my camp, there was a raid and nearly all of my men were wiped out by the Mau Mau—all five of them—my corporal and some of my best lads. I grew very bitter then . . . until one day T-B asked me (he always pronounced my name to sound like *lion*), 'What are you going to do now?' I told him I loved Kenya but I didn't want to stay in the police. 'Why don't you become a white hunter?'

"I had just turned twenty-four, had saved nearly five hundred pounds, and on deciding to become a white hunter I forfeited my passage home. I bought an old Land Rover and a rifle, and with another trainee, Jack Barrah, I killed and killed buffalo on game control for the game department until I was confident with myself. Then T-B recommended me to the firm of Selby and Holmberg as an assistant. I drove trucks, dug latrines and two years later, in December 1956, conducted my first professional hunt.

"And then there was Didi, but enough of that. She was proper English and we were married, had a fabulous boy and then we were divorced; and I won't say what it was she did to me, but I'm now dead set against marriage, and so now—I don't know—I can't see myself ever marrying again, just poking along as I am now, and it'll be fucking good. You're a dead man when you marry. Believe me. I know."

Just before the sun rises we set off once again, to beat the heat. . . .

FEBRUARY 7: Back at the base camp:

> Having one's own tent is the best solution to Kearney who is forever on the prowl for an audience. I drink a tamarind juice while learning from Malabu [one of Liam's permanent camp staff] that Mr. Kearney had words with his son last night and he is intending to spend the morning lying in bed. . . . [Now en route north on bad roads] Kearney, drunk as a lord, refers to himself as "Bullmoose" and then, overpowered by some sense of inadequacy starts fawning over Liam: "You're one hell of a man; you're a living legend." . . . He is embarrassing his son. . . .

FEBRUARY 8: Where do the flies come from?

> Having conducted an extraordinary search for the fabled Mrs. Grey's lechwe, hired a river steamer in Malakal, proceeded to a vast grassy meadow by the bank of the Nile, spotted the animals from a great distance, stalked them only to hear at the last minute the report of another gun. The region's game warden had himself just shot a trophy Mrs. Grey's. Today's hunt is now over for us and we return back to our steamer, disappointed and confused:

FEBRUARY 10: Tom Kearney is enraged when he hears the news. He obviously has been dipping into the sauce while we were out hunting, and he has built himself into a fine rage. He addresses the game warden and the captain of our steamer as "pig-fucker"—a term of double contempt since both men are Muslim. All we can do is quiet him and hope that if we go to bed early he will too. The next time I visit the Sudan, I shall pick my own friends. Liam has been very quiet recently. He lies on his bed, staring at the rotting beams overhead. "This is a whore's job," he says to me not all that quietly, hoping perhaps that Kearney will hear him, "and Kearney's a disgrace to Ireland."

FEBRUARY 11: We depart as morning black changes to purple. The old Arab sits forlornly in the folds of his robe on the deck-house roof, chewing on memories of food with memories of teeth. Papyrus boats (à la Kon-Tiki) are paddled along-side, their Shilluk owners not even casting glances our way. We see few Mrs. Greys—just a handful of females at a great distance, as we attempt to go farther upstream. Soon we are stuck in mud. Hands dip into our last remaining can of pine-apple chunks, and I bury myself in Noel Coward's *Bon Voyage* (my seventh book since we have been with the Kear-neys). Strange how in moments of indecision we all resort to the exotica. Now, however, we must set off on foot, while Kearney stays on board. I jump in and, with boots squelching, sluice through twenty feet of mud, matted grass and then dead water hyacinth before I reach firm ground. And ahead, yet another tributary to negotiate. Miles of empty grassland with a distant trace of a herd of Mrs. Grey's. We approach slowly, carefully, and once again discover the herd is female. The sun grows hot. The Shilluk guides fan out in little clusters toward horizon villages, and after someone suggests how absurd this chase has become, we slowly work our way back to the boat. I think to myself I have once again performed my service to conservation. Kearney booms, "Let's return to Juba."

We are the first whites in years to visit the Imatong Moun-tains, a legendary country for buffalo in the old days:

FEBRUARY 15: When the morning is still cool, butterflies flit through high grass and pye-dogs from the village sniff our now cool cooking fire. A note has arrived from a place called Itibol saying that buffalo have been sighted, and soon we are seated in the Diki Diki, rattling down the splattered road through a teak forest. A good-natured Bari called Ogunya, dressed in green coveralls, waits for us at Itibol. He carries a .303 Enfield and is accompanied by two bare-chested Letuhos with reedy muscles. Each of them carries a bow, metal-tipped arrows and two spears. They never travel through this forest unarmed. We drive a distance up a logging road until it vanishes, and then we continue on foot. We have barely gone a quarter of a mile when Kearney admits he can walk no farther because of his heart. Being second-in-command, I must stay with him, to keep him company. We sit on a log and talk nonsense . . .

Again Kearney demands that we abort the hunt. Returning to Juba we are stopped as usual by police, this time in Torit:

FEBRUARY 11: The police keep us waiting for half an hour [outside their dilapidated headquarters] until finally Liam rushes up to the corporal and says: "If you want to arrest me, charge me. Show me the sentence. I was a police officer myself once and I know the form. I'm either under arrest or not under arrest but you can't hold me indefinitely. Here in the Sudan I've been harassed ever since I arrived. You police have evidently been instructed to make it as difficult as possible for visitors. You can be absolutely sure that when I reach Juba I'll make a full report to your government. I'll tell your commanding officer that the police in Torit are harassing visitors, and I'll tell them your name . . ."

"But you misunderstand, Mr. Lynn . . ."

"Listen, don't interrupt."

"But, Mr. Lynn, you must not be so vexed." The officer promptly sees us off with all his best wishes. Liam clearly feels better that he has been allowed to let off steam. We drive down the Loronyo road. The moon is so bright we hardly need the headlamps . . .

One of the hunters, Alan Price, who had been on our original convoy from Kenya, had had difficulties in Torit a month earlier with the police on his return to Kenya. He was driving an ancient Chevrolet four-wheel-drive van, carrying several of Liam's staff back to Kenya. My notes of February 7 tell the story as I heard it many weeks later:

Alan drove through Torit not knowing that he was supposed to check in with the police. They chased him in the
only car in town—an old Land Rover. Since the Chev made
a din on these bad roads, Alan never knew he was being
followed for the first ten miles. Suddenly, he looked out of
his side window and saw the police vehicle beside him, trying
to overtake him, weaving around trees through the bush.
Alan veered to miss an obstacle; so did the police, and their
vehicle overturned. When he ran back to see what had happened, he found two men in uniform badly injured. He pried
them out of the wreckage and raced them back to Torit for
medical help. Immediately, on entering the town, he was
thrown into prison by a drunken game warden. After three
days, the police colonel in charge of the two injured men
(who were improving rapidly at the hospital) became
charmed by Alan's witticisms and allowed him to stay under
house arrest in more comfortable quarters. For two days,
Alan negotiated his sentence, and in a mood of remorse the
police chief let him go with a fine of £5. "That's very kind,"
said Alan. "Unfortunately I don't have any Sudanese
money."

"Well," the colonel replied. "Pay me the next time you come
through Torit."

"I don't know when that will be. Maybe not for several
years."

"No matter, I can wait." Such is Sudanese hospitality.

Two days later, when Alan crossed the Kenya border at
Lokichoggio he ran into more trouble. The commander of
the Kenya police saw Alan's headlights approaching near
midnight, and since the officer had never seen a car coming
from that direction before, he naturally believed he was being
besieged by a Sudanese mounted force. He opened fire at
the Chevrolet, a few inches over the windshield. Alan
jammed on the brakes and ordered all his men to jump out
with their hands in the air. Once again, Alan was under arrest, but by dawn, as soon as the commandant had overcome his fright, Alan was allowed to continue.

We wait until afternoon to look for buffalo, sitting in the heat near a village where all its inhabitants seem to be suffering from elephantiasis. One has a scrotum the size of a soccer ball:

FEBRUARY 17: Kearney will not join us in the stream since he is sure it is the source of the elephantiasis. We slip on the cool mud, shave and shout. Kearney, searching for something to say, finally announces: "I've set a quarter past two aside to clean my fingernails."

In the late afternoon Liam conducts Randy Kearney on a successful buffalo hunt. His father is overjoyed and claims the buffalo must be a world record.

All evening we must listen to the postmortem of the hunt, celebrating with Kearney's gin, smiling and laughing and saying how proud we are of the kid.

We have returned to base camp. Kearney has bought himself another bottle of gin. The flies are thick. Randy is growing more impatient with his father, with only a few more days of the safari left. Kearney has heard that today is my birthday, and he has allegedly contracted for local Murli to serenade us around the campfire in the evening. Liam meanwhile is doing everything he can to pretend Kearney does not exist:

FEBRUARY 19: A drunken game warden approaches me in camp and demands to see a permit for the buffalo. Liam overhears the conversation, puts his arm around the shoulder of the poor game warden, drawing him aside to whisper that I have just been released from a mental institute for the weekend. "Please don't upset him," Liam cautions the game warden. "It will only make him worse." The gulled game warden shakes Liam's hand feverishly to thank him for his help and walks away, glancing back from time to time to check my condition.

"Just as well," Liam added, returning to his tent. "We didn't have a permit for the buffalo."

The flies thin, the moon rises, a red yolk in a scorched sky, and the drumming explodes from a distant village, brought to us on a wind bitter with woodsmoke.

By sunset Kearney has already had two drinks. He addresses us all as "candy asses," and then he drills Liam with a regular epiphany: "If we lived in the age of armor and chariots we'd either have had it out—killed each other—or be steadfast friends."

"Absolutely, Tom," Liam replies, not listening. Finally, when the conversation shows no sign of improving, Liam adds: "You know, Randy has a better approach to hunting than you do, you old fart. A finer spirit. A sense of grandeur. Pity you don't have 'em." Far from being offended, Kearney leans across the table to hear Liam better. "Goddamn the youth, Tom. They're always better. You know what we should do? Why don't you and I get into the corner and take on those two bastards? We'll smash the hell out of them. Yes, that's right. Us two old bastards can handle them any day."

Liam's words are pure inspiration for Kearney who, for a few moments, until he leaves the tent, seems even sober.

When he returns, there clearly is going to be trouble. Allegedly, he had given Malabu, one of Liam's staff, a hundred shillings to hire the drummers, and now he claims Malabu has cheated him. Malabu, his slender outline etched by the background fire, quietly murmurs he only received twenty shillings.

"Someone isn't telling the truth," Liam intones, uncomfortable as a disciplinarian.

"Are you accusing me of lying?" Kearney barks across the table.

"Well, not exactly, but if you insist you gave a hundred shillings, then I must fire Malabu, who's one of my best men."

"I don't care if you do fire him. You called me a liar."

Liam had always hoped he could fake his way through the safari, but now he must look into the eyes of the man who is paying $400 a day to be his friend. "Christ, you're a selfish bastard, Kearney."

Tom Kearney rushes from the mess tent, headlong into the night, his embarrassed son, trying to stroll, but at the same time running, and then their two voices, from beyond the fire, alternately plaintive and gruff, plainsong and strident, mixing with the distant drums. Liam and I are alone. He speaks to me: "Just as well you witness this, Sunshine. Now you know what can happen to a safari."

Kearney—just a shadow on the moonswept plain—yells, "Let's pack it up. Call it quits."

Liam: "Gladly." He turns to me, smiling for the first time in days. "It's not only the drink that makes them do it," he adds. "It's the smell of blood, a feeling that with a gun and a little success you own bloody Africa, the fucking world." Liam pours himself another orange squash. [I have never seen him so sober.] "Hunting's a magnificent sport. It's the hunters that ruin it." Just then both Kearneys return with apologies.

"I'll accept conciliation on one condition," Liam insists. "That you don't drink any more, Tom. You're a pretty awful fellow at the best of times, but when you're drinking, you're horrible."

"Please accept my apologies," Kearney pleads, resuming his seat. He pours himself another gin, as Liam sips the warm squash. "I'll tell you something," Kearney continues, as if nothing had happened. "There's no one I'd rather hunt with than you. You're one hell of a guy."

"Please let's not talk about me. Why not the troubles in Ireland? Why not the devalued dollar? Why is it always me?" A pause. "Let's talk about Randy."

Tom Kearney looks at his son, his mind switching gears with ease. "He's a great hunter, my Randy. I've got a hell of a respect for him. He'll never quit, will he? Not my Randy. He'll never quit, this boy."

At last the drummers arrive, but by now Tom Kearney has fallen asleep. Liam and I pull our chairs outside the tent to watch the moon, no longer in flames, but now a mere white hole in the sky. "Beautiful drumming," Liam notes, content at last. "Happy birthday, Sunshine."

Tonight I have made my first decision at age twenty-nine: My career as an assistant professional hunter will be concluded as of tomorrow.

FEBRUARY 20: Liam suffers from psychosomatic illness this morning and fails to get out of bed. The Kearneys have left, at last, and hopefully I shall have some time for my own exploration . . .

FEBRUARY 21: Liam still will not move.

FEBRUARY 21–MARCH 3: We try to repair Diki Diki's radiator as best as possible . . .

Liam, depressed for the last ten days, has just been invited by the fledgling Southern Sudan Game Department to serve as auctioneer for their cache of ivory collected during the revolution. Suddenly there is a transformation:

MARCH 4: Liam is dressed in his smartest shirt, in long stockings and elegant shorts. At breakfast he drinks two beers and announces to all: "The word of the day is legs and the motto of the day is spread the word."

Suddenly the sky turns red; the dust storm we had heard about over Radio Khartoum has finally reached us. Even our hands turn pastel orange. The sun looks like a full moon, a mere glowing sphere, and now the far bank of the Nile is only barely visible. In the mess tent Liam is preparing his opening statement as the auctioneer. "In this auction, ladies and gentlemen," he says to the camp, "there will be no discrimination. However, all Arabs, please step to the rear . . . You may be interested, ladies and gentlemen, to note some rather interesting items, in addition to the ivory, to be auctioned off. In particular, please note the Nubian nymphs.

Let me add how pleased we are to have Mr. Heminway in our midst. As you know, he is the last surviving American in the Sudan. [A few days previously the American Ambassador had been murdered in Khartoum by Arab extremists.] Here we have a special lot, straight from the kutch crotchy . . ." And so on.

Liam has not been in Juba for a few days and, like a phantom Gatsby in his Range Rover, he catches everyone's eye. All of Juba has been transformed for the upcoming festivities, celebrating one year of peace. Truckloads of Shilluk women, having just been supplied with Maidenform bras so as not to offend Muslim eyes, have been ferried to Juba for the evening's tribal dance. Streets are decorated with ornate posters reading: *Peace and love is ever our motto; Behold how good and pleasant it is when brothers dwell in unity; Long live Afro-Arab solidarity, African solidarity will defeat Imperialism.* "Lies, lies," says Liam softly as we arrive at the game department. "Reminds me of what they say in Northern Ireland."

This auction is one of a kind, conducted in the Animal Orphanage. Two baby buffaloes, one ostrich and a flock of Muscovy ducks mill among the thirty-one spectators until a game guard shoos them away. Liam; the Greek, George Zaphiro; Ian Parker and Alastair Graham, both from Nairobi; and I are the only Europeans. The Arabs, mostly from Omdurman, near Khartoum, inspect the goods with great suspicion. In the past they have generally dispensed with auctions, acquired through game control, and bought the ivory directly from the Southerners for a set price. Since the Southerners have long felt they were exploited, today they are going to right all wrongs. Traditionally ivory has sold for about $3 a pound. The Arabs try to make a deal with Liam. "No arguments," yells Isaiah, head of the game department. "On with the auction."

Before the Arabs can say another word, the first lot goes for 116 shillings a pound (about $16). The Arabs are in shock. They were sure that the sudden appreciation in the world value of ivory would have gone unnoticed in remote Juba.

No doubt part of the reason ivory prices have soared to new heights (an average of about $17 a pound) is because of Parker and Graham's competitive bidding. But after the event, Liam insists on taking much of the glory himself. Liam was surely at his best: Speaking with his quick Irish tongue, he had been able to confuse the Arabs time and again, always to the benefit of the game department. He had the natural cunning to force the price one piaster higher than the last bid, to shame everyone into being lavish. Every lot was of course his best lot, every stick of ivory somehow "majestic, flawless and worth a king's ransom." By the end of the auction, Liam is using a jumbo bottle of Blue Nile beer as his gavel, much to the consternation of the Muslims. He had been able to raise a total of £36,000 for the game department. Liam, who has given his time and talent free to the southern Sudan, is now treated as a national hero. Everyone must shake his hand. "A great day," he says, "for Belfast–Juba relations." And with that, he invites everyone to the Greek Club for Nile perch and a bottle of beer.

MARCH 5: The haboob reigns. The sky still red, with the dust covering even the ground sheet inside my tent with its nuclear fallout. Liam threatens to go to Nairobi, to await his next clients. . . .

MARCH 6: The stars have been out during the night, giving me hope the haboob has expired, but with dawn I can still not see the far fig trees, and the sun still rises rose pink and waferlike. Not sure why he must go to Nairobi for a week, I say farewell to Liam and then drive south to shoot game for camp. Every day Liam's men have been begging me for camp meat, and every day I have returned from my late-afternoon forays empty-handed.

My first sight of life (after leaving camp) is a beautifully marked serval cat, bent on some distant goal. Funny how the sight of a cat can convince me there must be plenty of game. I soon reach some lelwel hartebeest. I stalk them for a mile and a half on foot, from thicket to thicket, always believing I shall overtake them, they always ahead, knowing, it would seem, that I am in pursuit yet never actually acknowledging me with a glance. What a superb stalk! Although I never pull the trigger I am thrilled to be on my own and, at last, out on foot. Luckily I fall upon a slow-witted oribi, shoot him and carry him on my shoulders back to the vehicle. A sudden change in attitude of the men: I am suddenly back in their good graces. Now they would like me to shoot everything that moves. Wherever we walk the dust from the haboob rises explosively from each blade of grass. We cough incessantly and when I sneeze I sneeze mud.

Realizing that my hunting license entitles me to three elephants, I conclude that it is right I make a little money for a change, now that I have time to myself. I decide that the best place to start looking for elephant will be on the east bank, northeast of Mongalla:

MARCH 7: Mateo sits in the back of the open Land Rover Diki Diki, like an upright Tutankhamen. After three hours of driving, I leave the track. Soon I come upon a man riding a bicycle. Because few people in this country can afford a bicycle, I stop to say hello, only to discover the old man is a leper. I give him some of our water. He has no fingers, his thighs are frightfully scarred, his calves wrapped in puttees (no doubt to hold them together) and his canvas shoes are only half filled. I am stunned by his cheerfulness.

The farther into the bush we travel, the more evident birds of prey: first a grasshopper buzzard with diaphanous gray-brown wings and a wide fantail, followed closely by a shikra, flying erratically close to the ground, feeding, I suppose, on small birds. White-headed vultures squat about a nearly dry water hole, and near a deserted village hooded vultures peck and stare, peck and stare, as if they were the town council. Of course one becomes so inured to black African kites, so irritated at their persistent scavenging about camp, that one rarely pays them attention.

We continue farther northeast, stopping every few hundred yards to look for elephant sign. There's no doubt they cross this road most evenings but so far we see little evidence of

lone bulls. Occasionally I wonder if there's any moral justi-
fication for shooting an elephant at all, but out here one finds
thoughts of morality painful. . . .

Our camp is under an acacia tree in some sansevieria and
black cotton country, not far from the swamps where these
elephant seem to be feeding. When I arrive the sun is still
blasting, and so I wander to the river with a towel on my
arm, like a club man going to the steam room. My arrival
there is heralded by a six-foot croc plunging from the safety
of his bank into reeds. The water is covered with an electric
blue film, but once I have negotiated the reeds, I find pockets of clear water. A fish eagle screams, soaring just above
stall speed. I can see his head switching left to right and then
nearly backward, as he works the swamp.

In camp, food makes me tired, and squash makes me drink
more squash; instead, I read, waiting for the cool of darkness. Mosquitoes thereupon take up their evening vigil. A
hippo grunts and gurgles. I never know when I am sleeping
or not sleeping. I suppose I am awake when I can see
stars. . . .

MARCH 9: We leave camp early, soon after the last lion roars. I
am immediately disappointed by how few elephant tracks I
spot. Eventually I find myself back in our old stomping
grounds near the Badengellu swamps, just out of Mongalla.
My theory is that elephants here will be making a daily trip
back and forth from the Nile to inaccessible ground near the
swamps. We drive at right angles to the track, crossing occasional patches of burned ground, our passage leaving a
plume of black ash climbing into still air. At last I reach a
plain where there are many tracks of elephant, crisscrossing
each other, deeply embedded like smallpox in the ground.
At nightfall I throw my few belongings under a tamarind
tree, a tree so deserted I wonder how it survives. In the
branches above me lives a lone prunea—a tiny doomed bird
who refuses to leave his homestead even when I invade it.
In the Sudan, shade is as important as water. Both the prunea and I are in complete agreement at least on one point.

286

MARCH 10: The sky is overcast when I awake at 5:30, the most comfortable time of the day in the Sudan. The prunea has vanished, and our lone tree is even more abandoned on this great scalped plain. With my field glasses I scan the distance. On the edge of the plain where in more hospitable land I would expect a forest, there is a tree line of buffalo. Ill at ease, they stir dust and red-billed oxpeckers. Once I am behind the wheel in Diki Diki, the maneless zebra move aside, leaving just enough space for us to pass. The elephant tracks here are not as plentiful as they seemed last evening. Still, we have at last reached the legendary Peter Molloy landscape of tiang, lelwel hartebeest, reedbuck, oribi, duiker and giraffe—all ignorant, so it seems, of guns and vehicles. Perhaps the revolution never came this far.

I cannot understand why I itch so much to use the gun in the rack behind me. My camera will not do. I need to kill only one animal, and then be done with it forever (at least that is what I tell myself). Any one of these animals should do, yet wouldn't it be magnificent to kill an elephant? [Later, recalling this moment, I thought of the leopard who sometimes kills and kills, slapping at hocks, hamstringing there, eviscerating here, and at the end, walking away from the carnage because he really had not been hungry at all.]

On another plain, under two distant trees, I see the elephants: six bulls, their ears ompf-ompfing against their shoulders. Mateo and I both scan them with our glasses, and a while passes before either of us speaks. My mind is on how I can execute them. I must use the brain shot. The elephant on the left I can kill between the eyes. As he falls, the one immediately to his right will present a lateral view of his head. I will not shoot the third from the left, nor the fourth; but the fifth, the one looking my way now, may charge and, as he does, I shall shoot him through the roof of his mouth. I can feel my pulse skipping as I absently pick away at the scratches on the wood receiver of the .458, so long in disuse. Mateo clucks once and shakes his head.

As long as I have known him—some ten years—his eyes have always been bloodshot, no doubt from years spent in the smoky huts. He bears two cicatrices on his left cheek, reminders of a now-forgotten custom of the wa-Kamba. They were gouged into his cheek sometime during what he describes as the time the wa-Ingereza, the English, were fighting the wa-Deitchi, the Germans. He can even remember hearing the German bullets hitting home, for he was herding his father's goats, and herdboys often saw more than everyone else. He has seen lots of killing since then—wildlife by poachers, wildlife by rich white people, poachers by the game department, blacks during Mau Mau, blacks after Mau Mau. Killing is, for Mateo, an everyday matter.

He looks at the elephants without a blink. I am ready when he gives the nod to shoot. He puts down the glasses, spits a yellow stream onto the ground and shakes his head. *"Hakuna meno"*—"No ivory worth taking."

I plead with Mateo. I explain the ivory market. I tell him that even if each tusk weighs only twenty pounds, these elephants constitute a considerable fortune. Mateo avoids looking into my eyes although he surely could use the money. He spits again. If he could hum, I am sure he would.

Five minutes later, retracing our morning's tracks in Diki Diki, with the unused gun safely back in its holder, I begin to shake. I can hear blood pumping in my head, practically feel my arteries swelling. I brake to a halt and dash behind a bush where I hope Mateo will not hear me vomit. I wonder if he knows how much I once loved elephants. . . .

MARCH 13: I tried reaching Liam on the radiotelephone last night, but Swedish missionaries seem to control all the channels. I fell asleep listening to their singsongy complaints about broken half-shafts. . . .

Driving is such a bore, but hunting keeps me watchful. Swallow-tailed bee-eaters are fairly common here and long-crested hawk eagles perch always on the topmost branches with the wind cocking their crests. Such conceit, I think. My eyes glint with the rising sun, sorting out a shadow from a movement and the lie of a tree, the glint of a coppery bush from a lelwel's back, and later on foot, a snort from the scrape of my sandals on rock. Now that I need to shoot plains game for camp meat, wildlife has suddenly become rare . . . Every time I come within range of a particularly large lelwel hartebeest, it springs behind cover. Mateo is clucking again, this time at my ineptitude. When finally I have a chance at a shot of the male, I miss. I search for a metaphor to describe my performance, and Mateo suggests "like a woman." Good old Mateo. Not a dishonest bone in his body.

When I stop to ask questions of the Dinka along the road, I notice they prefer to slap hands rather than shake. In late afternoon I resort to the final indignity: I buy the men a chicken from some villagers. And in the evening, in a sad little camp, without any shade at all, I finally succeed in reaching Liam on the radiotelephone some thousand miles away in Nairobi, through the crackling of an intervening storm. He is "far too busy" to return to the Sudan just yet. When he mentions that the Kearneys have now left Africa for good, I can detect pleasure in the way he frames his words. I suppose he has already had his first beer of the evening, and what really gives him pleasure is not having to think of spare parts for the Range Rover, supplies in Juba and this debilitating heat.

MARCH 14: I have heard much about the game on the east bank of the Nile next to Chief Karpeta's village. While my information is some twenty years old, surely there is no harm in having a look. The track to the chief's village is at Mile 83, south of the ferry to Juba. It will bring me, according to the accounts, into a valley pregnant with game. But at Mile 83 there is no track as promised. After asking several passersby, one old man seems to remember Chief Karpeta. He points to a footpath, then changes his mind and suggests another track farther down the road. But when asked whether he has in fact been to Chief Karpeta's he shakes his head. Still, I take the track and proceed slowly and precariously into some of the most desolate country I have yet seen . . . Lunch in splendor under a fig tree where I watch soldier ants spiriting away the tinfoil of my Gruyère cheese. We drive on, with

Mateo, seated as our oracle, scouting the route from his perch on the Land Rover's hood. Feeding the men and myself is, at best, an honest occupation, so when I finally spot the lelwel hartebeest I reach for the 7 mm rifle without qualms and bound into the bush. Even Mateo's protean form froze for a moment—a sure sign that he too approved. I creep after the animal, thinking about the other men waiting back in the car. The hartebeest grazes in a westerly direction. I pretend to find cover behind each blade of grass, finally making my final stalk on my stomach. Even though I hear the whumpf of my shot striking flesh, Mateo is not convinced. He shakes his head, sure that I have let him down once again, and he barely looks for blood spoor.

The hartebeest is lying behind a bush, having gone about ten yards before dying. I try not to see Mateo's face or to let the relief show too visibly on mine, but I am willing to admit to myself that today is one of the happiest days yet in the Sudan. I feel that I shall never have to shoot again.

By nightfall we are lucky to find the only water hole we have yet seen all day. It is the color of Scotch broth—the Sudan's equivalent of Poland Spring water. I string the antenna for the radiotelephone and stack our few tin boxes around the fire. Sweat digs furrows along my dusty forehead long after the sun sets and even after the Southern Cross starts revolving on its axis. The canvas shower bucket, already beginning to rot after its one season in the Sudan, is strung from a tree and, delighting to the feel of cool dirty water mixing with my sweat, I sing a song of nakedness and peace bloody peace, listening to laughter mixing in two African tongues. The hartebeest steak, eaten on top of the radiotelephone, is tough and acrid with bile, yet it is all I need. For mindless pleasure I listen to the radio conversations of Kenyan white hunters ordering Omo and Vim and spare tires, and to their wives telling them about work permits that were not renewed.

These hunters have difficult clients too. They also intimate by the code language of their conversations that, as in Liam's case, Africa today is too exhausting a quarry for even them, a no-man's-land, a place where white roots never "take." Everything is slipping through their fingers and the specter of that little cottage in Dorset is fast becoming real. "Why wasn't the flour on today's shipment?" they ask. (The crackling of a storm) ". . . strike in town," the wife replies from Nairobi. A long pause. "Love to the kids. Over and out."

Villagers, having heard about the meat, fill our camp with their plainsong chatter. Mateo guards the cache, talking in a bastard Swahili that seems to work over much of East Africa. Pye-dogs quiver by the edge of the firelight, ready to leap for a scrap.

Mateo brings me a cup of muddy coffee. "After all these years of hunting," he says, "first as Tumbo Moto's ["Hot Stomach," Liam's nickname] client, now as his assistant, you are no longer thought by us as a foreigner. You are *'mutu ya Afrika,'* part of Africa." When Mateo is done, I look into his kindly old eyes, reflecting the fire's phosphorescence. Of course, I do not believe him. The old man who tended goats during World War I is lying to me for the first time.

At midnight I awake, thinking that I had forgotten to turn off the pressure lamp, but the light is from the moon rising.

MARCH 16: I allow myself a short diversion before bringing the meat back to base camp. On the way here I had noticed an impressive track leading off the main Nimule to Juba road. I have been warned not to travel on unused roads because of the possibility that mines, planted by Anya Nya revolutionaries, had not yet been removed [I had even heard talk about one stretch of road littered with the carcasses of elephants, killed en masse by these land mines]. But I can see relatively fresh vehicle tracks ahead.

In a few miles: a clearing and in the middle, a cathedral so huge I must jam on the brakes and proceed slowly on foot, a mouse in terror of a cat. Built of red brick, fitted with a large columned entrance and a vaunting bell tower, it is the most impressive human monument I have yet seen in the country. The empty clearing, the deserted cathedral, the smell of overripe potatoes from somewhere make me uneasy. Inside, I see that all the pews have been used for firewood. The statues of the Virgin and the saints are shoulder to shoulder, arms akimbo, jammed into a closet in the vestry, as if assembled for a macabre cocktail party. A few have had their eyes gouged out and two are beheaded. By the altar on a slab of exquisite rose marble, brought no doubt from Italy, lies a dead bat.

Outside, once my eyes have cleared, I see a white woman standing by the Land Rover. She introduces herself as a Norwegian, and she tells me that the cathedral was built by the Verona fathers who, in the early part of the civil war, were expelled from the country for allegedly fomenting trouble (or, in real language, for taking sides with the blacks against the Muslim Northerners). The woman is astonishingly beautiful. She explains that she and her husband have been here on a foreign aid project for the last six months. They have no budget, no car and, so far, no success either in learning the language or helping the locals in any way.

I hurry to leave. I am astonished by my own shyness. I fumbled with words, I was barely able to look her in the eye and, at the first opportunity, I extended my hand to say good-bye. Normally a pretty woman would have been a good reason to invite myself for lunch. Back on the road, I realize she was the first white person I have seen in over a week. I much prefer the company of these blacks. Here I am distinct in command, unquestioned by virtue of skin color. I know how to make them laugh, how to engage their esprit de corps. We think of water, food, wildlife and our dwindling supply of petrol. The cool of evenings, a little orange squash or a Blue Nile beer is all we need of luxury. That white woman was complicated.

In the open car with my hair long, blond and knotted like an addict's, I realize the time has come for me to leave the Sudan. I am Samuel Baker, Emin Pasha, Captain C. H. Stigand, Peter Molloy and all the others who did not want to leave. For all its discomforts, this Sudan is hardly the world.

My last foray in the Sudan is north of Juba on the west bank, near a place called Terakeka where Mateo, the other men and I are put under arrest because I took a photograph of a Mondari woman doing her early-morning toilette in the village square. After sitting in the shade of a mango tree for about five hours, I notice another police officer arriving.

MARCH 18: The first police officer begins to assume a look of groveling meekness. "You can go," he says.

"But why?" I query, bewildered by the sudden switch.

"We do not have enough food to feed you." Suddenly, I realize the first officer did not have any authority in the first place. He is merely the police radio operator. . . . With a guide, we continue north, I driving Diki Diki, laughing with Mateo. All I need is mention the word "Sudan" and he very nearly collapses with hysteria on the floor of the car. After one hour of driving along footpaths and fallow fields, through thornbushes and over giant pig holes, between trees withered and dead, I ask the driver how much farther until we begin seeing game. So far I have not seen one head of anything. "How much farther?" I repeat. He waves his hand casually. I stop the car. "How much farther?" Again he gestures across 180 degrees of country. "Will we be there in half an hour?" I ask. He thinks for a moment, then looks at the sky. Finally he shakes his head.

"In a half-hour," he replies, "we will still not be halfway there."

Since I have no more tire patches, since Liam returns tomorrow and since I must leave the Sudan the day following, I wheel the car around and return toward Terakeka and Juba.

I try to imagine what someday my Sudan tale will be. I am discovering every foreigner's bitter puzzle: It is natural to be interested in this country, these fabulous people, but how does one mobilize that curiosity? How does one convey authority without becoming an arrogant Colonial? How does one assimilate and not lose one's identity? How does the generous white man accept that the only way to experience the true Sudanese experience is through a massive compromise of one's background? Perhaps the most powerful lessons are those learned through a resistance to the land. The mere effort of maintaining standards here reveals much about those standards, much about the alternatives. No wonder this country demands us to be in a continuous state of motion—a constant coming, self-conscious decisions, rigid schedules. Almost every white I have met here in the Sudan is searching for a mission. Even grown men scratch around the country, convinced they are in an important land but not sure what to do with it. . . .

While driving through Terakeka with a one-eyed smelly lady as a hitchhiker, I am approached by a boy holding a young duiker [a very small antelope]. I certainly do not want to join the *Born Free* fraternity. "How much do you want?" I inquire all the same.

"One pound."

"No. I'd only give you fifty piasters for it."

The boy sticks out his hand for the money and presents me with the duiker. I am flabbergasted. I did not want the animal. I must be insane. How will I bring it to Nairobi?

Mateo holds on to the antelope during the return trip. Occasionally its hooves beat out a frightened rhythm on the floor plates.

Once in camp I name the duiker Chinese Gordon and decide that he is everything the great General was not: He likes older men, he enjoys company (following me from tent to tent like a gust of wind) and he has no intention of giving up his life for anything. I am enchanted. Sadly, we cannot find fresh milk to feed him, so I must settle for Coffee-Mate, a milk substitute. Tonight is my last night alone in camp and I am terrified someone will drive in and destroy the tranquillity. Each of the staff comes into the mess tent, one by one, voicing complaints or telling stories. It is an evening of great Swahili, a moment of communication between old friends who have known each other in so many curious places throughout Africa. At the end, it is Mateo who tells the best story—one about Tumbo Moto. Told with respect, warmth, humor, it ends with a chill note: "But that was nearly ten years ago."

MARCH 19: A great storm has tangled the fig tree above my tent, and all through the night, rain mixed with hard nuts pelted onto the canvas, keeping me from sleep. Beside the tent, the Nile brews and spits, not its usual self. Chinese Gordon has made a considerable mess on the groundsheet. I watch him out of one eye. Behind him through the mosquito netting a steady stream of people passes, en route for the river. All the women, including young girls, balance tins, cradled on reed halos, on their heads. Poking at hoops, naked boys [only boys go naked] scatter like dust in a whirlwind and then reconvene by the river's edge, settling down with poles and bent pins [for fish hooks] to catch the tiny and delicious *alestes*. The Nile is everyone's club: under one tree the men talk; under another, discreetly obscured by ground cover, the women bathe and do their washing. Nobody mixes.

One last look around is all I need before collecting Liam at the Juba airfield. Strange how Chinese doesn't want his milk formula this morning. Am I imagining that he seems unsteady on his hooves? I haven't yet climbed the hill behind the camp—the hill from which the camp takes its name— Rejaf. This place has always been prime camping. Baker mentioned the hill, and so too the Belgians who briefly controlled this region.

As part of my research on the southern Sudan, I had read "The Wanderings of an Elephant Hunter" (*Country Life*, 1923), in which its author, "Karamojo" Bell, talks of this site as the headquarters of what was known as L'Enclave de Lado, a huge region of the Sudan that at the turn of the century was privately leased to Leopold, king of the Belgians, for the duration of his life and for six months after his death:

Close to our camp lived the Chef de Zone and each evening he entertained his subordinate Belgians—these he regarded as "scum"—in a peculiar house: the mess room . . . was a large thatched roof stand-

ing on many pillars of sun-dried brick. In place of walls nothing more than mosquito netting interposed itself between the diners and the gaze of the native multitude . . . This system of architecture suits the climate admirably, its sole drawback being its publicity. For when the inmates of such a structure have the playful habits of our forefathers, without their heads, and try to drink each other under the table, and when, moreover, the casualties are removed by native servants from that ignominious position one after the other, speechless, prostrate and puking, naturally the whole affair becomes a kind of "movie" show, with sounds added for the native population. When, for instance, the Chef de Post, whose image is intimately connected in most of the spectators' minds with floggings, ambitiously tries to mount the table, fails and falls flat, the "thunders of applause" of our newspapers best describe the reception of his downfall by the audience.

Not far from camp is a graveyard, the only memory of those halcyon days. Most of the crosses are cast-iron and ceramic. I can only read the names on three graves: I wonder if sous-officier Bienaime, sous-lieutenant Peyans and chevalier Skerkove fell from the famous table, never to awake . . . Beside the individual graves there is a mass burial, and beside that an unusual flat rock suspended by a pillar of earth. Countless Arab slavers, I am told, have slept under this rock and built fires on its edge.

The great hill of Rejaf has shadowed me for the last weeks; from a distance it appears a minor climb, but I do not reach the top until well past noon. The rock at the top here is decorated in Arabic, the only European to inscribe his name being an Ernst Schmidt in 1910. The wind blows fiercely, and I must sit to steady myself for a view of the Acholi Hills, to the southeast, and Mount Lado, beyond Juba, far to the north. Here before me is what Hemingway described as "miles and miles of bloody Africa"—parchment gray with hardly a dimple. It emerges this year from sacrifice, war and anonymity. Other hunters will come in droves; so too will planners, administrators, builders, social workers, ecologists. They will find a use for this country. But why, I ask myself, the wind making my eyes water, must a use for it be found at all?

On the hotel veranda in Juba, the rain has collected in puddles where the mason forgot to use his level. The usual Europeans are seated in the uncomfortable metal chairs, dodging rays of sticky sun. There is, still, no beer in town, so the choice today ranges between orange squash, tamarind juice and gin. The usual refrain: no petrol, no building materials, no cooperation. A neat Englishman, eating Nile perch by himself in a direct ray of sun, quietly murmurs to himself: "Welcome to Africa."

Liam arrives shortly. Dressed in his green shorts, and weighing slightly more than he did when he left, he claims to be happy to be "home in the Sudan."

Liam believes the occasion warrants a party. In the evening, in camp after one beer, he tells the three assembled guests collected from the hotel that he plans to study for the priesthood. "Is there any chance," he inquires, "that an Irishman can become Pope?"

Next to the mess tent, in his cardboard box, comes a sharp cry from Chinese Gordon. He is having a convulsion. I try to feed him more of the quasi-milk but he is not interested. He shrieks again—a terrible, childlike cry, and then he dies, his head falling back against my bush jacket . . . Some irreconcilable change is coming over our lives and I wish I knew what it is . . .

MARCH 20: Rain splatters on me through the windows of the tent. It stretches guy ropes, rattles the flaps and clears the outside table of my papers and toothbrush. The bed, resting on the groundsheet, moves with the wind, scuttling up and down, trying to throw me. Murmurs come from the staff quarters and a light is lit, moving through the restless night. Tent poles hump the ground and then fall rattling onto stones. When finally dawn creeps across the river, the camp seems born again, the same color of the Sudan, ragged and aged. The day stays gray for many hours, like indecisive dawn.

All the men come with Liam to the airport to see me off. On the wet tarmac, they stand at attention with a formality I have never before witnessed. "No good-byes," I say to Liam.

"Live forever," he replies.

The Sudan, for all my imaginings, was never my last safari. It was only, for me, the end of the hunt. Liam stayed on. One month later, one of his drivers drove Big Buster off a bridge and into a dry river. The lorry, I am told, is still there today. Several weeks later, while conducting another hunt, he suffered yet another setback to his career in the Sudan. He had allowed his client to drive the Range Rover while he sat in the back with the client's girl friend, playing backgammon. She rolled a five and a two. When her boyfriend turned around to advise her about the play, the Range Rover skidded off the road and flipped into a ditch. While no one was injured, the car was damaged beyond repair. "It was the worst five and two I ever saw played," was Liam's only comment. Two years later, he had given up hunting altogether and had fallen onto a "foolproof money-maker"—driving truckloads of Tusker Export beer from Nairobi to Juba. Even then he asserted that giving up hunting was the best decision he ever made. And when he gave up hunting, he unwittingly gave up the only Africa in which he could survive. The beer never sold in Juba, and like all of us who love Africa but never know the next step, Liam returned home claiming all the time that Africa had changed.

The engines catch, the wind pours through the vents and soon we are airborne. I can see my friends for quite a while— one white man, dressed in bright green shorts, surrounded by seven blacks. They all seem so small, against the bitter landscape of the Sudan . . . Soon the sweat that has been my shell for the last two months dries on my face. Needles of rain hiss against the windscreen. I see the old watercourse I followed after that hartebeest. The Imatong Hills are green and wild, the Acholis gray. I can even spot a yellow dog wandering through a Madi village. Imagine these tracks, built more than fifty years ago by the finest civil service in the British Empire. Or the slave traders who pillaged villages for fifty miles on either side of the river. Or the explorers who, not even a century ago, cruised up this river to claim they were the first. Africa was old even then.

ABOUT THE AUTHOR

John Heminway has traveled extensively in Africa since childhood. He attended Princeton University and then became a writer/ producer for ABC Sports, winning an Emmy from the National Academy of Television Sciences. He has worked as a documentary filmmaker for years, and has made several films on African wildlife and anthropology for Anglia's "Survival" series. He is currently directing and producing a PBS film series on the human brain. The author of one previous book on Africa, *The Imminent Rains,* he divides his time between New York and a ranch in Montana.